10th Edition

Incorporate Your Business

Attorney Anthony Mancuso

TENTH EDITION	JUNE 2019
Editor	LINA GUILLEN
Cover Design	SUSAN PUTNEY
Production	SUSAN PUTNEY
Proofreader	ROBERT WELLS
Index	UNGER INDEXING
Printing	BANG PRINTING

ISSN 2326-6465 (print)
ISSN 2326-6457 (online)

ISBN 978-1-4133-2639-0 (pbk)
ISBN 978-1-4133-2640-6 (ebook)

This book covers only United States law, unless it specifically states otherwise.

Please note

We believe accurate, plain-English legal information should help you solve many of your own legal problems. But this text is not a substitute for personalized advice from a knowledgeable lawyer. If you want the help of a trained professional—and we'll always point out situations in which we think that's a good idea—consult an attorney licensed to practice in your state.

Acknowledgments

Thanks to Lina Guillen for editing this edition of the book and to all the Nolo people for their help in making this book a reality.

About the Author

Anthony Mancuso is a California corporations and limited liability company expert. A graduate of Hastings College of the Law in San Francisco, Tony is an active member of the California State Bar, writes books and software in the fields of corporate and LLC law, and has studied advanced business taxation at Golden Gate University in San Francisco. He has also been a consultant for Silicon Valley EDA (Electronic Design Automation) and other technology companies. He is currently employed at Google in Mountain View, California. Tony is the author of many Nolo books on forming and operating corporations (both profit and nonprofit) and limited liability companies. Among his current books are *The Corporate Records Handbook*; *How to Form a Nonprofit Corporation*; *Form Your Own Limited Liability Company*, and *LLC or Corporation?* His books have shown over 500,000 businesses and organizations how to form a corporation or LLC. He also is a licensed helicopter pilot and has performed for years as a guitarist.

Table of Contents

Appendixes

Forms for Incorporating

Request for Reservation of Corporate Name

Iowa Articles of Incorporation With Instructions

Nebraska Articles of Incorporation With Instructions

Cover Letter for Filing Articles

Bylaws

Incorporator's Statement

Minutes of First Meeting of Board of Directors

Forms for Issuing Shares of Stock

Stock Certificates

Bill of Sale for Assets of a Business

Receipt for Cash Payment

Bill of Sale for Items of Property

Receipt for Services Rendered

Contract for Future Services

Promissory Note

Cancellation of Debt

Forms for Postincorporation Tasks

Notice of Incorporation Letter

General Minutes of Meeting

Your Legal Companion for Incorporating

Incorporating your business may sound like a task you should hand over to a lawyer just as quickly as you can—after all, isn't there a lot of paperwork and filings, and complicated corporate and tax laws to learn? There is paperwork, and it will take some work on your part, but the truth is, you can do it yourself. Forming a corporation is actually a fairly simple, straightforward process. Thousands of people have gone through the entire process of incorporating on their own with this book to guide them.

You may still be wondering why you should go through the hassle of incorporating. As the owner of a business, incorporating can give you the legal liability protection you need so that you—personally—are shielded from the debts, obligations, and lawsuits of your business. In today's volatile business world, this type of protection is more needed than ever. You don't want to be personally exposed in the event your business gets in trouble and can't pay bills as they become due. Forming a corporation can give you the peace of mind you need to keep going with your business in these turbulent economic times.

This book explains, in plain English, how to incorporate in any state and get your newly formed corporation up and running. We show you how to:

- prepare and file articles of incorporation in any of the 50 states
- prepare bylaws for your corporation
- prepare minutes for your first board meeting
- issue shares of stock to your initial investors, and
- take care of postincorporation filings and tasks.

Appendix A explains how you can contact state offices online to obtain the latest incorporation forms and information. If a state does not provide a fill-in-the-blanks or sample incorporation form, we provide a form you can use that meets your state's statutory requirements. Two states (Iowa and Nebraska) currently do not provide their own articles form. Appendix C contains articles with instructions for these two states.

This book also contains a wealth of legal and tax information in a way that you can understand and use.

During the incorporation process, there may be decisions you need to make where you should seek professional advice. We'll let you know when you need outside help. And even if you do decide to hire a lawyer to handle some of the work for you, the information in this book will help you be an informed client—and get the most for your money.

We know that any legal process can be challenging. We hope this book, with its step-by-step and state-by-state approach to incorporation, will help you through the legal hoops and over the hurdles of incorporating your business. Congratulations on taking your first steps toward success in your new enterprise!

Get Forms, Updates, and More Online

This book contains useful forms, including articles of incorporation, ready-to-use bylaws, minutes of first board meeting, and others. You can download any of the forms in this book at:

www.nolo.com/back-of-book/NIBS.html

(See Appendix B for complete instructions on how to download and use the electronic forms.) All the forms in this book are also included in Appendix C.

Choosing the Right Legal Structure for Your Business

Is a Corporation Right for You and Your Business?

Over the past several decades, new forms of doing business have been added to the mix of business entities available to entrepreneurs who want to limit their liability, but maintain tax advantages. New state law entities, such as hybrid nonprofit corporations that can pursue both business and nonprofit objectives (see "Do-Good LLCs and Corporations" in Chapter 2) are appealing to only a small number of new business founders and stakeholders. In contrast, the limited liability company (LLC) has gained significant market share over the last several decades among entrepreneurs as a way to limit liability for business debts, while allowing the business to be taxed as either a sole proprietorship or partnership.

Despite these developments, the corporate form still has a strong attraction to start-ups seeking investment capital and a more formal business structure, as well as to employees looking to participate in equity (stock) ownership in the enterprise.

To help you decide if forming a corporation is the best choice for your business, go through the first three chapters of this book to get a sense of how corporations work and to learn about the legal and tax rules that apply to them. If the corporate form seems a bit much for you and your business now, the LLC form may be a better fit. But keep this book handy—you may want to convert your unincorporated business to a corporation later. The information in these pages should help make the transition to the corporate form easier when you decide the time is right.

To make sure that forming a corporation is the best legal and tax approach for your business, this chapter compares the corporation to other small business legal structures, such as the sole proprietorship, the partnership, and the popular limited liability company. A corporation, like a limited liability company, protects your personal assets from business creditors. But the corporation stands apart from all other business forms due to its built-in organizational structure and unique access to investment sources and capital markets. It also uniquely answers a need felt by many business owners who are attracted to the formality of the corporate form, a quality not shared by the other business structures.

 SKIP AHEAD

If you know you want to incorporate your business. If you've already considered the different types of business structures available to you and are certain that you want to form a corporation, there's no need to read this chapter. Skip ahead to Chapter 2, *How Corporations Work*.

The Different Ways of Doing Business

There are a number of legal structures or legal forms under which a business can operate, including the sole proprietorship, partnership, limited liability company, and corporation.

These basic structures have important legal and tax variants. For example, the partnership form has spawned the limited partnership and the registered limited liability partnership—two special types of partnership legal structures. And the corporation can be recognized, for tax purposes, as either a standard C corporation, in which the corporation and its owners are treated as separate taxpaying entities, or as an S corporation, in which business income passes through the corporate entity and is taxed only to its owners on their individual tax returns. Finally, the limited liability company can adopt corporate tax status if it wishes to obtain some of the tax benefits available to the C corporation. We know all of this may sound confusing. Take comfort: These legal and tax differences will become clear as you read through the material below.

Choosing the initial legal structure for your business is one of the most important decisions you'll make when starting a business. Often, business owners start with the simplest, least expensive legal form (the sole proprietorship), then move on to a more complicated business structure as their businesses grow. Other businesspeople pick the legal structure they like best from the start, and let their businesses grow into it. You are not stuck with the legal entity with which you start out—you can change your legal and tax structure from one form to another during the life of your business. However, there are tax consequences when you change your business entity, so you'll want to consider that decision as carefully as your initial business entity choice. The analysis we present here, which includes examples of businesses that choose each of these types of business structures, should help you make a good decision about what business entity makes the most sense for you.

Sole Proprietorship

A sole proprietorship is the legal name for a one-owner business. A sole proprietorship has the following general characteristics.

Ease of formation. The sole proprietorship is the easiest business form to establish, in the sense that it requires few formalities to get started. Just hang out your shingle or "Open for Business" sign, and you have established a sole proprietorship. Sure, there are other legal steps you may wish or be required to take— such as registering a fictitious business name if your business won't use your personal name or registering for a business license or sales tax permit—but these steps are not necessary to legally establish your business.

Personal liability for business debts, liabilities, and taxes. In this simplest form of small business legal structures, the owner, who usually runs the business, is personally liable for its debts, taxes, and other liabilities. This means that personal assets—for example, cash in a bank account, equity in a home or car, or a personal stock portfolio—can be used to satisfy a court judgment entered against the business. Also, if the owner hires employees, the owner is personally responsible for legal claims—for example, an auto accident—made against these employees acting within the course and scope of their employment.

Simple tax treatment. All business profits and losses are reported on the personal income tax return of the owner each year (Schedule C, *Profit or Loss From Business*, filed with the owner's 1040 federal income tax return). And this remains true even if a portion of this money is invested back in the business—that is, even if the owner doesn't pocket business profits for personal use.

Businesses Co-Owned by Spouses

In the past, a husband and wife who worked together in an unincorporated business and shared the profits and losses were considered co-owners of a partnership and had to file a partnership tax return for the business. The only exception was for spouses who lived in a community property state. They could elect to classify their business as a sole proprietorship by filing a single Schedule C listing one spouse as the sole proprietor.

Under current law, spouses in all states can elect to be taxed as a "qualified joint venture." Having this status means that the couple gets treated as a sole proprietor for tax purposes. To qualify, the couple must be the only owners of the unincorporated business and they must both "materially participate" in the business. The spouses must also file a joint Form 1040, with two separate Schedule Cs showing each spouse's share of the profits. Each spouse must include a self-employment tax schedule (Schedule SE) and pay self-employment tax on his or her share of the profits. If the couple qualifies for this exception, each spouse gets Social Security credit for his or her share of earnings in the business.

What if a couple jointly owns their business as an LLC? In this case, the spouses will normally be treated as partners and must file a partnership tax return for the LLC. However, if the couple lives in one of the nine community property states (Arizona, California, Idaho, Louisiana, Nevada, New Mexico, Texas, Washington, and Wisconsin), they have the option of treating their business as a sole proprietorship. They do this by filing an IRS Form 1040 Schedule C for the business, listing one of the spouses as the owner. There is no requirement that both spouses materially participate in the business so this election is easier than the qualified joint venture status described above.

Alaska: If you have adopted a community property election for your Alaskan spousal business, ask a tax consultant about options for IRS treatment of your business.

Only the listed spouse pays income and self-employment taxes on the reported Schedule C net profits. This means only the listed Schedule C owner-spouse will receive Social Security account earning credits for the Form SE taxes paid with the 1040 return. For this reason, some eligible spouses will decide not to make this Schedule C filing and will continue to file a partnership tax return for their jointly owned spousal LLC. Also, the IRS treats the filing of a Schedule C for a jointly owned spousal LLC as the conversion of a partnership to a sole proprietorship, which can have tax consequences.

Finally, if one spouse manages the business and the other helps out as an employee or volunteer worker (but does not contribute to running the business), the managing spouse can claim ownership and treat the business as a sole proprietorship.

For more information on spousal businesses, see "Forming a Partnership" in IRS Publication 541 and "Husband and Wife Business" and other information on the IRS website at www.irs.gov. In all cases, be sure to check with your tax adviser before deciding on the best way to own, file, and pay taxes for a spousal business.

TIP

A corporate comparison. Earnings retained in a corporation are not taxed on the owner's individual income tax return. Instead, this money is taxed at separate corporate income tax rates. Because corporate tax rates are sometimes lower than individual income tax rates, business owners who leave earnings in their businesses often save tax dollars by incorporating. We discuss this feature of corporations—called income splitting—in "The Corporation," below.

Legal life same as owner's. On the death of its owner, a sole proprietorship simply ends. The assets of the business normally pass under the terms of the deceased owner's will or trust, or by intestate succession (under the state's inheritance statutes) if there is no formal estate plan.

CAUTION

Don't let business assets get stuck in probate. Probate—the court process necessary to "prove" a will and distribute property—can take up to one year or more. In the meantime, it may be difficult for the inheritors to operate or sell the business or its assets. Often, the best way to avoid having a probate court involved in business operations is for the owner to transfer the assets of the business into a living trust during his or her lifetime. This permits business assets to be transferred to inheritors promptly on the death of the business owner, free of probate. (For detailed information on estate planning, including whether or not it makes sense to create a living trust, see *Plan Your Estate*, by Denis Clifford (Nolo), or Nolo's *Quicken WillMaker Plus*, software that allows you to prepare your own living trust.)

Sole proprietorships in action. Many one-owner or spouse-owned businesses start small, with very little advance planning or procedural red tape. Let's look at an example. Celia Wong is a graphic artist with a full-time salaried job for a local book publishing company. In her spare

time, she takes on extra work using her home computer to produce audiocassette and CD jacket cover art for musicians. These jobs are usually commissioned on a handshake or over the phone. Without thinking much about it, Celia has started her own sole proprietorship business. Celia should include a Schedule C in her yearly federal 1040 individual tax return, showing the net profits (profits minus expenses) or losses of her sole proprietorship. Celia is responsible for paying income taxes on profits, plus self-employment (Social Security) taxes based on her sole proprietorship income. (IRS Form SE is used to compute self-employment taxes and is attached to a 1040 income tax return.) If Celia has any business debts, she is personally liable for the money owed. For example, she usually owes on a charge account at a local art supply house, or a disgruntled client successfully may sue her in small claims court for money paid for a job she failed to complete. She can't simply fold up her business and walk away from these debts, claiming that they were the legal responsibility of her business only.

TIP

Put some profits aside to buy business insurance. Once Celia begins to make enough money, she should consider taking out a commercial business insurance policy to cover legal claims against her business. While off-the-shelf insurance normally won't protect her from her own business mistakes—for example, failure to perform work properly or on time or to pay bills—it can cover many risks, including slip-and-fall lawsuits and damage to her or a client's property, as well as fire, theft, and other casualties that might occur in her home-based business.

Running her business as a sole proprietorship serves Celia's needs for the present. Assuming her small business succeeds, she will want to put it on a more formal footing by establishing a separate business checking account, possibly coming up with a fancier name and filing a fictitious business name statement with the county clerk, and, if she hires employees, obtaining a federal Employer Identification Number (EIN) from the IRS. At some point, Celia may also feel ready to renovate her house to separate her office space from her living quarters. Besides the convenience this might offer, it can also help to convince the IRS that the portion of the mortgage or rent paid for the office is deductible as a business expense on her Schedule C.

Celia can quit her day job, expand her business, and still keep her sole proprietorship legal status. Unless her business grows significantly or she takes on work that puts her at a much higher risk of being sued—and, therefore, being held personally liable for business debts—it makes sense for her to continue to operate her business as a sole proprietorship.

RESOURCE

More information about starting and running a sole proprietorship. A great source of practical information on how to start and operate a small sole proprietorship is *The Small Business Start-Up Kit*, by Peri H. Pakroo (Nolo). Also, see *Tax Savvy for Small Business*, by Frederick W. Daily (Nolo), a small business owner's guide to taxes that includes a full discussion of setting up a home-based business and deducting its expenses.

Partnership

A partnership is simply an enterprise in which two or more co-owners agree to share the profits. No written partnership agreement is necessary, though it's a good idea to make one. If two people go into business together, they automatically establish a "general partnership" under state law unless they incorporate, form a limited liability company, or file paperwork

Partnerships Can Choose to Be Taxed Like Corporations

Unlike regular partnerships, where profits pass through the business and are taxed to the individual owners, corporations are taxed as separate entities. (This is explained in detail below in "The Corporation.") If they choose, partners can elect to change the normal pass-through taxation their partnership receives and have the IRS tax the business like a corporation. Specifically, the "check-the-box" federal tax rules, also followed in most states, let partnerships (and LLCs) elect to be treated as corporate tax entities by filing IRS Form 8832, *Entity Classification Election*. This election means that partnership income will be taxed at the entity level at corporate tax rates, and the partners pay individual income tax only on profits actually paid out to them (in the form of salaries, bonuses, and direct payouts of profits).

Most smaller partnerships will not wish to make this election, preferring instead to have profits divided among the partners and then taxed on their individual tax returns.

But this is not always true. For example, some partnerships—especially one that wants to reinvest profits in expanding the business— may prefer to keep profits in the business and have them taxed to the business at the lower initial corporate tax rates. (For a discussion of corporate tax income splitting, see "The Corporation," below.) Your tax adviser can tell you if this tax strategy makes sense if you're considering forming a partnership or an LLC. We believe that any partnership seriously considering making a corporate tax election should also consider converting to a corporation (instead of filing a corporate tax election for the partnership) to get the additional capital benefits that a corporation provides.

Why You Need a Written Partnership Agreement

Although it's possible to start a partnership with a verbal agreement—or even with no stated agreement at all—there are drawbacks to taking this casual approach. The most obvious problem is that a verbal agreement may be remembered and interpreted differently by different partners. (And, of course, having no stated agreement at all almost always means trouble.) Also, if you don't write out how you want to operate your partnership, you lose a great deal of flexibility. Instead of being able to make your own rules in a number of key areas—for example, how partnership profits and losses are divided among the partners—the lack of a written agreement means that, by default, state partnership law will come into play. These state-based rules may not be to your liking—for example, state law generally calls for an equal division of profits and losses, regardless of partners' capital contributions.

Other problems with doing business without a written partnership agreement come up when a partner wants to leave the business. Here are just a few of the difficult questions that can arise:

- If the remaining partners want to buy out the departing partner, how will the partner's ownership interest be valued?

- Assuming you agree on how much the departing partner's interest is worth, how will the departing partner be paid for that interest—in a lump sum or in installments? If payment will be made in installments, how big will the down payment be, how many years will it take to pay the balance, and how much interest will be charged?

- What happens if none of the remaining partners wants to buy the departing partner's interest? Will your partnership dissolve? If so, can some of the partners form a new partnership to continue the partnership business? Who gets to use the dissolved partnership's name and client or customer list?

Partnership law, which is written in generalities, does not provide context-specific answers to these questions, meaning that in the absence of a written partnership agreement, you may face a long legal battle with a partner who decides to call it quits.

To avoid these and other problems, a basic partnership agreement should, at a minimum, spell out:

- each partner's interest in the partnership

- how profits and losses will be split up between or among the partners

- how any buyout or transfer of a partner's interest will be valued and handled, and

- how the former partners can continue the partnership's business if they want to.

---

with the state to establish a special type of partnership, such as a limited partnership. (See "Limited Partnerships," below, for more on special partnerships.) A general partnership, simply stated, is one where each of the partnership owners is legally entitled to manage the partnership business.

General partnerships are governed by each state's partnership law. But since all states have adopted a version of the Uniform Partnership Act, general partnership laws are very similar throughout the United States. Mostly, these laws contain basic rules that provide for a division of profits and losses among partners and set out the partners' legal relationship with one another. These rules are not mandatory in most cases. You can (and should) spell out your own rules for dividing profits and losses and operating

Limited Partnerships

Most smaller partnerships are general partnerships, where all owners agree to manage the partnership together, and each partner is personally liable for partnership debts. However, there are two other fairly common types of partnerships: limited partnerships and registered limited liability partnerships (RLLPs). Each of these is quite different from a general partnership.

The limited partnership. Owners use the limited partnership structure when one or more of the partners are passive investors (the "limited partners") and another partner runs the partnership (the "general partner"). You must file a Certificate of Limited Partnership with the secretary of state (or a similar state filing office) to form a limited partnership, and pay a filing fee. The advantage of a limited partnership is that, unlike a general partnership, where all partners are personally liable for business debts and liabilities, a limited partner is allowed to invest in a partnership without the risk of incurring personal liability. If the business fails, all that the limited partner can lose is a capital investment—that is, the amount of money or the property that partner paid for an interest in the business. However, in exchange for this big advantage, the limited partner normally is not allowed to participate in the management or control of the partnership. A partner who does so can lose limited liability status and can be held personally liable for partnership debts, claims, and other obligations. This disadvantage has caused many a business owner who might form a limited partnership to turn to the limited liability company (LLC). LLCs offer pass-through tax status, limited liability protection, *and* the ability to participate fully in the management of the business. We discuss LLCs just below.

Typically, a limited partnership has several limited partner investors and at least one general partner who is responsible for partnership management and is personally liable for its debts and other liabilities.

The registered limited liability partnership. This is a legal structure allowed in most states and designed specifically for professionals (attorneys, accountants, architects, engineers, and other licensed businesspeople). An RLLP is formed by filing a Registration of Limited Liability Partnership form with the secretary of state (or another state agency that handles business filings). An RLLP relieves professional partners from personal liability for claims against another partner for professional malpractice. However, professionals in an RLLP remain personally liable for their own professional malpractice.

EXAMPLE: Martha and Veronica operate a two-person accounting partnership, registered as an RLLP. Each has her own clients. Suppose Martha loses a malpractice lawsuit, and Veronica did not participate in providing services to the client who won the suit. If partnership insurance and assets are not sufficient to pay the judgment, Martha's personal assets, but not Veronica's, are subject to seizure to pay the money due. In a general partnership practice that's not an RLLP, both Martha and Veronica could be personally liable for either CPA's individual malpractice.

RESOURCE

For more LP and RLLP information. To determine the forms and procedures necessary to set up a limited partnership or an RLLP in your state, go to your state's business filing office website. (See Appendix A.)

your partnership in a written partnership agreement. If you don't prepare your own partnership agreement, all provisions of state partnership law apply to your partnership.

A general partnership has the following characteristics.

Each partner has personal liability. Like the owner of a sole proprietorship, each partner is personally liable for the debts and taxes of the partnership. In other words, if the partnership assets and insurance are insufficient to satisfy a creditor's claim or legal judgment, the partners' personal assets are subject to attachment and liquidation to pay the debt.

The act or signature of each partner can bind the partnership. Each partner is an agent for the partnership and can individually hire employees, borrow money, sign contracts, and perform any act necessary to the operation of the business in which the partnership engages. All partners are personally liable for these debts and obligations. This rule makes it essential that the partners trust each other to act in the best interests of the partnership and each of the other partners.

Partners report and pay individual income taxes on profits. A partnership files a yearly IRS Form 1065—called *U.S. Return of Partnership Income*—that includes a schedule showing the allocation of profits, losses, and other tax items to all partners (Schedule K-1). The partnership must mail an individual Schedule K-1 to each partner at the end of each year, showing the items of income and loss, credits, and deductions allocated to each partner. When partners file individual income tax returns, the partners report their allocated shares of partnership profits (taken from the partners' Schedule K-1) and pay individual income taxes on these profits. As with the sole proprietorship, partners are taxed on business profits even if the profits are plowed back into the business,

unless the partners elect to have the partnership taxed as a corporation. In that case, the corporate entity is taxed separately. (See "Partnerships Can Choose to Be Taxed Like Corporations," above.)

Partnership dissolves when a partner leaves. Legally, when a partner ceases to be involved with the business of the partnership (when the partner withdraws or dies), the partnership is automatically dissolved as a legal entity. However, a properly written partnership agreement provides for these eventualities and allows the partnership to continue by permitting the remaining partners to buy out the interest of the departing or deceased partner (see "Why You Need a Written Partnership Agreement," above). Of course, if one person in a two-partner business leaves or dies, the partnership must end; you need at least two people to have a partnership.

RESOURCE

A partnership resource. For a thorough look at the legal and tax characteristics of partnerships, and for a clause-by-clause approach to preparing a partnership agreement, see *Form a Partnership*, by Denis Clifford and Ralph Warner (Nolo).

Partnerships in action. George and Tamatha are good friends who have been working together in a rented warehouse space where they share a kiln used to make blown glass pieces. They recently collaborated on the design and production of a batch of hand-blown halogen light fixtures, which immediately became popular with local lighting vendors. Believing that they can streamline the production of these custom pieces, they plan to solicit and fill larger orders with retailers, and look into wholesale distribution. They shake hands on their new venture, which they name Halo Light Sculptures. Although they obtain a business license and file a fictitious name statement with the county clerk showing that they are working together as Halo Light Sculptures, they don't bother to write up a partnership agreement. Their only agreement is a verbal one to equally share in the work of making the glass pieces, splitting expenses and any profits that result.

This type of informal arrangement can sometimes be justified in the early exploratory days of a co-owned business where the owners, like George and Tamatha, have yet to decide whether to commit to the venture. However, for the reasons mentioned earlier, from the moment the business looks like it has long-term potential, the partners should prepare and sign a written partnership agreement. Furthermore, if either partner is worried about personal liability for business debts or the possibility of lawsuits by purchasers of the fixtures, then forming a limited liability company (LLC) or a corporation probably would be a better business choice.

Tax update. Under the 2018 federal Tax Cuts and Jobs Act, owners of sole proprietorships, partnerships, LLCs, and S corporations may be eligible to deduct up to 20% of business income on their federal tax returns. Limitations and exceptions apply. See Chapter 4 and ask your tax adviser for more information.

The Limited Liability Company (LLC)

The limited liability company (LLC) is the new kid on the block of business organizations. It has become popular with many small business owners, in part because it was custom-designed by state legislatures to overcome particular limitations of each of the other business forms, including, in some contexts, the corporation. Essentially, the LLC is a business ownership structure that allows owners to pay business taxes on their individual income tax returns like partners (or, for a one-person LLC, like a sole proprietorship). In addition, owners get the legal protection of personal limited liability for business debts and judgments as if they had formed a corporation. Put another way, with an LLC you simultaneously achieve the twin goals of pass-through taxation of business profits and limited personal liability for business debts.

All states allow an LLC to be formed by one or more people. LLC members need not be residents of the state where they form their LLC, or even of the United States, for that matter, and other business entities, such as a corporation or another LLC, can be LLC owners.

Here is a look at the most important LLC characteristics.

Limited Liability

Under each state's LLC laws, the owners of an LLC are not personally liable for the LLC's debts and other liabilities. This personal legal liability protection is the same as that offered to shareholders of a corporation.

Pass-Through Taxation

Federal and state tax laws treat an LLC like a partnership—or, for a one-owner LLC, like a sole proprietorship. Again, this means that LLC income, loss, credits, and deductions are reported on the individual income tax returns of the LLC owners. The LLC entity itself does not pay income tax. However, as with partnerships, there are "check-the-box" tax rules that let an LLC elect corporate tax treatment if its owners wish to leave income in the business and have it taxed at separate corporate income tax rates. We explain how corporate tax treatment works in Chapter 3.

RESOURCE

Finding your state's LLC tax rules. Some states impose an annual fee or tax on LLCs, in addition to individual income tax that owners pay on the LLC profits allocated to them each year. To find out whether your state imposes an LLC tax, go to your state's tax department website. (See Appendix A.)

Because a co-owned LLC is taxed as a partnership, it files standard partnership tax returns (IRS Form 1065 and Schedules K-1) with the IRS and state, and the LLC owners pay taxes on their share of LLC profits on their individual income tax returns. (Each owner gets a Schedule K-1 from the LLC, which shows the owner's share of LLC profits and deductions. The owner attaches the K-1 to the owner's individual income tax return.) A sole-owned LLC is treated as a sole proprietorship for tax purposes. The owner includes profits or losses from LLC operations, as well as deductions and credits allowable to the business, on a Schedule C included with the owners' individual income tax returns. In essence, for a sole LLC owner, the Schedule C works much like the K-1 schedule filed by the owners of a co-owned LLC.

If a sole-owner or multiowner LLC elects corporate tax treatment, the LLC is treated and taxed as a corporation, not as a sole proprietorship or partnership. The LLC files corporate income tax returns, reporting and paying corporate income tax on any profits retained in the LLC. The LLC members report and pay individual income tax only on salaries paid to them or distributions of LLC profits or losses. However, as is true for partnerships, LLCs that may benefit from electing corporate tax treatment normally decide to go ahead and incorporate. By doing so, they get corporate tax treatment plus the other advantages the corporation provides, such as access to capital, capital sharing with employees, tax deductible employee fringe benefits, and built-in management formalities. (To learn more, see "The Corporation," below.)

Management Flexibility

LLCs are normally managed by all the owners (also called members)—this is known as "member-management." But state law also allows for management by one or more specially appointed managers, who may be members or nonmembers. Not surprisingly (but somewhat awkwardly), this arrangement is known as "manager-management." In other words, an LLC can appoint one or more of its members, or one of its CEOs or even a person contracted from outside the LLC, to manage its affairs. This manager setup is somewhat atypical and normally only makes sense if one person wishes to assume full-time control of the LLC, with the other owners acting as passive investors in the enterprise.

Formation Requirements

Like a corporation, an LLC requires paperwork to get going. You must file articles of organization with the state business filing office. And if the LLC is to maintain a business presence in another state, such as a branch office, you must also file registration or qualification papers with the other state's business filing office. LLC formation fees vary, but most are comparable to the fee each state charges for incorporation.

Like a partnership, an LLC should prepare an operating agreement to spell out how the LLC will be owned, how profits and losses will be divided, how departing or deceased members will be bought out, and other essential ownership details. If you don't prepare an operating agreement, the default provisions of the state's LLC Act will apply to the operation of your LLC. Since LLC owners will want to control exactly how profits and losses are apportioned among the members as well as other essential LLC operating rules, they need an LLC operating agreement.

> **EXAMPLE:** Barry and Sam jointly own and run a flower shop, Aunt Jessica's Floral Arrangements, which specializes in unique flower arrangements. (The name stems from the fact that Barry used to work for his Aunt Jessica, who taught him the ropes of floral design.) Lately, business has been particularly rosy, and the two men plan to sign a long-term contract with a flower importer to supply them with larger quantities of seasonal flowers. Once they receive the additional flowers, they will be able to create more floral pieces and wholesale them to a wider market. Both men are sensitive to the fact that they will encounter more risks as their business grows. Accordingly, they decide to protect their personal assets from business risks by converting their partnership to an LLC. They could accomplish the same result by incorporating, but they prefer the simplicity of paying taxes on their business income on their individual income tax returns—rather than splitting business income between themselves and their corporation and filing both corporate and individual income tax returns. They also realize that if they begin making more money than each needs to take home, they can convert their LLC to a corporation later to obtain lower corporate income tax rates on earnings kept in the business or, as an alternative, make an IRS election to have their LLC taxed as a corporation without having to change its legal structure at all.

Creditors' Attempts to Reach an LLC Interest

Most of the time, the LLC's limited liability shield protects LLC owners' personal assets from claims, lawsuits, and money judgments arising out of LLC business operations. However, this protection doesn't always work the other way: An LLC owner's interest in LLC business assets is not necessarily protected from creditors seeking to satisfy personal debts or judgments against the LLC owner.

In most states, if an LLC owner defaults on a personal debt or is hit with a personal money judgment, the owner's interest in the LLC can be reached to satisfy the claim or debt. Personal creditors (such as credit card companies and mortgage lenders) can obtain a "charging order," or a lien, against the LLC owner's personal business interests, including a partnership interest, LLC interest, or stock in a corporation. This charging order allows the creditor to receive profit payments that would otherwise go to the LLC owner.

> **EXAMPLE:** Sam defaults on a personal bank loan unrelated to his LLC business, and the bank obtains a charging order against Sam's LLC membership interest. This order allows the bank to receive profits that would otherwise go directly to Sam under the terms of the LLC's operating agreement.

However, a charging order may not do a creditor much good if an LLC does not regularly distribute profits to its owners. In that case, if state law permits, the creditor may be able to convince a court to allow it to foreclose on (become the new legal owner of) the LLC owner's interest. The foreclosing creditor becomes a "transferee" or "assignee" and is entitled to all economic rights associated with the LLC interest, including a share of any profits paid out on the interest and the value of the interest, if and when the business is sold or liquidated.

Under most state laws, a creditor that forecloses on an LLC interest cannot manage the LLC, become a full voting member, or assume any other membership rights granted to full members.

The Series LLC—A Rising Star on the Business Entity Horizon

A new type of LLC is taking shape under state LLC laws: the series LLC. States are still in the process of developing their series LLC statutes and it will take time for them to coordinate the laws, fees, and tax treatments. Once this happens, however, and the courts settle some of the legal nuances of series LLCs, the series LLC may become the new big thing in business entity formations. A handful of states have adopted a series LLC formation statute. Go to your state's online business entity filing office (see Appendix A) to see if your state has jumped on the series LLC bandwagon.

The main characteristic and advantage of the series LLC is that it allows you to set up one or more series of assets within a single LLC. The business and assets of each series can be managed and operated separately—for example, each series can have separate owners and managers, a separate operating agreement that specifies a separate division of profits and losses associated with the series, and other separate formation and operation characteristics. And, under some state statutes, there is also a separation of legal liability between each series within an LLC.

A number of series LLC states allow for this separation of legal liability between each series within an LLC. In these states, assets such as real estate can be put into separate series within an LLC, and, if done properly, each property should be subject only to its own financing obligations. This consolidation of assets in one LLC coupled with a separation of liability between the assets

in each series can be an advantage to organizers who want to set up one LLC to develop, encumber, and sell multiple parcels of real estate.

Before you decide to form a series LLC, however, there are certain things you should keep in mind. For one, a state that does not have a series LLC statute may not respect the characteristics of a series LLC formed in another state. And, because these entities are so new, there are other uncertainties. For example, it is not clear that a federal bankruptcy court will respect the separateness of each series within an LLC.

Finally, forming a series LLC may seem like a good way to avoid paying a lot of formation and annual fees for multiple LLC entities. However, some states may not be willing to forgo these filing fees so easily. In California, for example, the Franchise Tax Board assesses an $800 franchise tax payment, plus an annual added gross receipts fee of up to $12,000 per year on each LLC formed or operated within the state. The Board has stated that it will treat each series in many out-of-state LLCs as separate LLCs (see FTB Form 568 and FTB Publication 689 at www.ftb.ca.gov). This means that a Delaware series LLC that operates or owns property in California may have to pay the annual California franchise and any added tax for *each* series within the LLC. Similarly, when you go to register your series LLC in a state that does not have a series LLC statute, the state may decide that you owe a registration fee for each series in your LLC, not just one for the whole LLC.

In exceptional cases, such as when an LLC member has committed a fraud on a creditor, a court may grant the creditor more leeway in recovering any resulting debt, particularly where the court is dealing with a single-member LLC. For example, if a member of a single-member LLC committed fraud during a transaction with a creditor, a judge may allow the assignee creditor to become a full member, with voting rights, including the right to force a sale of the LLC. After all, with a single-member LLC, there is no risk that other members' rights will be compromised.

This area of law is complex and developing rapidly. If you're worried about how a charging order may affect your interest in an LLC, please contact an experienced business lawyer to learn about relevant laws in your state.

Tax update. Under the 2018 federal Tax Cuts and Jobs Act, owners of sole proprietorships, partnerships, LLCs, and S corporations may be eligible to deduct up to 20% of business income on their federal tax returns. Limitations and exceptions apply. See Chapter 4 and ask your tax adviser for more information.

Beware of Exceptions to the Rule of Limited Personal Liability

In some unusual situations, corporate directors, officers, and shareholders can be held responsible for paying money owed by their corporation. Here are a few of the most common exceptions to the rule of limited personal liability; these exceptions also apply to other limited liability business structures, such as the LLC.

Personal guarantees. Often when a bank or other lender lends money to a small corporation, particularly a newly formed one, it requires the principal corporate owners (shareholders) to agree to repay the loan from their personal assets if the corporation defaults. In some instances, shareholders may even have to pledge equity in a house or other personal assets as security for repayment of the debt.

Federal and state taxes. If a corporation fails to pay income, payroll, or other taxes, the IRS and the state tax agency are likely to attempt to recover the unpaid taxes from "responsible persons"—a category that often includes the principal directors, officers, and shareholders of a small corporation. The IRS and states sometimes succeed in these tax collection strategies. Therefore, paying taxes should be a top priority for all businesses.

Unlawful or unauthorized transactions. If you use the corporation as a means to defraud people, or if you intentionally make a reckless decision that results in physical harm to others or their property—for example, you fail to maintain premises or a worksite properly when you've been warned of the probability of imminent danger to others, or you deliberately manufacture unsafe products—a court may hold you individually liable for the monetary losses of the people you harm. Lawyers call this "piercing the corporate veil," meaning that the corporate entity is disregarded and the owners are treated just like the owners of an unincorporated business.

Fortunately, most of these problem areas can be avoided by following a few commonsense rules—rules you'll probably follow anyway:

- Don't do anything dishonest or illegal.
- Make sure your corporation does the same, by getting necessary permits, licenses, or clearances for its business operations.
- Pay employee wages, and withhold and pay corporate income and payroll taxes on time.
- Try not to become personally obligated for corporate debts unless you decide that the need for corporate funds is worth the personal risk.

The Corporation

A corporation is a statutory creature, created and regulated by state law. In short, if you want the "privilege"—that's what the courts call it—of turning your business enterprise into a corporation, you must follow the requirements of your state's Business Corporation Law or Business Corporation Act (BCA). What sets the corporation apart, in a theoretical sense, from all other types of businesses is that it is a legal and tax entity separate from any of the people who own, control, manage, or operate it. The state corporation and federal and state tax laws view the corporation as a legal "person." This means the corporation is capable of entering into contracts, incurring debts, and paying taxes separately from its owners.

Advantages of Incorporating

Let's start by looking at the advantages that flow from this separate entity treatment of the corporation. The first and foremost is built-in legal limited liability protection.

Limited Personal Liability

Like the owners of an LLC or the limited partners in a limited partnership, the owners (shareholders) of a corporation are not personally liable for business debts, claims, or other liabilities. Put another way, this means that people who invest in a corporation—shareholders—normally stand to lose only the amount of money or the value of the property that they have paid for its stock. As a result, if the corporation does not succeed and cannot pay its debts or other financial obligations, creditors cannot seize or sell the corporate investor's home, car, or other personal assets.

EXAMPLE: Rackafrax Dry Cleaners, Inc., a corporation, has several bad years in a row. When it finally files for bankruptcy it owes $50,000 to a number of suppliers and $80,000 as a result of a lawsuit for uninsured losses stemming from a fire. Stock in Rackafrax is owned by Harry Rack, Edith Frax, and John Quincy Taft. Fortunately, the personal assets of these people cannot be taken to pay the money Rackafrax owes.

Corporate Tax Treatment

Unlike other business forms, a corporation is a separate tax entity, distinct from its owners. This means that the company itself is taxed on all profits that it cannot deduct as business expenses. This separate-entity tax treatment brings certain benefits to a corporation—for example, it permits income splitting between the corporation and its owners, and also allows the owners to be classified as "employees" of their own business, making them eligible to receive tax-deductible employee fringe benefits. (Employee benefits are discussed below in "Corporate Employee Benefits and Employee Incentives.")

Income splitting. Because a corporation is a separate taxpayer, it has its own income tax rate and files its own tax returns, separate from the tax rates and tax returns of its owners. This double layer of taxation allows corporate profits to be kept in the business and taxed at the corporate tax rate, which can be lower than the tax rates of the corporation's owners. (See "Federal Corporate Income Tax Treatment" in Chapter 3.) Income splitting between the corporation and its owners can result in an overall tax savings for the owners, compared to the pass-through taxation that is standard for sole proprietorships, partnerships, and LLCs.

EXAMPLE: Jeff and Sally own and work for their own two-person corporation, Hair Looms, Inc., a mail-order wig supply business that is starting to enjoy popularity with overseas purchasers. To keep pace with sprouting orders, they need to expand by investing a portion of their profits in the business. Since Hair Looms is incorporated, only the portion of the profits paid to Jeff and Sally as salary is reported and taxed to them on their individual tax returns—let's assume, at the top individual income tax rate of 37%. By contrast, profits left in the business for expansion is reported on Hair Looms's corporate income tax return and is taxed at the corporate tax rate of only 21%.

RESOURCE

LLCs and partnerships can elect corporate tax treatment. Income splitting is no longer a unique aspect of corporate life. As mentioned earlier in this chapter, partnerships and LLCs can elect to be taxed as corporations if they wish to keep money in the business to be taxed at corporate rates. (See "Partnerships Can Choose to Be Taxed Like Corporations," above.) However, partnerships and LLCs that can benefit from doing this normally decide to incorporate instead of electing corporate tax status for their unincorporated business. By changing to a corporate legal entity, they get corporate income tax splitting plus the other advantages the corporation provides, such as access to capital, capital sharing with employees, tax-deductible employee fringe benefits, and built-in management formalities. (See below for more on these advantages.)

How Small Corporations Avoid Double Taxation of Corporate Profits

What about the old bugaboo of corporate double taxation? Most people have heard that corporate income is taxed twice: once at the corporate level and again when it is paid out to shareholders in the form of dividends. In theory, the Internal Revenue Code says that most corporations are treated this way (except S corporations, whose profits automatically pass to shareholders each year; see below). In practice, however, double taxation seldom occurs in the context of the small business corporation. The reason is simple: Employee-owners don't pay themselves dividends. Instead, the shareholders, who usually work for their corporation, pay themselves salaries and bonuses, which are deducted from the profits of the corporate business as ordinary and necessary business expenses. The result is that profits paid out in salary and other forms of employee compensation to the owner-employees of a small corporation are taxed only once, at the individual level. In other words, as long as you work for your corporation, even in a part-time or consulting capacity, you can pay out business profits to yourself as reasonable compensation, and you avoid having your corporation pay taxes on these profits.

S corporation tax election. Just as partnerships and LLCs have the ability to elect corporate tax treatment, corporations can choose the type of pass-through taxation of business profits that normally applies to partnerships and LLCs. (But there are some technical differences that lend an advantage to partnerships and LLCs.

See "A Comparison of LLC, Partnership, and S Corporation Tax Treatment," below.) You can do this by making an S corporation tax election with the IRS and your state tax authority.

If your corporation files an S corporation tax election, all profits, losses, credits, and deductions pass through to the shareholders, who report these items on their individual tax returns. Each S corporation shareholder is allocated a portion of profits and losses of the corporation according to that person's percentage of stock ownership in the corporation. For example, a 50% shareholder reports and pays individual income taxes on 50% of the corporation's annual profits. These profits are allocated to the shareholders whether the profits are actually paid to them or kept in the corporation.

Why would a corporation want to elect S corporation status, given that the separate taxability of the corporation (which the S corporation eliminates) is normally a primary advantage of the corporation? The answer is that there may come a time during the life of an existing corporation when pass-through taxation makes sense, for tax or other reasons. One example occurs when the incorporators expect start-up losses. In a regular corporation, these losses are normally locked into the business; they can be used only to offset future corporate profits. But if an S tax election is made, the losses may qualify to be used to offset other individual income earned by the owners from business activity outside the corporation—for example, salaried income they receive from another business.

As another example, if corporate shareholders who do not work in the business decide it's time for them to receive their share of corporate profits, but the corporation doesn't want to pay out nondeductible dividends, an S corporation election can be made to automatically allocate profits to shareholders—the S corporation itself pays no income tax on the passed-through allocated profits. (The corporation may, however, owe taxes at the time it converts to an S corporation.)

When Forming an S Corporation Doesn't Make Sense

S corporation tax status is normally elected for special reasons by existing corporations, to achieve pass-through tax status for shareholders. In other words, if you really want pass-through tax treatment throughout the life of your business (and you haven't yet formed your corporation), don't incorporate. Instead, form an LLC. You'll get pass-through taxation plus limited liability protection, just like an S corp—in fact, the pass-through benefits of an LLC are even better. (See "A Comparison of LLC, Partnership, and S Corporation Tax Treatment," below.)

A corporation must meet certain requirements to qualify for S corporation status. It must have 100 or fewer individual shareholders who are U.S. citizens or residents (not entities, except for a few special types), and it must have only one class of stock. The shares may have different voting rights, but otherwise all corporate shares must have the same rights and restrictions. You can revoke an S corporation election to go back to regular C corporation tax treatment, but then you cannot reelect S corporation status for another five years. After you make an S corporation election with the IRS, you can make the election with your state tax agency as well. (Many states automatically recognize your federal S corporation election once it is filed.)

A Comparison of LLC, Partnership, and S Corporation Tax Treatment

S corporation tax status, though similar to the pass-through tax treatment given to LLC and partnership owners, is not quite as good. Specifically, LLC owners and partners are not required to allocate profits in proportion to ownership interests in the business. They can make what are known as "special allocations" of profits and losses under the federal tax code, but S corporation shareholders can't do this. Also, the amount of losses that can be passed through to an S corporation shareholder is limited to the total of the shareholder's "basis" in his stock (that is, the amount paid for stock plus and minus adjustments during the life of the corporation—plus amounts loaned personally by the shareholder to the corporation). Losses allocated to a shareholder that exceed these limits can be carried forward and deducted in future tax years (if the shareholder qualifies) to deduct the losses at that later time.

In contrast, LLC owners and partners may be able to personally deduct more business losses on their tax returns in a given year. LLC members and partners get to count their pro rata share of all money borrowed by the business, not just loans personally made by the member or partner, when computing how much of any loss allocated to the member by the business can be deducted in a given year on an individual income tax return.

Given these differences, you might think that the owners of a regular corporation who wish to receive pass-through taxation of business income should dissolve the corporation and form an LLC or partnership, rather than electing S corporation tax treatment. But this may not be the case. This type of conversion (from a corporation to an LLC or partnership) can be expensive in terms of taxes and legal fees. In other words, it may be best for an existing corporation to elect S corporation tax status if it wants pass-through tax treatment, even if the S corporation election does not provide full pass-through tax benefits. (Even here, however, the corporation may owe taxes when it converts to an S corporation.) This is a complex tax issue; you should check with an expert tax adviser if you are considering S corporation status.

TIP

S corporation status can reduce self-employment taxes. There is one area where S corporations do better than LLCs or partnerships: self-employment taxes. Although the current federal tax rules are not specifically written for LLCs, tax experts generally advise their clients that LLC managing owners and managing partners must pay self-employment taxes on their share of business profits. The self-employment tax bite can be hefty: over 15% of taxable income. However, the owners of an S corporation pay self-employment taxes only on compensation (salaries and bonuses) paid to them, not on profits automatically allocated to them as a shareholder. To take advantage of this benefit, some corporate owners elect S corporation tax treatment, then pay themselves a low salary—this means that remaining S corporation profits (which are automatically allocated to the shareholders) are not subject to self-employment tax. This is an aggressive tax strategy, and the IRS may challenge S corporation owners who keep their salaries below a reasonable level simply to avoid self-employment taxes. Again, ask your tax adviser for guidance.

Built-In Organizational Structure

A unique benefit of forming a corporation is the ability to separate management, executive decision making, and ownership into distinct areas of corporate activity. This separation is achieved automatically because of the unique legal roles that reside in the corporate form: the roles of directors (managers), officers (executives), and shareholders (owners). Unlike partnerships and LLCs, the corporate structure comes ready-made with a built-in separation of these three activity levels, each with its own legal authority, rules, and ability to share in corporate income and profits. To understand how this works, consider a couple of examples.

EXAMPLE 1: Myra, Danielle, and Rocco form their own three-person corporation, Skate City, Inc., a skate and bike shop. Storefront access to a heavily used Rollerblade, skating, and bike path makes it popular with local Rollerbladers and cyclists. Needing more cash, the three approach relatives for investment capital. Rocco's brother, Tony, and Danielle's sister, Collette, chip in $30,000 each in return for shares in the business. Myra's Aunt Kate lends the corporation $50,000 in return for an interest-only promissory note, with the principal amount to be repaid at the end of five years.

Here's how the management, executive, and financial structure of this corporation breaks down.

Board of directors. The board manages the corporation, meeting once each quarter to analyze and project financial performance and to review store operations. The board consists of the three founders, Myra, Danielle, and Rocco, and one of the other three investors. Under the terms of Skate City's bylaws, the investor board position is a one-year rotating seat. This year Tony has the investor board seat, next year it goes to Collette, the third year to Aunt Kate—then the pattern repeats. Directors have one vote apiece, regardless of share ownership; this is a common approach for small corporations and one that is legally established in Skate City's bylaws. This means the founders can always get together to outvote the investor vote on the board, but it also makes sure that each of the investors periodically gets to hear board discussions and have a say on major management decisions.

Executive team. The officers of the corporation are charged with overseeing day-to-day business; supervising employees; keeping track of ordering, inventory, and sales activities; and generally putting into practice the goals set by the board. The officers are Myra (president) and Danielle (vice president). Rocco fills the remaining officer positions of secretary and treasurer of the corporation, but this is a part-time administrative task only. Rocco's real vocation—or avocation—is blading along the beach and training to be a professional, touring Rollerblader with his own corporate sponsor (maybe Skate City if profits continue to roll in).

Participation in profits. Corporate profits, of course, are used to pay salaries, stock inventory, pay rent on the storefront, and pay all the other usual and customary expenses of doing business. The two full-time executives, Myra and Danielle, get a corporate salary, plus a year-end bonus when profits are good. Rocco gets a small stipend (hourly pay) for his part-time work. Otherwise, he and the investor shareholders are simply sitting on their shares. Skate City is not in a position yet to pay dividends—all excess profits of the corporation are used to expand the store's product lines and add a new service facility at the back of the store. Even if dividends are never paid, the shareholders know that their stock will be worth a good deal if the business is successful. They can cash in their shares when the business sells or when they decide to sell their shares back to the corporation—or, who knows, if Skate City goes public someday. Aunt Kate, the most conservative of the investment group, will look to ongoing interest payments as her share in corporate profits, getting her capital back when the principal amount of her loan is due.

As you can see from this example, the mechanisms used to put this custom-tailored management, executive, and investment structure into place are built into the Skate City corporation. To erect it, all that is needed is to fill in a few blanks on standard incorporation forms, including stock certificates, and prepare a standard promissory note. To duplicate this structure as a partnership or LLC would require a specially drafted partnership or LLC operating agreement with custom language and plenty of review by the founders and investment group—and, no doubt, their lawyers. The corporate form is designed to handle this division of management, day-to-day responsibilities, and investment with little or no extra time, trouble, or expense.

There is a potential downside to this division of corporate positions and participation in profits. Some businesspeople—particularly those who run a business by themselves or who prefer to run a co-owned business informally—feel that the extra activity levels of corporate operation and paperwork are a nuisance. That's why incorporating may be a bit of an overload for small start-up companies. These may be better and more comfortably served by the less formal business structures of the sole proprietorship or partnership, or, if limited legal liability is an overriding concern, by the LLC legal structure.

EXAMPLE 2: Leila runs a lunch counter business that provides her both a decent income and an escape from the cubicled office environment in which she was once unhappily ensconced. Business has been slow, but Leila has a new idea to give the business more appeal, as well as make it more fun for her. She changes the decor to reflect a tropical motif, installs a saltwater aquarium facing the lunch counter, adds coral reef (metal halide) lighting and light-reflective wall paneling,

and renames the business The Tide Pool. The standard lunch counter fare is augmented with a special bouillabaisse soup entrée and a selection of organic salads and fruit juice drinks, and a seafood and sushi dinner menu is added to cater to the after-work crowd. Leila has her hands full, doing most of the remodeling work herself and preparing the expanded menu each day.

The new operation enjoys great success, and a major newspaper favorably reviews The Tide Pool in an article on trendy eating spots. Patronage increases, so Leila hires a cook and adds three waiters to help her.

A local entrepreneur, Sally, who represents an investment group, asks Leila if she would be interested in franchising other Tide Pools throughout the country. Sally says the investment group would help develop a franchise plan, plus fund the new operation. Leila would be asked to travel to help set up franchise operations for the first year, and she would receive a managerial role and a stake in the new venture.

Leila likes the idea. True, she'll have to get back into the workaday world, but on her own terms, and as a consultant and business owner. Besides, she's not feeling comfortable running the business side of The Tide Pool by herself, and it would be a relief to have the new venture take over. The investment group wants a managerial role in the franchise operation, plus a comprehensive set of financial controls. Leila and the investment group agree to incorporate the new venture as Tide Pool Franchising, Inc. The corporate business structure is a good fit. Leila will assume a managerial role as director of the new company, along with Sally and a member of the venture capital firm. The new firm hires two seasoned small business owners, one as president and one as treasurer, to run the new franchise operation. Business begins with the original Tide Pool as the first franchise, and Leila gets started working for a good salary, plus commission, setting up other franchise locations.

If the new venture makes a go of it, Leila and the investment group can either sell their shares back to the corporation at a healthy profit, or, if growth is substantial and consistent, take the company public in a few years. They will sell their stock in the corporation at a sizable profit, once a market has been established for the corporation's publicly held shares.

This example highlights the flexibility of the corporate form and its ability to provide an infrastructure to handle changes in corporate management and ownership. When you want to redesign your corporate mission and make management and capital changes, the built-in activity layers of the corporation are ready to meet your needs.

Raising Money—Corporate Access to Private, Venture, and Public Capital

Corporations offer a terrific structure for raising money from friends, family, and business associates. There is something special about stock ownership, even in a small business, that attracts others. The corporate structure is designed to accommodate various capital interests. For example, you can:

- issue common, voting shares to the initial owner-employees

- set up a special nonvoting class of shares to distribute to key employees as an incentive to remain loyal to the business, and

- issue a "preferred" class of stock to venture capitalists willing to help fund future expansion of your corporation. (Preferred stock puts investors at the front of the line when dividends are declared or when the corporation is sold.)

Corporate capital incentives also attract creditors who are more willing to help finance a promising corporate enterprise in return for an option to buy shares.

What's more, owners of a small corporation can set their sights someday on making a public offering of shares. Even if your corporation never grows large enough to interest a conventional stock underwriting company in selling your shares as part of a large public offering, you may be able to market your shares to your customers or to individual investors by placing your company's small offering prospectus on the Internet. This strategy has been approved by the federal Securities and Exchange Commission (SEC). And the good news is that no matter how you market your shares, the possibility of handling your own small direct public offering (DPO) is much more available than it was even a few years ago. The reason is that federal and state securities laws have been liberalized to help smaller corporations raise from $1 million to $10 million annually by making a limited public offering of shares.

Of course, raising equity capital by selling stock is not the only way that corporations shine. Incorporated businesses also have an easier time in obtaining loans from banks and other capital investment firms, assuming a corporation's balance sheet and cash flow statements look good. That's partially due to the increased structural formality of the corporation (discussed in the previous section). In addition, loans can be made part of a package where the bank or investment company obtains special rights to choose one or more board members or has special voting prerogatives in matters of corporate management or finance. For example, a lender may require veto power over expenditures exceeding a specified amount. The variety of capital arrangements possible, even for a small corporation, is almost limitless, giving the corporation its well-known knack for attracting outside investment.

EXAMPLE: Rara Avis Investment Group lends Eagle Eye Management Corporation $1 million under the terms of a standard commercial promissory note. However, an added kicker to the deal that helps Rara reach its decision to lend the funds is a warrant agreement (much like a stock option grant) that lets it buy future shares of Eagle at its current low share price of $1. Rara expects Eagle to use the funds wisely to increase corporate profitability and raise its share price well above the current $1 level. If so, Rara will exercise its warrant and buy shares at the $1 price, then sell them for a profit.

TIP

Employees often prefer to work for corporations. Don't forget that key employees are more likely to work for a business that offers them a chance to profit through the issuance of stock options and stock bonuses if future growth is strong—and that these financial incentives are built into the corporate form. See the next section for a brief discussion. (For more details, read Chapter 3, which covers the benefits and tax treatment of each of the main types of employee equity plans.)

Corporate Employee Benefits and Employee Incentives

Another advantage of the corporate structure is that business owners who actually work in the business become employees. This means that you, in your role as an employee, become eligible for reimbursement for medical expenses and up to $50,000 of group term life insurance paid for by your business. These perks are not available to employees of unincorporated businesses. (For further information on standard employee fringe benefits, see "Tax Treatment of Employee Compensation and Benefits" in Chapter 3.)

Owners can also establish tax-favored equity-sharing plans, such as stock option, stock bonus, and stock purchase plans, for nonowner employees. As a corporation grows, these employee equity-sharing plans motivate employees by giving them a piece of the corporate ownership pie—at a low cash cost to the business. (See "Employee Equity Sharing Plans" in Chapter 3 for detailed treatment of each of the most common types of corporate employee equity plans.)

EXAMPLE: Henry incorporates his sole proprietorship, Big Foot Shoes. He now works as a full-time corporate employee, and is entitled to tax-deductible corporate perks. He also attracts talented employees by setting up a qualified incentive stock option (ISO) plan. Under the plan, employees are granted stock options with a strike (purchase) price of $1 per share (their current fair value as determined by the board). Employees pay nothing for the options, and the corporation itself neither pays for nor deducts any money for the option grants. After the options vest, an employee may exercise the option and buy the shares. Then the employee can sell them for a gain—that is, for more than $1 per share—and get taxed at capital gains rates that are lower than standard individual income tax rates. (To do this, the employee must hold the stock options for one year after buying them, and other conditions must be met.)

Perpetual Existence

A corporation is, in some senses, immortal. Unlike a sole proprietorship, partnership, or LLC, which may terminate on the death or withdrawal of an owner, a corporation has an independent legal existence that continues despite changeovers in management or ownership. Of course, like any business, a corporation can be terminated by the mutual consent of

Does It Make Sense to Incorporate Out of State?

You no doubt have heard about the possibility of incorporating in another state, most likely Delaware, where initial and ongoing fees are lower and regulations may be less restrictive than in other states. Does this make sense? For large, publicly held corporations looking for the most lenient statutes and courts to help them fend off corporate raiders, perhaps yes. But for a small, privately held corporation pursuing an active business, our answer is probably no—it is usually a very poor idea to incorporate out of state.

The main reason is that you will probably have to qualify to do business in your home state anyway. This process takes about as much time and costs as much money as filing incorporation papers in your home state in the first place. You'll also need to appoint a corporate agent to receive official corporate notices in the state where you incorporate and open the corporate bank account.

It is also important to realize that incorporating in another state with a lower corporate income tax isn't likely to save you any money. That's because if your business makes money from operations in your home state, even if it is incorporated in another state, you still must pay home-state income taxes on this income.

EXAMPLE: Best Greeting Card, Inc., plans to open a Massachusetts facility to design and market holiday greeting cards throughout the country. If it incorporates in Delaware, it must qualify to do business in Massachusetts, and pay Massachusetts corporate income tax on its Massachusetts operations. It also must hire a registered agent to act on its behalf in Delaware. It decides to incorporate in Massachusetts.

Unless you plan to open up a business with offices and operations in more than one state and, therefore, have a real reason to compare corporate domiciles, you normally should stay where you are and incorporate in your home state. Check with your tax adviser for guidance.

the owners for personal or economic reasons. In some cases it is terminated involuntarily, as in corporate bankruptcy proceedings. Nevertheless, a corporation does not depend for its legal existence on the life or continual ownership interest of a particular individual. This encourages creditors, employees, and others to participate in the operations of the business, particularly as the business grows.

Downsides of Incorporating

Just about everything, including the advantages of incorporating, comes at a price. Let's look at two of the primary disadvantages.

Fees and Paperwork

The answer to the question "How much does it cost?" is an important factor to weigh when considering whether to incorporate your business. For starters, a corporation, unlike a sole proprietorship or general partnership, requires the filing of formation papers—articles of incorporation—with the state business filing office. Incorporation fees are modest in most states—typically, $50 to $100—and fees are commonly based on the number of shares authorized for issuance in your articles. By the way, incorporation, limited partnership, and LLC fees and paperwork are about the same in terms of cost and complexity in most states.

The ongoing paperwork that is necessary to keep your corporation legally current is generally not burdensome. But, unlike other business forms, you must pay particular attention to holding and documenting annual meetings of shareholders and directors, and keeping minutes of important corporate meetings. Creating this paper trail is a good way to show the IRS (in case of an audit) or the courts (in case of a lawsuit) that you have respected the corporate form and are entitled to hide behind its insulating layer of limited personal liability.

Tax Consequences of Corporate Dissolution

A significant downside to forming a corporation is the tax burden that may result from a dissolution or sale of the business. The general rule is that when a corporation is sold or dissolved, both the corporation and its shareholders are subject to the payment of income taxes on assets held by the corporation. Generally, here's how it works.

When a corporation dissolves, the corporation pays tax on the difference between the market value of a corporate asset and its tax basis in the asset. The corporation's basis in the asset is generally what it paid for the asset, minus any depreciation it has deducted on the asset during ownership. Corporations pay taxes on this spread—the difference between market value and the corporation's basis—according to the corporate tax rate schedule.

> **EXAMPLE:** If your corporation buys a building for $400,000 and deducts $100,000 in depreciation during five years of ownership, it has a $300,000 basis in the property. When the company liquidates and sells the building for $500,000, it pays corporate income taxes on the difference between the basis and the sale price—in this case, $200,000.

Now, here's the second part: When the corporation liquidates its assets—that is, converts them to cash to distribute to shareholders—technically, it is buying back its shares of stock from the shareholders. As you probably know, any sale of property by an individual is subject to income tax, and this "stock sale" is no exception. This means that, in the example above, a portion of the $500,000 sales proceeds is taxed again to the shareholders when the corporation distributes cash to them. (Shareholders may qualify for lower capital gains tax rates, rather than individual tax rates, if they held their shares for more than one year. See "Employee Equity Sharing Plans" in Chapter 3.) The taxable amount for each shareholder is determined according to the shareholder's individual basis in that person's shares.

> **EXAMPLE:** Let's assume that Sharon is the sole shareholder of the dissolving corporation from the previous example. Let's also assume she paid $100,000 into her corporation at the beginning to capitalize it. This amount represents her basis in her shares—that is, is the amount she paid for her corporate stock. When Sharon receives $500,000 from the sale of the building, she must pay individual income tax on $400,000 (the $500,000 her corporation distributes to her for her shares, minus her $100,000 basis). Because Sharon owned her shares for more than one year (her corporation existed for five years), she qualifies for capital gains tax rates when she computes how much she pays on the $400,000 taxable amount. (In fact, she probably qualifies for special small business stock rates, as explained in "Tax Concerns When Stock is Sold" in Chapter 3.)

If a business owner incorporates by transferring to the corporation tangible property—such as equipment, land, or a building—the owner gets a basis in stock equal to the owner's existing basis in the transferred assets, instead of cash. (This is governed by Internal Revenue Code Section 351, which applies to the incorporation of most small businesses. See "Tax Treatment When Incorporating an Existing Business" in Chapter 3.)

> **EXAMPLE:** Continuing with our example, assume Sharon transfers a building to her corporation (instead of cash) for her stock. She paid $100,000 for the building, but it is worth $400,000 when she transfers it to her corporation. Her individual basis in her shares is $100,000—the amount she paid for the building—even though she transfers it to her corporation for its current $400,000 market value. When her corporation liquidates and sells the building for $500,000, Sharon pays tax on the $400,000 difference between the $500,000 distributed to her and her $100,000 basis in her shares. What's more, the corporation pays corporate income taxes on $400,000, too. When Sharon transferred the building at the time of incorporation, it received her $100,000 basis in the property as its basis. So when the corporation liquidates the building at the time of dissolution, it pays corporate income tax on $500,000 minus its $100,000 basis in the property ($400,000).

You do not have to master these rules—your tax adviser does. But now you know enough to notice the following: Sharon probably should not have transferred the building to the corporation when she incorporated. Why not? Because, when the building is sold, she pays taxes on $400,000 twice: She pays once as a shareholder, and her corporation pays a second time. Each follows slightly different rules to compute taxable amounts, and each pays at different rates, but each pays tax on the same transaction.

Here are two general points to keep in mind if you think your corporation will own significant assets that are likely to appreciate or otherwise be sold for more than their income tax basis:

- If your business plans to own significant assets that will appreciate, you may save yourself a lot of tax when the business is sold by doing business in an unincorporated form—for example, as an LLC, which also provides limited liability protection.

- If the nontax benefits, such as the corporate capital and employee equity-sharing incentives discussed above, make incorporation a top priority, your tax adviser can help you conduct your incorporation so that existing assets that are likely to appreciate are not transferred to the corporation. For example, you may decide to sell business assets prior to incorporation, then use cash to capitalize the corporation. You will pay tax on the sale of property, but you will avoid the double tax consequences that follow from having your corporation own it. Or you may decide to lease the property to the corporation.

SEE AN EXPERT

Ask your tax adviser before you incorporate about the tax consequences of dissolving your corporation. Ask your tax adviser up front whether a major tax cost is likely when you sell or transfer shares in your corporation or sell its assets later. One of the most important preincorporation services your tax adviser can provide is to make sure that the possible dissolution or sale of your corporation will not result in an unexpectedly hefty tax bill for you or the business. If a huge bill looks unavoidable, your adviser will probably steer you away from incorporating and advise the formation of an LLC instead.

Where Does a Business With a Website or a Web-Based Business Need to Incorporate and Qualify?

Like many businesses, yours probably has a website. Or, your business may operate solely through your website, without a brick-and-mortar operation. In either case, you may be wondering whether the website affects your decision on where to incorporate, and whether you need to "qualify to do business" in other states as well. In addition to incorporating in one state, a corporation may need to qualify to do business in other states where it has significant business contacts (for example, engaging in transactions beyond merely shipping goods into the state).

A business incorporates where the majority of its work and operations take place. This can be a little tricky to figure out when you're running a website-only business. But it's likely that you operate your business website from a physical location, such as your home or an office. Of course, you may use network servers (computers that process requests and deliver data to other computers via the Internet) that are located somewhere else, but you and your employees have a physical setting where you do business related to the website (such as maintaining the site, taking and fulfilling orders, and answering customer email). This location likely represents your primary physical place of business, and most small business owners would reasonably decide to incorporate in the state where this workplace is located.

Now, given that people across the U.S. can load your Web pages into their Internet browser and possibly order merchandise from your site, should you qualify to do business in other states besides the state of incorporation? In most cases, no. The general rule is you don't have to qualify to do business in another state unless you have either a physical presence in that state (such as a sales office or warehouse), or you have certain types of repeated and successive business transactions within that state (for instance, your website enters into agreements with companies in that state).

Of course, this is a very general analysis, and the answer will depend on the location, type, and amount of your company's website-related activity and each state's qualification laws. (If you want to learn more about the issues surrounding operating an Internet business, see Chapter 5 ("Doing Business Out of State") of *LLC or Corporation?*, by Anthony Mancuso (Nolo).)

Business Entity Comparison Tables—Legal, Financial, and Tax Characteristics

	Sole Proprietorship	General Partnership	Limited Partnership	C Corporation	S Corporation	LLC
Who owns business?	sole proprietor	general partners	general and limited partners	shareholders	same as C corporation	members
Personal liability for business debts	sole proprietor personally liable	general partners personally liable	only general partner(s) personally liable	no personal liability for shareholders	same as C corporation	no personal liability for members
Restrictions on kind of business	may engage in any lawful business	may engage in any lawful business	same as general partnership	can't be formed for banking or trust business and other special business	same as C corporation— but excessive passive income (such as from rents, royalties, interest) can jeopardize S tax status	same as C corpo-ration (in a few states, like California, certain professionals cannot form an LLC)
Restrictions on number of owners	only one sole proprietor (a spouse may own an interest under marital property laws)	minimum two general partners	minimum one general partner and one limited partner	one-shareholder corporation allowed in all states	same as C corporation, but no more than 100 shareholders permitted, who must be U.S. citizens or residents	all states allow the formation of one-member LLCs
Who makes management decisions?	sole proprietor	general partners	general partner(s) only, not limited to partners	board of directors	same as C corporation	ordinarily members, or managers if LLC elects manager-management
Who may legally obligate business?	sole proprietor	any general partner	any general partner, not limited partners	officers	same as C corporation	any member if member-managed or any manager if manager-managed
Effect on business if an owner dies or departs	dissolves automatically	dissolves automatically unless otherwise stated in partnership agreement	same as general partnership	no effect	same as C corporation	some LLC agree-ments (and some default provisions of state law) say that LLC dissolves unless remaining members vote to continue business; otherwise LLC auto-matically continues
Limits on transfer of ownership interests	free transferability	consent of all general partners usually required under partnership agreement	same as general partnership	transfer of stock may be limited under securities laws	same as C corporations— but transfers to nonqualified shareholders terminate S tax status	most LLC agree-ments require membership consent to admit new member (absent such consent, transferee gets economic, not voting, rights in the transferor's membership)

Business Entity Comparison Tables—Legal, Financial, and Tax Characteristics (continued)

	Sole Proprietorship	General Partnership	Limited Partnership	C Corporation	S Corporation	LLC
Amount of organizational paperwork and ongoing legal formalities	minimal	minimal required, but partnership agreement recommended	start-up filing required, partnership agreement recommended	start-up filing required; bylaws recommended; annual meetings of directors and shareholders recommended	same as C corporation	start-up filing required, operating agreement recommended
Source of start-up funds	sole proprietor	general partners	general and limited partners	initial shareholders; in some states, shareholders cannot buy shares by promising to perform future services or promising to pay for shares later (promissory notes)	same as C corporation— but cannot issue shares of different classes of stock with different dividend or liquidation rights	members
How business usually obtains additional capital	sole proprietor's contributions; working capital loans backed by personal assets of sole proprietor	capital contributions from general partners; business loans from banks backed by partnership and personal assets of partners	investment capital from limited partners; bank loans guaranteed by general partners	flexible; issuance of new shares to investors, bank loans (backed by personal assets of major shareholders if necessary)	generally same as C corporation —but can't have foreign or entity shareholders and cannot issue special classes of shares to investors (differences in voting rights are allowed)	capital contributions from members; bank loans backed by members' personal assets if necessary
Ease of conversion to another type of business	may change form at will to partnership (if a new owner is added), corporation, or LLC	may change form to limited partnership, corporation, or LLC	may change to corporation or LLC	may change to S corporation by filing simple tax election; change to LLC can involve tax cost	generally same as C corporation— may terminate S tax status to become C corporation, but cannot reelect S status for five years	may change to general or limited partnership or to corporation
Is establishment or sale of ownership interests subject to federal and state securities laws?	generally, no	generally, no	yes	yes	yes	generally, no, if all members are active in the business

Business Entity Comparison Tables—Legal, Financial, and Tax Characteristics (continued)

	Sole Proprietorship	General Partnership	Limited Partnership	C Corporation	S Corporation	LLC
Who generally finds this the best way to do business?	sole owner who wants minimum red tape and maximum autonomy	joint owners who are not concerned with personal liability for business debts	joint owner with passive investors who want limited liability protection and pass-through tax status (and prefer not to form an LLC); some real estate syndicates prefer to set up LPs rather than LLCs because they are accustomed to the LP form	owners who want the limited liability, formal structure, and capital incentives of the corporate form and the ability to split business income to reduce overall income taxes	owners who want the formal structure of the corporation form but want pass-through taxation of business profits (note: owners who want limited liability protection plus pass-through taxation should usually set up an LLC instead of an S corporation); some owners form an S corporation simply to minimize the owner's self-employment taxes	owners who want limited liability legal protection and pass-through taxation of business profits
How business profits are taxed	individual tax rates of sole proprietor	individual tax rates of general partners (unless partnership elects corporate tax treatment) May be eligible for 20% business income deduction	individual tax rates of general and limited partners (unless partnership elects corporate tax treatment) May be eligible for 20% business income deduction	profits are split up and taxed at the 21% corporate rate and individual tax rates of employee-shareholders	individual tax rates of shareholders May be eligible for 20% business income deduction	individual tax rates of members May be eligible for 20% business income deduction
Tax-deductible employee benefits available to owners who work in the business?	generally, no, but owner may deduct medical insurance premiums and establish IRA or Keogh retirement plan	same as sole proprietorship (unless partnership elects corporate tax treatment)	same as sole proprietorship (unless partnership elects corporate tax treatment)	tax-deductible fringe benefits, including corporate retirement and profit-sharing plan as well as tax-favored stock option and bonus plan for employee-shareholders; may reimburse employees' actual medical expenses; group term life insurance also deductible within limits	same as sole proprietorship	same as sole proprietorship (unless LLC elects corporate tax treatment)

Business Entity Comparison Tables—Legal, Financial, and Tax Characteristics (continued)

	Sole Proprietorship	General Partnership	Limited Partnership	C Corporation	S Corporation	LLC
Automatic tax status	yes	yes; can elect corporate tax status by filing IRS Form 8832	yes, on filing certificate of limited partnership with state filing office; can elect corporate tax status by filing IRS Form 8832	yes, on filing articles of incorporation with state filing office	no; must meet requirements and file tax election form (IRS Form 2553)	yes; sole owner LLC automatically treated as sole proprietorship, co-owned LLC as partnership; can elect corporate tax status by filing IRS Form 8832
Deductibility of business losses	generally, owner may deduct losses from active business income on individual tax return	partners active in the business may deduct losses from active business income on individual tax returns	limited partners not active in the business cannot use losses to offset active business income, but may be able to use them to offset other investment income; limited partners normally get the benefit only of nonrecourse debts—those for which general partners are not at risk; check with your tax adviser	corporation, not individual shareholders, deducts business losses; shareholders who sell their stock for a loss may be able to deduct part of the loss from ordinary income	shareholders receive pro rata amount of corporate loss to deduct on their individual income tax returns, subject to special loss limitation rules	generally, same as general partnership, but subject to special rules—see your tax adviser
Tax level when business is sold	personal tax level of owner	personal tax levels of individual general partners	personal tax levels of individual general and limited partners	two levels: shareholders and corporation are subject to tax on liquidation	normally taxed at personal tax levels of individual shareholders, but corporate-level tax sometimes due if S corporation formerly was a C corporation	personal tax levels of individual members

Comparing Business Entities

In the table above, we highlight and compare general and specific legal and tax traits of each type of business entity. Should any of the additional points of comparison seem relevant to your business, we encourage you to talk them over with a legal or tax professional.

Nolo's Small Business Resources

Nolo offers plenty of guidance for small business owners who want to set up a new venture and keep it running smoothly. The best place to start is Nolo's website at www.nolo.com. There, you'll find dozens of free articles to help you do everything from picking a good location to paying taxes. The following sections offer a partial list of Nolo's most popular small business publications.

Starting and Running Your Business

The Small Business Start-Up Kit, by Peri H. Pakroo (national and California editions), helps you launch a business quickly, easily, and with confidence. Among other topics, the book shows you how to write an effective business plan, file for necessary permits and licenses, and acquire and keep good accounting and bookkeeping habits.

Legal Guide for Starting & Running a Small Business, by Fred S. Steingold, is a comprehensive business owner's guide that provides in-depth coverage of topics ranging from raising start-up money and negotiating a lease to adopting the best customer policies, hiring workers, and avoiding legal problems.

Business Buyout Agreements: Plan Now for All Types of Business Transitions, by Anthony Mancuso and Bethany K. Laurence, helps you ensure a smooth transition following the departure of a business partner by writing a buy-sell agreement at the start of your business relationship. The book carefully explains each step of the process, providing all the tax and legal information you need to draft your own agreement.

Tax Savvy for Small Business, by Frederick W. Daily and Jeffrey A. Quinn, lays out year-round tax saving strategies for business owners that show you how to claim all legitimate deductions, maximize fringe benefits, and keep accurate records to avoid trouble with the IRS.

Deduct It! Lower Your Small Business Taxes, by Stephen Fishman, is a comprehensive guide to tax deductions for small business owners.

The Employer's Legal Handbook, by Fred S. Steingold, is a complete, plain-English guide to employee benefits, wage laws, workplace safety, and more.

Nondisclosure Agreements is an online form on the Nolo website (www.nolo.com) that can protect your confidential information from future competitors.

Partnerships

Form a Partnership, by Denis Clifford and Ralph Warner, thoroughly explains the legal and practical issues involved in forming a partnership and shows you how to write a comprehensive partnership agreement.

LLCs

LLC or Corporation? How to Choose the Right Form for Your Business, by Anthony Mancuso. This book explains the different legal and tax rules that apply to each entity and provides examples showing when it makes the most sense to form an LLC or to incorporate instead. The book isn't only relevant at the formation stage—it includes comprehensive treatment of the legal and tax effects of converting from one form of business to another as your business grows.

Nolo's Quick LLC: All You Need to Know About Limited Liability Companies, by Anthony Mancuso, teaches you the basics of limited liability companies and helps you figure out whether forming an LLC is the right thing to do.

Your Limited Liability Company: An Operating Manual, by Anthony Mancuso, shows you how to maintain the legal validity of your LLC. The book explains how to prepare minutes of meetings; record important legal, tax, and business decisions; handle formal record keeping; and set up an LLC records book.

Nonprofit Corporations

How to Form a Nonprofit Corporation, by Anthony Mancuso, shows you step by step how to form and operate a tax-exempt corporation in all 50 states. (California readers should see *How to Form a Nonprofit Corporation in California*, which gives more detailed advice to nonprofiteers in the Golden State.) Both books include step-by-step instructions on how to prepare IRS Form 1023 or 1023EZ—the tax exemption application that must be filed with the IRS.

Starting & Building a Nonprofit: A Practical Guide, by Peri Pakroo, offers nuts-and-bolts advice on issues like finding people to run your organization, holding board meetings, bookkeeping, marketing, and more.

Effective Fundraising for Nonprofits: Real-World Strategies That Work, by Ilona Bray, is a comprehensive guide to fundraising planning and methods, including proposal writing, individual and major donor cultivation, special events, Internet outreach, earned income strategies, planned giving, and more.

Nonprofit Meetings, Minutes & Records, by Anthony Mancuso, shows you how to call, notice, hold, and prepare minutes for your nonprofit corporation's director, committee, and membership meetings.

Running a Corporation

The Corporate Records Handbook, by Anthony Mancuso, shows you how to establish the essential paper trail of your corporation's legal life: corporate meeting minutes. The book contains forms to help you call and document meetings, including more than 80 individual resolutions that you can customize and include in your minutes when appropriate.

RESOURCE

For more information about LLCs. See Nolo's *LLC or Corporation?* by Anthony Mancuso, for a comprehensive comparison of the legal and tax rules that apply to LLCs and corporations and to help you decide which form is better for your business. See *Form Your Own Limited Liability Company*, by Anthony Mancuso (Nolo), for instructions on how to form an LLC in each state, how to prepare an operating agreement, and how to handle all other LLC formation requirements. You can also learn more about LLC formation procedures and fees for your state by visiting your state's business filing office website. (To find the Web address of your state's business filing office, see Appendix A.) ●

How Corporations Work

This chapter introduces you to the structures, procedures, and legal rules you need to know to form a profit-making corporation and keep it running.

To help you understand where a business corporation fits in the corporate landscape, we begin by briefly describing other types of corporations, including nonprofit, professional, and close corporations. Then we cover the basic legal paperwork and procedures that you must undertake to form and operate a business corporation, including the issuance of shares to your initial shareholders. This background information will help you follow the specific instructions we provide in the later chapters for preparing corporate articles, bylaws, and minutes, and making your first stock issuance. This chapter also helps you understand any corporate or securities statutes you may wish to browse in your state's Business Corporation Act or Securities Act.

Understanding and paying corporate taxes is covered in the next chapter, Chapter 3.

Kinds of Corporations

State law classifies and regulates different types of corporations. This book shows you how to form a business corporation (a few states call it a "profit corporation"). Essentially, a business corporation is one that engages in any lawful business that is not specially regulated under state law (such as the insurance, banking, or trust business).

Before discussing the rules that apply to business corporations—the type most readers of this book will want to form—let's look at a few other types of corporations that are set up and operated under special state rules. You must follow unique procedures to form one of these types of corporations, which are not covered in this book.

Domestic Versus Foreign Corporations

When browsing your state's corporate statutes, you may run into the terms domestic corporation and foreign corporation. A domestic corporation is one that is formed under the laws of your state by filing articles of incorporation with the state's corporate filing office. A corporation that is formed in another state, even though it may be physically present and doing business in your state, is classified as a foreign corporation in your state's corporation statutes. In this context, foreign means out of state, not out of the country.

Nonprofit Corporations

A nonprofit corporation (in some states called a not-for-profit corporation) is formed under a state's Nonprofit Corporation Act for nonprofit purposes. In other words, its primary purpose is not to make money for its founders, but to do good work—for example, to establish child care centers, shelters for the homeless, community health care clinics, museums, hospitals, churches, schools, or performing arts groups. Most nonprofits are formed for purposes recognized as tax-exempt under federal and state income tax laws. This means that the nonprofit doesn't have to pay corporate income tax on its revenues, that it is eligible to receive tax-deductible contributions from the public, and that it qualifies to receive grant funds from other tax-exempt public and private agencies.

State law as well as federal tax-exemption requirements typically prohibit a nonprofit corporation from paying out profits to nonprofit members, except in the form of reasonable salaries to those who work for it. When a nonprofit dissolves, the members are normally not allowed to share in a distribution of the nonprofit's assets. Instead, any assets remaining after the nonprofit dissolves must be distributed to another tax-exempt organization. Special types of nonprofits may be recognized under state law that allow people to own, in one fashion or another, corporate assets, so they can receive a portion of these assets when the nonprofit dissolves. For example, a nonprofit homeowners' association or nonprofit trade group may give each member a proprietary interest in the assets of the nonprofit. But these special nonprofits do not enjoy the same benefits as a qualified tax-exempt nonprofit. They may be eligible for an income tax exemption, but they normally do not qualify to receive tax-deductible contributions or public or private grant funds.

Nonprofit corporations, like regular business corporations, have directors who manage the business of the corporation. The nonprofit corporation can also collect enrollment fees, dues, or similar amounts from members. Like regular corporations, a nonprofit corporation may sue or be sued; pay salaries; provide various types of employee fringe benefits; incur debts and obligations; acquire and hold property; and engage, generally, in any lawful activity not inconsistent with its nonprofit purposes and tax-exempt status. It also provides its directors and members with limited liability for the debts and liabilities of the corporation and continues perpetually unless steps are taken to dissolve it.

There are key differences between forming and operating a nonprofit and a regular business corporation:

- To form a nonprofit, in most states you must file special nonprofit articles of incorporation. These are normally available for downloading from your state corporate filing office website. (See your state sheet for contact information.)

- Nonprofit bylaws typically contain provisions similar to those of business corporations. However, nonprofits typically set up a number of special committees to handle nonprofit operations, and nonprofits routinely schedule more frequent meetings of directors than their commercial counterparts. Also, nonprofits replace shareholder provisions with member provisions, which specify the rules for membership meetings and the qualifications, responsibilities, and rights of members. Of course, nonprofit bylaws do not contain provisions relating to payouts of profits (payment of dividends). The state Nonprofit Corporation Act typically follows or is in close proximity to the state Business Corporation Act in the corporate statutes. So you can usually use the citation to your state's Business Corporation Act to help you locate the Nonprofit Corporation Act. (A few states include nonprofit as well as business corporation statutes in a consolidated General Corporation Act.) (See Appendix A for information about locating corporate laws.)

- A critical part of forming and operating a nonprofit is obtaining a federal and state income tax exemption and making sure to operate the nonprofit in a way that meets the tax exemption requirements. The requirements for obtaining a state income tax exemption should be posted on your state tax agency website. (See Appendix A.)

RELATED TOPIC

For more information about nonprofit corporations. For all the forms and instructions you need to organize a nonprofit corporation in your state, including step-by-step instructions on preparing nonprofit articles and bylaws and applying for and obtaining your federal 501(c)(3) nonprofit tax exemption, see *How to Form a Nonprofit Corporation*, by Anthony Mancuso (Nolo). (California readers should see Nolo's *How to Form a Nonprofit Corporation in California*, also by Anthony Mancuso.)

Do-Good LLCs and Corporations

A number of states allow people to form LLCs and corporations that are for-profit, yet exist in order to be socially beneficial. These are known as "hybrid" entities. For example, some states authorize the formation of a "low-profit LLC" (also called an "L3C"), which is a for-profit business entity that has a socially conscious mission, such as supporting education or charitable giving. Ironically, states initially created this hybrid entity to allow foundations to easily distribute funds to a qualified social-purpose organization, but the IRS has not yet formally approved L3Cs for this purpose.

Corporations, too, now have hybrid options in some states. "Flexible purpose corporations" and "benefit corporations" are established to perform good works as well as make money. The advantage of these hybrid entities is that they allow the principals to spend time and money on charitable works, without having to worry about upsetting stakeholders who might sue them for not focusing exclusively on profits.

Because hybrids are profit-making entities, they are not likely to qualify for 501(c)(3) tax-exempt status; this is reserved for organizations that are established and operated exclusively for nonprofit purposes.

Hybrid entities are sometimes mistakenly referred to as "B corporations," which leads people to believe that only these special hybrids are "B corporations." However, the "B corporation" term is nothing more than a label, which refers to a type of certification any corporation or entity (profit, nonprofit, hybrid) can seek.

Specifically, the B corporation term refers to a privately issued certification given by B Labs, which a socially responsible entity can seek to show others that they meet B Labs' certification requirements.

There are many other sustainability certifications available, including GRI (GRI Global Reporting Initiative) and ULE 880 (a sustainability standard developed by UL Environment, an Underwriters Laboratories initiative). You can locate the websites for the organizations that confer B corporation, GRI, and ULE 880 certifications by searching for these terms online. Some of the issues surrounding socially sustainable certification are discussed in more detail in "Answering to a Broader Class of Stakeholders—Do You Need a Socially Sustainable Certification?" (later in this chapter).

Professional Corporations

Most states have special requirements for forming a corporation whose owners will provide state-licensed professional services. The list of particular professions to which these rules apply varies from state to state, but typically lawyers, doctors, other health care professionals, accountants, engineers, and architects must follow these special rules when they incorporate. Other professionals ranging from acupuncturists to massage therapists may also be included.

TIP

How to find out whether you must form a professional corporation. If you plan to form a corporation to render professional services, check your state's corporate filing office website (see Appendix A) to see what professions must incorporate as professional corporations. If this information is not posted, send the office an email asking if your profession must incorporate as a professional corporation. If your profession is not on the state's professional corporation list, you can establish a regular business corporation—the type this book shows you how to form.

Professionals That May Have to Incorporate Under Special Rules

Here is a typical list of professions that must incorporate as professional corporations, rather than as regular business corporations, in many states:

Accountant

Acupuncturist

Architect

Attorney

Audiologist

Clinical social worker

Dentist

Doctor (all medical doctors including surgeons)

Marriage, family, and child counselor

Nurse

Optometrist

Osteopath (physician or surgeon)

Pharmacist

Physical therapist

Physician's assistant

Podiatrist

Psychologist

Shorthand reporter

Speech pathologist, and

Veterinarian.

If your profession is on the professional corporation list in your state, you must file special professional corporation articles of incorporation to form your corporation, not the standard articles for a business corporation discussed in this book. In many states, professional corporation articles are available for downloading from the corporate filing office website. (See Appendix A for information on how to find your state's website.)

In addition to the rules set out in this book that apply to business corporations, the following rules and requirements typically also apply to the formation and operation of professional corporations:

- The name of a professional corporation normally must include a special designator such as "Professional Corporation," "P.C.," or the like, and must meet any additional professional business name requirements imposed by the state licensing board that oversees the profession.

- In addition to professional corporation articles, you may be required to file a certification from the state licensing board showing that all shareholders hold current professional state licenses.

- Generally, the corporation must be formed to render only one professional service, but some professions are allowed to form a corporation to render more than one professional service in related fields. For example, a licensed surgeon may be allowed to incorporate a professional corporation together with a licensed orthopedist.

- The corporation must render professional services only through licensed members, managers, officers, agents, and employees.

- Each licensed professional must carry the amount of liability insurance specified under the rules that apply to the profession.

- Generally, licensed shareholder/employees of professional corporations remain personally liable for their own negligent or wrongful acts, or acts of those under the professional's direct supervision or control, when performing professional services on behalf of the corporation. The limited liability shield of the corporation does, however, normally protect professionals from personal liability for the negligent acts of other professionals in the incorporated professional practice. (And, as for other corporations, the liability shield protects professional shareholders from personal liability for the regular commercial debts and other business liabilities of the corporation.)

The Registered Limited Liability Partnership (RLLP): An Alternate Choice for Professionals

All states allow certain professionals to form a Registered Limited Liability Partnership (RLLP). The RLLP is similar to a regular general partnership, legally and for tax purposes, but it also provides each RLLP partner with the limited liability protection of a professional corporation. Specifically, like a professional corporation, the RLLP gives its partners immunity from personal liability for the malpractice of other partners in the firm—though each professional partner remains personally liable for that partner's own negligence. The RLLP also may protect its owners from personal liability for the regular commercial debts and other liabilities of the business, depending on state law. Owners of an RLLP are taxed individually on business profits (like sole proprietors or nonprofessional partners), while a corporation is a separate taxable entity. If you are considering incorporating a professional practice but may prefer pass-through taxation of business profits, give the RLLP your consideration (and consult your tax adviser). Forms and instructions for creating an RLLP should be available from your state's corporate filing office website. (See Appendix A.)

The Close Corporation

Many states have enacted laws, usually as part of their Business Corporation Act, that allow for the organization of a special type of business corporation, called a "close corporation" or "statutory close corporation." These laws permit corporations with a small number of shareholders —usually no more than 35—to operate without a board of directors according to the terms of a specially prepared shareholders' agreement. In other words, the owners of a close corporation can dispense with normal corporate formalities and operate their corporation under a shareholders' agreement, similar to the way in which owners of a partnership operate their business under the terms of a partnership agreement.

Close Versus Closely Held Corporations: Confusing Legal Jargon Made Simple

Don't confuse the legal term "close corporation," discussed in this section, with the term "closely held corporation." The latter is a loosely used business term, not found in corporate statutes. "Closely held corporation" is usually used to describe any small, privately held corporation owned and operated by a closely knit group of founders, such as a family or small group of business associates. Put another way, a closely held corporation is simply an incorporated small business, not one that has adopted special rules allowing shareholders to proceed without corporate formalities. However, the term closely held corporation does have a special tax meaning. Under Internal Revenue Code §§ 469(j)(1), 465(a)(1)(B), and 542(a)(2), a closely held corporation is defined as one where more than 50% of the value of the corporation's stock is owned by five or fewer individuals during the last half of the corporation's tax year. This special tax classification has no connection to state corporate statutes.

Operating a close corporation under a shareholders' agreement can provide business owners with a great deal of flexibility. For example, the shareholders' agreement can dispense with the need for annual directors' or shareholders' meetings, corporate officers, or even for the board of directors itself, allowing shareholders to manage and carry out the business of the corporation without having to put on their director or shareholder hats. And, as in a partnership, profits can be distributed without regard to capital contributions (stock ownership); thus a 10% shareholder could, for example, receive 25% of the profits (dividends). Special tax rules apply to this sort of special allocation of business profits; your tax adviser can fill you in on the details if you want to know more.

Despite the benefits of informality and flexibility, most incorporators don't want to form close corporations. Indeed, it is estimated that less than 2% of all business corporations are formed as close corporations. Why hasn't the close corporation business form caught on in the states that allow it? There are a number of reasons.

To begin with, most incorporators do not want to operate their corporation under informal or nonstandard close corporation shareholder agreement rules and procedures. In fact, many incorporators form a corporation to rely on the traditional corporation and tax statutes that apply to regular business corporations. (By doing so, they know what is expected of directors, officers, and shareholders—for example, they can simply follow the rules set out in their state Business Corporation Act to call and hold meetings of directors and shareholders without having to design their own procedures.) Second, shares of stock in a close corporation normally contain built-in restrictions on transferability, and most incorporators do not want their shares

to be restricted in this way. Third, it is costly and time-consuming to prepare a shareholders' agreement. It's much simpler and less expensive to adopt standard corporate bylaws.

RELATED TOPIC

For more information about close corporations. Your state corporate filing office website should tell you whether you can form a close corporation in your state and, if so, how to do it. Typically, you must add special provisions to your articles of incorporation to elect close corporation status, prepare and adopt a special shareholders' agreement that follows the requirements set out in your state's Business Corporation Act, and prepare special stock certificates that contain language that limits the transfer of the shares represented by the certificate.

The Business Corporation

This is the type of corporation that this book shows you how to form. In the remainder of this chapter we'll review the statutes (laws), required documents, state offices, and other features on the legal landscape you'll encounter on your way to forming your own business corporation.

Corporate Statutes

Each state has many laws that regulate the organization and operation of a business corporation. The portion that governs most areas of corporate operation is the state's Business Corporation Act (BCA). Appendix A explains how you can locate your state's corporate statutes online. This section simply provides a summary of how the state BCA and other business laws will affect your corporate life and tells you how to locate the laws if you need to look something up.

The Model Business Corporation Act

The basic corporate statutes of many states contain the same, or quite similar, rules for organizing and operating business corporations. The reason for this uniformity is that a number of states have adopted some, most, or all of the provisions of a standard law: the Model Business Corporation Act. The Act undergoes periodic changes, which states are free to enact.

Business Corporation Act

Most of the laws that govern corporations are contained in your state's business corporation statutes, usually titled the "Business Corporation Act" (BCA) or "Business Corporation Law." The BCA spells out the essential rules for forming and operating a corporation. For example, the BCA explains the requirements for preparing and filing articles of incorporation to form the corporation, the rules for preparing and changing corporate bylaws, and the basic rights and responsibilities of corporate directors, officers, and shareholders. The BCA explains when and how directors and shareholders meet to approve corporate decisions, and how much leeway a corporation has in setting its own rules that vary from the BCA requirements. We cover BCA director, officer, and shareholder rules in more detail in the remaining sections of this chapter.

Other Laws

In addition to the Business Corporation Act, other state laws regulate special areas of corporate activity. These include the following:

Securities act or blue-sky law. This law contains each state's rules and procedures for offering, issuing, selling, and transferring shares of corporate stock and other securities within the state. The term "blue-sky law" is derived from the sometimes underhanded, and often colorful, practices of corporate con artists who, in return for an investment in their latest get-rich-quick undertaking, would promise the "blue sky" to unsuspecting investors. The securities laws of each state attempt, through registration and disclosure requirements, to tone down the picture painted by stock promoters to a more realistic hue.

Appendix A shows you how to find the Web address of your state's securities law office, where you can usually find a link to your state's securities law.

For more information on securities laws and procedures, see "Stock Issuance and the Securities Laws," below.

State Tax or Revenue Code. Most states impose corporate income or franchise taxes that are based on the amount of taxable income earned in the state by a corporation. Your corporation pays these taxes in addition to federal IRS income taxes. Each state's Tax or Revenue Code typically contains the state's income or franchise tax rules.

Tax statutes are even more off-putting than legal statutes. We think you'll get the most useful information directly from your state's tax publications, forms, and other instructions posted on your state's tax agency website. Appendix A shows you how to find your state's tax office online.

Other state and local laws. Other state laws affect the operations of all businesses, whether or not they are incorporated. For example, state and local building codes, professional and occupation licensing, environmental laws, local ordinances, zoning laws, and other laws and regulations may apply to your business and its operations.

RELATED TOPIC

Laws that apply when forming a business. For an excellent resource on the various state laws and regulations that apply to forming all types of businesses, corporate and noncorporate, see *The Small Business Start-Up Kit*, by Peri H. Pakroo (Nolo), available in both national and California editions.

Corporate Filing Offices

Each state has a corporate filing office where you file paperwork (and pay fees) to create or dissolve a corporation. Typically, this filing office handles all state business filings, including limited partnership and limited liability company (LLC) filings as well as business corporation and nonprofit corporate filings. Throughout this book, we refer to the office that accepts corporate filings as *the corporate filing office.* Typically, the official name of this office is the Corporations Division of the Secretary (or Department) of State. The main corporate filing office is located in each state's capital city. Some states maintain branch offices in secondary cities as well.

Appendix A explains how to locate your state's corporate filing office online. The best way to obtain the latest corporate filing and fee information and the latest corporate filing forms is to visit your state's corporate filing office website. Most state corporate filing office websites provide corporate statutory forms such as Articles of Incorporation, Amendment of Articles, Change of Registered Agent, or Registered Office Address, and the like. Many state websites also contain links to the state's corporate tax office and state employment, licensing, and other agencies.

TIP

For a faster response, contact the filing office via email. Corporate filing offices typically respond to email inquiries much faster than they respond to snail mail or telephone messages. (It's not uncommon to have to wait a day or more to get a telephone call through to a busy state filing office.) In short, if your question is not answered on the filing office website, send the office an email inquiry. (You will find the email address on the state filing office website.)

Corporate Documents

The primary corporate legal documents are articles of incorporation, bylaws, stock certificates, and minutes of meetings. This section introduces you to each in turn.

Articles of Incorporation

The key corporate organizing documents are the articles of incorporation. In some states, the articles go by a different name, such as the corporate charter or certificate of incorporation. A corporation comes into existence when its articles of incorporation are filed with the state corporate filing office. *The filing of articles is the only legal filing necessary to create a corporate entity.* However, you'll want to follow up after filing articles by preparing and adopting bylaws, holding a first meeting of directors, and issuing stock to your initial shareholders. These additional steps are necessary to make sure the legal organization of your corporation is complete.

The articles normally contain basic structural information, such as the name of the corporation, the names and addresses of its directors, its registered agent and registered office address, and the corporation's capital stock structure. The information that must be included is typically established by a section of the state Business Corporation Act titled "Contents of Articles of Incorporation." Standard state articles forms contain all required provisions. State articles statutes also normally list optional provisions that you can include in your articles, such as provisions to implement a complex stock structure with different classes or series of shares. (We discuss adding optional provisions to articles in Chapter 4.)

EXAMPLE: The Equine Equity Investors Corporation adds an optional provision to its articles that sets up a multiclass stock structure consisting of Class A Voting shares and Class B Nonvoting shares. Another optional provision is added that requires a vote of two-thirds of each class of stock for the approval of amendments (changes) to the corporation's articles or bylaws.

Most corporate filing office websites provide a downloadable, ready-to-use articles of incorporation form that you can use to establish your business corporation. This book provides an articles form for use in Iowa and Nebraska, the only states that do not offer a standard articles form. For those two states, we include specific instructions to help you fill in the forms.

Bylaws

After articles of incorporation, a corporation's bylaws are its second-most important document. You do not file bylaws with the state. They are an internal document that contains rules for holding corporate meetings and carrying out other formalities according to state corporate laws. Bylaws typically specify

how often the corporation must hold regular meetings of directors and shareholders, as well as the call, notice, quorum, and voting rules for these meetings. Also, bylaws usually contain the rules for setting up and delegating authority to special committees of the board of directors, the rights of directors and shareholders to inspect corporate records and books, the rights of directors and officers to insurance coverage or indemnification (reimbursement by the corporation for legal fees and judgments) in the event of lawsuits, plus a number of other standard legal provisions.

Use Bylaws Instead of Articles for Corporate Operating Rules

Some states let corporations choose whether to place corporate operating rules and procedures in the articles of incorporation or bylaws. It's always better to use the bylaws because you can change them easily—without the need for filing your changes with the state. For example, many states allow you to place super majority quorum or voting rules for directors' or shareholders' meetings in either document. If you use the bylaws for this purpose, you can change these provisions by amending your bylaws at a directors' or shareholders' meeting. But if you put these provisions in your articles after the directors or shareholders approve the changes, you must file a formal amendment to the articles with your state's corporate filing office.

Many of the procedures set out in corporate bylaws are controlled by statutes in your state's Business Corporation Act. For example, most states require corporations to hold an annual meeting of shareholders to elect or reelect the board of directors to a one-year term of office. In your bylaws, you set the date of this annual meeting. Similarly, most states require written notice of shareholders' meetings to be delivered to each shareholder no less than ten nor more than 60 days prior to the date of the meeting. In your bylaws, you can specify the exact number of days required for providing notice of shareholders' meetings. If you do, your notice period must fall within this ten-to-60-day range.

This book provides fill-in-the-blanks bylaws (see Appendixes B and C) that you can use for your corporation.

Stock Certificates

A new corporation issues stock to its founders and initial investors. Stock ownership is usually documented by stock certificates given to each shareholder. Today, many states do not require the actual completion and delivery of paper stock certificates to shareholders, but we think it continues to make sense to issue certificates. A stock certificate is tangible evidence of a person's ownership rights in your corporation, and most founders and investors expect to receive one after buying shares in a new corporation.

State law sets out the very basic content requirements for stock certificates. Normally, the minimum information necessary is the name of the corporation, the state where the corporation was formed, the name and number of shares issued to the shareholder, and the signature of two corporate officers. We provide ten stock certificates. (See Appendixes B and C.) Blank certificates that comply with your state's requirements may be available in local stationery stores. If you want custom-printed certificates, a local legal printer will prepare your certificates for a higher cost. We provide specific information on how to issue the initial shares of your corporation in "Sale and Issuance of Stock," below.

Minutes of the First Directors' Meeting

After filing articles and preparing bylaws, the initial board of directors meets to formally approve the bylaws, approve the issuance of stock to initial shareholders, appoint corporate officers, and handle other essential corporate start-up tasks. If the initial members of the board are not named in the articles, the incorporator—the person who signed and filed your articles—prepares a written "Incorporator Statement" in which the incorporator appoints the initial board members prior to its first meeting. Once the board has been named— either in the filed articles or the incorporator statement—the board of directors can hold its first meeting. The actions taken by the board at its first meeting should be documented by written minutes that are filed in the corporate records book.

Chapter 4 of this book shows you how to prepare an incorporator statement (if you need one) and minutes of your first board meeting. (This book contains forms you can use for both purposes.)

RESOURCE

For help with corporate minutes. For simple forms that you can use to record subsequent board and shareholders' meetings, together with more than 80 resolutions you can adopt to handle the approval of standard legal, business, and tax decisions reached at these meetings, see Nolo's *The Corporate Records Handbook*, by Anthony Mancuso.

Corporate Powers

Each state's Business Corporation Act gives business corporations carte blanche to engage in any lawful business activity. In legalese, "lawful" doesn't just mean noncriminal; it means not otherwise prohibited by law. Generally this means that a corporation can do anything that a natural person can do. However, in most states, it is not lawful for a regular business corporation to engage in the banking, trust, or insurance business. If you want to set up one of these special financial corporations, you will need to follow special procedures—for example, obtain the written approval of your state's banking or insurance commission, and prepare and file special articles of incorporation with the state.

Here's a partial list of things that a business corporation may do. These powers do not need to be listed in your articles and bylaws:

- Engage in any lawful business.

- Adopt, amend, and repeal bylaws.

- Qualify to do business in any other state, territory, dependency, or foreign country.

- Issue, purchase, redeem, receive, or otherwise acquire, own, hold, sell, lend, exchange, transfer, or otherwise dispose of, pledge, use, and otherwise deal in and with its own shares, bonds, and other securities.

- Assume obligations, enter into contracts, incur liabilities, borrow and lend money, or otherwise use its credit, and secure any of its obligations, contracts, or liabilities by mortgage, pledge, or other encumbrance of all or any part of its property, franchises, and income.

- Make donations for the public welfare or for community fund, hospital, charitable, educational, scientific, or civic or similar purposes. (Like individuals, business corporations are allowed to make charitable donations.)

- Establish and carry out pension, profit-sharing, stock-bonus, share-pension, share-option, savings, thrift, and other employee retirement, incentive, and benefit plans.

- Participate with others in any partnership, joint venture, or other association, transaction, or arrangement of any kind, whether or not such participation involves the sharing or delegation of control with, or to, others.

- Adopt, use, and alter a corporate seal. (A corporate seal is simply a stamped or embossed design showing the name of the corporation and its state of formation.) Although state law does not require the use of a corporate seal, some corporations use the seal on formal corporate documents, such as stock certificates, to signify formal approval of the document by the corporation.

TIP

Your corporation can engage in more than one line of business. Although state BCAs don't specifically say so, it is clear that a business corporation can engage in as many lines of business as management sees fit. You do not need to set up a separate corporation for each line of business.

Corporate People

While a corporation is considered a legal "person," capable of making contracts, paying taxes, and otherwise enjoying the legal rights and responsibilities of a natural person, of course it needs real people to carry out its business. State BCAs classify corporate people in the following ways:

- incorporators
- directors
- officers, and
- shareholders.

As we explain below, state statutes—and occasionally courts—give each of these corporate people different rights and responsibilities.

One Person Can Wear Several Corporate Hats

In all states, one person may simultaneously serve in more than one corporate capacity. For example, if you form your own one-person corporation (most states allow this), you necessarily will be your corporation's only incorporator, director, and shareholder, and you will fill all the required corporate officer positions. Exception: In a handful of states, the corporate president and secretary offices must be filled by different individuals. Check your state's filing office website to see whether your state follows this specific rule, or look under "Number of Officers" in your state's Business Corporation Act. (See Appendix A.)

In all states, a business corporation may have just one director and one shareholder. However, in some states, the number of directors cannot be less than the number of shareholders if the corporation has three or fewer shareholders. In these states, if your corporation has three or more shareholders, you must have at least three directors, and if you have two shareholders, you need at least two directors. If you have just one shareholder, then you could have just one director. Check your state's filing office website. The state-specific instructions for creating Articles of Incorporation should contain this information.

Don't Start Business Until You File Articles

If you act as an incorporator for your corporation and do not limit your activities to preparing and filing articles, be careful. State courts usually say that a corporation is not bound by the incorporator's contracts with third parties prior to actual formation of the corporation, unless the contracts are later ratified by the board of directors or the corporation accepts the benefits of a contract—for example, uses office space under a preincorporation lease signed by an incorporator. Worse, the incorporator may be personally liable on these preincorporation contracts unless the incorporator signs the contract in the name of the corporation only and clearly informs the third party that the corporation does not yet exist, may never come into existence, and, even if it does, may not ratify the contract.

So, a suggestion: If you must arrange for office space, hire employees, or borrow money before you form the corporation, make it clear that any commitments you make are for and in the name of a proposed corporation and are subject to ratification by the corporation when, and if, it comes into existence.

The other party may, of course, refuse to do business with you under these conditions and tell you to come back after the corporation is formed. Again, this is usually the best approach to preincorporation business, anyway—namely, to postpone business until after your articles have been filed and approved by the state. Once this happens, all contracts should be signed in the name of the corporation by a corporate director, officer, or employee. (See "How to Sign Corporate Documents From Now On" at the end of Chapter 4.)

Incorporators

Your incorporator is the person who signs your articles of incorporation and files them with state corporate filing office. The incorporator is not required to be an initial director, officer, or shareholder of the corporation—nor must the incorporator be a resident of the state. The only legal requirement for incorporators is that, in many states, the incorporator must be at least 18 years old.

Even though it is not required, we recommend that you pick one of your initial board members as your incorporator. This helps to ensure that the entire board of directors, which must pick up the reins of management immediately after the corporation is formed, is in the corporate formation loop right from the start. It also means that any correspondence between your new corporation and the state corporate filing office will reach at least one director.

Directors

Under each state's Business Corporation Act, directors are given the authority and responsibility for managing the corporation. Let's look at some of the common features of state law that apply to directors.

Director Qualifications

State law does not impose residency or stock ownership requirements on directors. Your directors can come from any state and need not be shareholders. The only director requirement in some states is an age requirement—in these states, directors usually must be at least 18 years old (which is a good idea anyway, to make sure your director can legally make decisions).

When Do Directors Meet?

In a small, closely held corporation, the directors meet mostly to satisfy the state BCA's minimal meeting requirements. This normally means an annual meeting at which the newly elected or reelected board members accept their positions for the upcoming year and approve appropriate business objectives or strategies for the upcoming year. Many small boards also call special meetings during the year to conduct business in a formal setting, or when board approval must be sought under the BCA to make legal decisions, such as amendments to corporation articles or bylaws, issuance of corporate shares, declarations of dividends, appointments of officers, and the like. Other items of business necessary to run the corporation from day to day are normally handled by board members outside the boardroom in their capacities as corporate officers or in other supervisory corporate capacities. The holding of a minimal number of board meetings is the rule in sole-owner or family-managed corporations.

In larger corporations the board typically meets more frequently to review corporate performance and goals, not just to satisfy state BCA legal requirements. For example, the board of a larger corporation may meet quarterly or even monthly to discuss corporate policies and objectives and to establish and hear back from board committees. Since members of larger boards often come from outside corporations and financial institutions that have invested in the corporation, frequent meetings of the board help the corporations keep these investor representatives informed on current corporate performance.

The directors meet and make decisions collectively as the board of directors. In all states, the board may consist of one or more individuals. Many state BCAs specifically say that a director must be a natural (real) person, as opposed to another corporation or limited liability company (LLC). Even if your state's BCA doesn't say this, it is understood in all states that only real people may be elected as board members.

Director Meetings

In most states, directors must meet at least once each year. One reason for this requirement is that most state BCAs specify that directors must be elected (or reelected) for a one-year term at an annual meeting of shareholders. (See "Shareholders," below.) Once the board is voted in or continued in office at the annual shareholders' meeting, the newly elected or reelected board holds its annual meeting. At this meeting, board members accept their election to the board, then transact any business planned for the meeting.

The date, time, and place of the annual directors' meeting is normally specified in the bylaws. State BCAs usually allow the annual meeting to be held without having to give each director prior written notice of the meeting, but we think it's a good idea to provide written notice of all meetings, including annual board meetings. Directors, particularly newly elected ones, may not note or remember the annual director meeting date specified in the bylaws. Of course, boards often meet more frequently than once per year, particularly in larger corporations with multimember boards. (See "When Do Directors Meet?" above.)

Additional meetings are called special meetings. State law typically requires that directors receive written notice of the date, place, and purpose of all special meetings of directors.

Director Voting

Under state law, board members are given one vote each when making board decisions at directors' meetings. The BCA in most states normally sets the quorum requirement for board meetings—that is, the number of directors who must be present to hold a board meeting—at a majority of the full board. However, in most states, your bylaws can change this default rule and specify a greater- or less-than majority quorum rule for directors' meetings. State law also typically provides a majority-voting rule for the approval of board decisions at a meeting. This means that the board approves decisions at a meeting by the "yes" vote of at least a majority of the directors present at the meeting. Again, this majority rule is usually a default state rule; you are normally allowed to specify a different director approval rule in your bylaws.

> **EXAMPLE:** Tie-Dyed RetroFitters, Inc., is a retro clothing store owned and managed by its four founders. The corporate bylaws establish a four-person board, with a quorum for board meetings specified as a majority of the authorized number of directors. Therefore, to hold a directors' meeting, three of the four directors must attend. A majority of those present at a meeting must approve a decision—remember, at a minimum, a quorum must be present. If all four board members attend a meeting, three directors must approve a decision proposed at the meeting. If a minimum quorum of three attends, then two of the three must approve a decision proposed at the meeting.

CAUTION

Some states set a minimum quorum requirement for directors. In many states, your bylaws cannot establish a quorum of directors that is less than one-third the number of the full board. Look up your state's BCA in a section labeled "Directors' Meetings" to find out your state's minimum director quorum rule.

In addition to approving decisions at meetings, directors can also take action by written consent. Under state BCAs, this written voting procedure is allowed for all types of director action—that is, any type of action that directors can approve by voting in person at a real meeting. This means that the directors can individually or collectively date and sign a form that says they approve a particular item of business, without the need to hold a face-to-face meeting. State BCAs normally require the signature of *all* directors on a written consent form of this sort—obtaining the signed consent of a simple majority of directors is not sufficient under most state statutes. Look in your state BCA for a section with the title "Directors' Action by Written Consent" or "Directors' Action Without a Meeting" to see how many directors must sign a written consent form in your state.

Board Committees

In smaller corporations, the owners who also run the corporation as officers or other supervisory personnel make up the full board of directors. In larger corporations, the board may include individuals who are not involved with day-to-day corporate operations. These outside directors, who may be representatives of venture capital groups or financial institutions that have provided capital or financing to the corporation, rely heavily on reports of board committees to get the information necessary to make good decisions. For example, the compensation committee of a larger corporation may report regularly to the board to propose the granting of salary increases, bonuses, and stock options to deserving corporate employees. Similarly, a special finance committee may be established by the board to review corporate performance in one or more lines of its business.

State BCAs recognize the need for these committees to help the board get its work done. Here is a typical statute:

> *In performing the duties of a director, a director shall be entitled to rely on information, opinions, reports, or statements, including financial statements, prepared or presented by a committee of the board, as to matters within its designated authority, which committee the director believes to merit confidence.*

The above statute is typical in that it allows directors to rely on committees *if* the director is satisfied that a committee report merits confidence. State BCAs also allow a board to delegate its managerial authority to special types of committees, called executive committees of the board. These are committees made up of two or more board members, and often other corporate personnel such as officers, that take responsibility for one or more areas of board decision making. Larger corporations may set up one or more committees of this sort to handle ongoing areas of corporate management. The full board may meet less frequently to review overall corporate policy, while the committees of the board meet regularly to handle their assigned areas of responsibility.

State law limits the types of authority that can be delegated to an executive committee of the board. Typically, an executive committee cannot, without full board concurrence, amend the articles or bylaws, approve a corporate dividend, or take other specified major corporate actions. Here is a typical BCA statute covering executive committees:

Executive Committees of the Board: The board may, by resolution adopted by a majority of the authorized number of directors, designate one or more committees, each consisting of two or more directors, to serve at the pleasure of the board. Any such committee, to the extent provided in the resolution of the board or in the bylaws, shall have all the authority of the board except with respect to: (1) the approval of any action which also requires the approval of shareholders; (2) the filling of vacancies on the board; (3) the fixing of compensation of directors for serving on the board or any committee of the board; (4) a distribution by the corporation [typically, this is defined elsewhere in the Act as a dividend or other payment out of the profits and earnings of the corporation to shareholders]; *and (5) the establishment of other committees of the board or appointment of members to these other committees.*

Despite the restrictions, executive committees are permitted to handle a variety of corporate decision-making matters, including hiring and payroll decisions, corporate projects and operations, and a variety of management and overview tasks that would otherwise be handled by the full board.

Directors' Duties

Directors are required under state BCA statutes to exercise care in making management decisions and act in the best interests of the corporation. If a court decides that a director has violated these duties, the director may be held personally liable for any resulting financial loss to the corporation or its shareholders.

Duty of Care

The first and foremost duty owed by a director to a corporation is the statutory "duty of care."

Appointing an Executive Committee to Handle Employee Compensation

Designating a special executive committee of the board to handle employment compensation and payroll tax decisions can have a collateral tax benefit: It helps insulate directors who do not serve on the committee from personal liability for any unpaid corporate payroll taxes. We've already mentioned that potential personal liability for tax debts is one of the exceptions to corporate limited liability. (See "The Corporation" in Chapter 1.) Here's how this exception works.

Federal tax law permits the IRS and state income and payroll tax agencies to aggressively seek to collect unpaid corporate payroll taxes from "responsible persons" in a corporation. In its collection efforts, the IRS often claims that board members who approve of compensation to corporate employees, or specifically approve paying taxes to the IRS or state, are personally responsible for income or payroll taxes not paid by the corporation. Whether the IRS wins these arguments depends on the overall facts and the extent of a director's involvement in running the corporation. In a small, closely held corporation, it's difficult for a board member who also serves as a principal corporate officer to deny being a responsible person—after all, the board member probably has the power to make the corporation pay its taxes if it has the funds to do so. But in a larger corporation with outside directors on its board, the outside directors are less likely to be viewed as "responsible persons" if compensation and tax decisions are delegated to a special compensation or finance committee consisting of the more active board members. This helps them avoid personal liability in case of a payroll tax deficiency or dispute.

Here is a typical state BCA statute that defines, in general terms, a director's duty of care:

A director must act in good faith, in a manner the director believes to be in the best interests of the corporation and its shareholders and with such care, including reasonable inquiry, as an ordinarily prudent person in a like position would use under similar conditions.

This is a very broad standard. Courts interpret it to mean that a director is allowed to make mistakes that lead to financial loss for the corporation and its shareholders without fear of personal legal liability, as long as the director had good reason for making the decisions. And, as discussed in "Board Committees," above, one good reason may be that the director relied on the apparently reliable reports of a board committee.

The duty of care Is normally easy to fulfill. The standard for the directors' duty of care is fairly lenient. A director has to be negligent (careless), almost to the point of flagrant inattention or fraudulent disregard of the financial implications of board decisions, to violate the statutory standards. And in small corporations, even if the standard is violated, personal liability problems are rare. This is because the people who have legal standing to seek damages for a director's violation of the duty of care are those whose have been harmed financially by a director's bad decision making—namely, its shareholders. In a closely held corporation where all board members also are the corporation's only shareholders, it is unlikely that one director will sue another. But it's not unheard of, particularly if one or more directors officially disagreed with a corporate decision they felt was too risky and wrongheaded—and the value of their shares was diminished significantly because of it. But even if the disgruntled director-shareholders do bring suit against the other directors on behalf of the corporation, they will win only if they can convince a court that the directors had little or no business reason for their decision or that they made it simply to further their own personal financial interests, not those of the corporation.

In larger corporations with shareholders who are not members of the board of directors, chances increase that a disgruntled shareholder who has no voice in management may decide that the directors acted wrongly and should be held accountable for a major loss of share value. Even so, shareholder suits that seek to impose personal liability on a director are infrequent. They most often arise when a corporation is on the auction block—that is, when it is being sold or merged with another corporation. For example, courts have held the board personally liable to the shareholders for agreeing to a sale favored by a leading board member if the board did not adequately investigate the current market value of the corporation and seek counteroffers to the proposed sale.

CAUTION

How to avoid trouble. As a director, a court is more likely to find you in violation of your duty of care if you do not bother to attend and participate in board meetings, obtain information about the likely financial consequences of a board decision, or check alternative courses of action before going forward with an action that can affect share value. In other words, don't miss board meetings or simply attend and rubber-stamp proposals brought up by other board members for consideration, particularly if the decision involves a major commitment of corporate funds or resources. Another way of saying all of this is that it's okay for you to approve board decisions that put corporate capital or share values at risk as long as you are reasonably aware of the nature of these risks and decide they are worth taking to achieve a valid corporate business objective.

Many state BCAs underline the importance of a director's paying full attention to corporate decision making, rather than merely sitting back and letting others muscle their pet projects past the board. Under many BCAs, a director present at a meeting during which an action is approved is legally considered to have approved all decisions reached at the meeting unless the director speaks up and votes "no" to the decision or specifically requests that his or her dissent or abstention be entered in the minutes (or hands the chairperson a written abstention to the proposal).

Here's a typical statute that stresses the importance of taking an active stance as a director:

A director who is present at a meeting of the board of directors when corporate action is taken is deemed to have assented to all action taken at the meeting unless:

(a)   The director objects at the beginning of the meeting, or promptly upon his or her arrival, to holding the meeting or transacting business at the meeting and does not thereafter vote for or assent to any action taken at the meeting;

(b)   The director contemporaneously requests that his or her dissent or abstention as to any specific action taken be entered in the minutes of the meeting; or

(c)   The director causes written notice of his or her dissent or abstention as to any specific action to be received by the presiding officer of the meeting before adjournment of the meeting or by the corporation promptly after adjournment of the meeting.

EXAMPLE: A trustee in bankruptcy sued to recover from the estate of a corporate director a large sum paid as "loans" to the director's sons, who also sat on the board of a successful banking and insurance business. The court agreed that even though the director had not personally received the funds, she should not have deferred to the decisions of her sons without making her own inquiries. She had a duty to question any payouts made by the corporation, to examine financial statements, and to learn the requirements of corporate and insurance law that limited the making of the excessive insider loans. The court held the director's estate liable for payback of the loans, saying that "ornamental" or so-called "dummy" directors have the same responsibility to actively and attentively protect corporate assets as all active board members. (*Francis v. New Jersey Bank*, 87 N.J. 15, 432 A.2d 814 (1981).)

Some state statutes provide extra protection from shareholder suits. In recognition of the increased willingness of shareholders and their attorneys to sue directors—particularly when share values fall following action by the board—many state legislatures have added special director immunity provisions to their BCAs to help directors avoid personal liability when shareholders launch legal challenges to corporate management. This additional help comes in the form of special BCA provisions that let a corporation place language in its articles that limits or eliminates all personal liability of the board to the corporation or shareholders except in a few special cases. Typically, immunity cannot be provided where the board has acted unlawfully or where it can be shown the director purposefully acted against the best interests of the corporation or otherwise in flagrant disregard of the director's statutory duty of care.

If a state's BCA contains a provision of this sort, you'll likely find it in the section that specifies the optional provisions that may be included in your Articles of Incorporation. Here's a typical provision, extracted from California's "Articles of Incorporation—Optional Provisions" statute (California General Corporation Law, § 204(a)(10)):

The Articles of Incorporation may set forth provisions eliminating or limiting the personal liability of a director for monetary damages in an action brought by or for or in the right of the corporation for breach of a director's duties to the corporation and its shareholders, provided, however, that such a provision may not eliminate or limit the liability of directors (1) for acts or omissions that involve intentional misconduct or a knowing violation of law, (2) for acts or omissions that a director believes to be contrary to the best interests of the corporation or its shareholders or that involve the absence of good faith on the part of the director, (3) for any transaction for which the director derived an improper personal benefit, (4) for acts or omissions that show a reckless disregard for the director's duty to the corporation or its shareholders in circumstances in which the director was aware, or should have been aware, in the ordinary course of performing a director's duties, of a risk of serious injury to the corporation or its shareholders, or (5) for acts or omissions that constitute an unexcused pattern of inattention that amounts to an abdication of the director's duty to the corporation or its shareholders.

Again, it is probably unnecessary for a small business corporation where all shareholders will serve on the board of directors to adopt this type of provision. However, if you are worried about shareholder suits against your board—perhaps because you plan to have outside shareholders who may question risky policies the board must implement to achieve success in a competitive market—you may wish to look at your state BCA for this sort of director immunity provision. Adding this type of provision to your articles also makes sense if you want to reassure outsiders who serve on your board that they have the maximum legal protection possible. If you find an immunity statute in your state BCA, you can add the required language to your articles. A lawyer familiar with your state's BCA can help you get the job done right. (See Chapter 6.)

Duty of Loyalty

In addition to a director's statutory duty of care, state courts also say that a director has a duty of loyalty to the corporation. This duty of loyalty means a director must give the corporation a right of first refusal as to business opportunities the director becomes aware of while serving the corporation. If the corporation fails to take advantage of the opportunity after the board member discloses it, or if the corporation clearly would not be interested in it, the director can pursue it.

The duty of loyalty is simply a matter of fair dealing and common sense. No one wants a board member to take personal commercial advantage of an opportunity that arises within the corporate context unless the corporation itself is given first shot at it. If a board member violates the duty of loyalty, he or she can be held personally liable for the value of the commercial opportunity lost by the corporation.

EXAMPLE: A corporate director, who also works as an officer, is researching sites for new corporate headquarters when he discovers land being offered at a ridiculously low price. He buys the land for himself to launch his own sideline business without first reporting back to the full board and letting it decide whether to make an offer on the property. A court finds the director personally liable to the corporation for the value of the bargain the director appropriated for himself—that is, the difference between the bargain sales price and the higher prevailing market price the corporation ended up paying.

The duty of loyalty issue rarely presents a problem in a small corporation context where all directors are actively involved in the destiny of the corporation on a full-time basis; they don't have outside business interests that conflict with their corporation But in larger corporations with outside board members who have separate commercial interests, conflicts may more easily arise. For example, a board member with an outside business may discover a business opportunity that presents itself at a board meeting or as part of the reports or information the director reviews. This opportunity may provide a possible advantage to the director's outside business, as well as the corporation's. In this situation, board members can't blithely go ahead and use the opportunity for their outside business without first telling the board that they are interested in doing so and seeking the board's permission.

Conflicts of Interest

If you browse your state BCA, you'll probably find a law under the "Directors" heading that deals with board approval of transactions in which a director has a financial interest—for example, approval by the board of a lease of commercial real estate owned by a director. The title of this section may be "Directors' Conflict of Interests," "Board Approval of Self-Interested Transaction," or a similar title.

Throughout the states, these conflict of interest statutes share common provisions and features. In most states, the statute says that the full board is allowed to approve corporate business decisions that financially benefit one or more directors, as long as certain formalities are carried out. Typically, one way to approve such transactions is by the affirmative votes of a sufficient number of disinterested directors (those who will not benefit from the deal) after disclosure of the personal benefit to the interested director. The number of required votes is usually defined by statute as a majority of the full board without counting the vote of the interested director. (Most states allow you to count the interested director for purposes of obtaining a quorum for the meeting, but not to approve the deal.) Of course, in a small corporation it may not be possible to find a sufficient number of disinterested directors. For example, if two members of a three-person board financially benefit from a deal, the vote of the remaining one director will not constitute a majority of the full board.

Most states also allow the shareholders to approve a transaction that benefits a director. After full disclosure of the benefit to the director is made at a shareholders' meeting, a majority of shareholders must approve the transaction, not counting the votes of any shareholders who may benefit from the transaction. Again, in a small corporation, it may be difficult to obtain a sufficient number of disinterested shareholder votes, since the benefited directors may own most of the corporation's shares. Fortunately, most state statutes provide a third way to validate the decision. This alternative simply requires that the deal be fair to the corporation at the time it was approved by the board, even if it was approved in part by directors (or shareholders) who stand to benefit financially from the transaction.

Here are some points to keep in mind when considering rules relating to conflicts of interest:

- These rules normally come into play only if a board decision is later challenged in court by a disgruntled shareholder who sues the benefited director on behalf of the corporation. Typically, the suit will demand the benefited director pay back the amount of the undeserved benefit to the corporation—plus interest, legal fees, court costs, and possibly punitive damages. If your small corporation does not have outside shareholders, you do not need to worry about shareholder suits, provided all your director-shareholders agree to the decision.

- If your deal is fair to the corporation—that is, if the benefit that accrues to a director is the same financial benefit that would accrue to anyone doing business with the corporation in a similar deal—it should withstand challenge, regardless of how it was approved. Another way of saying this is that a director, just like any other person or company, is entitled to do business with your corporation as long as the deal is fair and commercially reasonable. In fact, executives from other businesses, such as bank managers, investment advisers, and CEOs from other companies, sit on the boards of promising small corporations, not just to give expert advice and guidance but to help facilitate business between their corporations. Again, as long as the corporation doesn't put together sweetheart deals that favor these outside board interests at the expense of the corporation and its shareholders, the deals should be considered fair.

Boards Can Approve Their Own Compensation

Most state BCAs specifically allow the board to set its own compensation. In other words, no matter what the state's director conflict of interest statute says, it's okay for the board to vote to pay itself fair compensation for doing its work. Normally, board members are simply paid a reasonable per diem amount for attending meetings, plus travel and lodging expenses if appropriate. Board members also get stock options—a way to buy shares at current prices to give them an incentive to manage the corporation successfully and raise its share value.

Director Approval of Shareholder Distributions

State BCAs impose limits on the payout of corporate profits and earnings to shareholders and other corporate insiders. Typically, these payouts are made in the form of dividends to shareholders. In small, closely held corporations, dividends are rarely paid, since they are subject to double taxation (even though under federal tax rules, dividends currently are subject to low individual tax rates).

However, other types of distributions that are subject to these BCA restrictions can occur—for example, the buyback of shares from a director/shareholder or the payback of a shareholder loan made by a corporate insider. If the board approves a shareholder distribution in violation of state BCA requirements, each director can be held personally liable for the amount not allowed under the state's BCA.

State requirements for shareholder distributions vary. Most apply what is called a solvency test, which requires that the corporation be able to meet its expected financial obligations after the distribution—that is, be able to pay its bills as they become due after the payout of funds to shareholders. Some states also add an assets test, which requires that corporate assets exceed liabilities by a specified amount or ratio.

To find your state's shareholder distribution requirements, browse your state BCA's Shareholder section, looking for a statute with the title "Dividends," "Distributions to Shareholders," or "Payments From Stated Capital."

> **CAUTION**
>
> **It doesn't pay to bankrupt your own corporation.** As a matter of practice, any payment approved by the board—whether to shareholders or to other corporate insiders, such as directors or officers—is likely to be subject to legal attack if it leaves a corporation insolvent. The reason: This type of overspending is likely to be challenged later on as a violation of the director's duty of care to the corporation. Court cases in this area show that even shareholders in small corporations can personally recover money from directors who approve a generous payout to corporate insiders—for example, a buyback of the founder's shares or repayment of a founder loan—when it leaves the corporation without sufficient funds to stay in business. And even though general corporate creditors don't normally have legal standing to sue directors for breach of their statutory duty of care to the corporation, in extreme cases state courts have found ways to let creditors recover money from directors personally. For example, when directors close down their corporation by raiding its remaining cash reserves to buy back their shares without first paying off creditors, state courts have required the directors to personally pay the creditors.

Personal Liability to Outsiders

So far, we've focused on a director's personal liability to insiders—that is, to corporate shareholders—for causing financial harm to a corporation by:

- breaching the duty of care or loyalty to the corporation
- entering into a preferential personal business deal with the corporation without full disclosure and approval by the other board members or shareholders, or
- approving an unlawful distribution of corporate funds.

But what about a director's liability to outsiders, such as banks, vendors, or suppliers? As you already know, the basic limited liability rule is that board members are not personally liable for corporate debts and liabilities owed to or claimed by outsiders. This means that if an outsider successfully sues a corporation for unpaid bills or for failure to pay or perform under a corporate contract, the directors are immune from personal liability arising from the dispute. However, as is almost always true in law, there are a few exceptions to this standard rule:

- **Personally signed loans and contracts.** In the early phase of corporate operations, a bank may ask corporate founders to cosign a corporate loan and personally guarantee repayment if the corporation defaults. It may also ask the founders to pledge their own personal assets—such as home equity—as security for the cosigned loan. If a director signs a bank loan or any other type of corporate contract in the director's own name, that director will be personally liable in the event of a default under the loan or contract—and any personal assets pledged as security are subject to seizure and liquidation.

- **Unpaid taxes.** If the corporation fails to pay corporate income or payroll taxes, the IRS and state tax agency can seek to hold any "responsible person," including a board member, personally liable for taxes plus interest and penalties. (See "Appointing an Executive Committee to Handle Employee Compensation," above.)

- **Personal liability statutes.** State and federal law may hold corporate directors personally liable for violations of special statutes—for example, repeated or flagrant violations of environmental or toxic cleanup laws, or intentional violations of securities statutes. As a director, your best defense against this sort of personal liability is to stay informed of any special legal rules that apply to your corporation, and to vote "no" if a board decision may give rise to a legal penalty.

- **Personal injuries.** Directors are personally liable for injuries and other damage they personally inflict on others. The legal way of saying this is that directors are personally liable for their own legal torts. In other words, if you, as a corporate director, hold a press conference and unlawfully libel and cause harm to a competitor's business, don't expect the shield of corporate limited liability to protect you. You are personally liable for any damage you cause to other people, other companies, and their property.

- **Corporate raiding.** As mentioned in "Director Approval of Shareholder Distributions," above, if you raid your corporate cookie jar—by approving an overly generous buyout of your shares or some other self-interested business deal that leaves your corporation unable to pay its bills—you may face a creditor lawsuit. In some states, a court will make you return the money to your corporation so the creditors can get paid—plus order you to pay lawsuit-related costs and attorneys' fees.

Director Indemnification and Insurance

As we've said, the directors of smaller, closely held corporations normally do not need to lose sleep worrying over whether they have met their statutory duty of care to their corporation. That's because corporate management and shareholders are normally the same people or, at the very least, are in close touch. Since directors and shareholders have the same information, even if corporate resources are used to implement risky corporate strategies that have lackluster financial results, shareholder lawsuits rarely follow.

But as a business grows and outside shareholders invest in the corporation's future, shareholder disputes can more easily arise. Outside shareholders are usually not aware of the nuances of board decisions. Even regular shareholder mailings and meetings may not be enough to educate shareholders about the wisdom of aggressive decisions made by the board to keep the corporation competitive. If the corporation loses money, one or more shareholders may file suit, seeking personal judgments from corporate directors for a failure to exercise their statutory duty of due care.

Fortunately, the laws of all states contain indemnification and insurance provisions that help a corporation protect its board members from having to pay money out of their own pockets, even if a shareholder suit succeeds or is settled on terms favorable to the shareholder. These statutes also help with other costs that must be paid even if the directors win, such as lawyers' fees and court costs (deposition costs and filing fees). Here's a brief rundown of how they work.

Indemnification

State BCAs contain indemnification statutes that cover some out-of-pocket lawsuit and settlement amounts a director may be asked to personally pay. "Indemnification" means that someone else promises to pay money to cover certain costs. BCA indemnification statutes specify the circumstances under which a corporation can agree to directly pay or reimburse a director for amounts that the director must pay because of an act—or failure to act—as a director.

If you browse your state's BCA, you'll find a corporate indemnification statute, titled "Indemnification," "Indemnification of Directors and Officers," or a similar title. These statutes tend to contain very similar provisions from state to state. Here's a summary of the provisions you're likely to find in your state's BCA:

- **If director wins.** Generally, if a director wins a lawsuit, corporations may indemnify—pay the director—legal costs incurred by the director, such as attorneys' fees and court costs. In many statutes, the corporation *must* pay these costs if the director succeeds in court.

- **If director loses or settles.** If a director loses a lawsuit or agrees to a settlement, the BCA normally allows the corporation to indemnify the director for legal judgments, settlements, attorneys' fees, and other costs if the director acted in good faith and in the best interests of the corporation. Typically, this determination must be made by a majority of the nonindemnified directors, by a majority of shareholders (not counting shares owned by the indemnified director), or by a court.

- **Limits on indemnity.** If the director loses a lawsuit or settles a controversy involving (1) the director's breach of the duty of care

or loyalty; (2) the receipt of an improper personal benefit by the director; or (3) the payment of unlawful distributions to shareholders, the statutes normally prohibit any indemnification. These prohibitions make sense. In each of these situations, the director has unlawfully caused financial harm to the corporation. If the director pays the corporation for its loss and then the corporation reimburses the director for this payment, the corporation has won nothing at all—it is left in a losing position, and the director is off the hook financially. Here's another way of saying this: A corporation cannot indemnify a director for unauthorized financial harm the director causes to the corporation; the director has to personally pay these amounts.

This is a very general summary. If indemnification is important to you, make a point to look at your BCA indemnification statute. Each state's law is different, and even small differences in wording can make a huge financial difference to your corporation and its directors if they are sued. You will probably want to ask a lawyer to help you understand the statute.

Insurance

Most state BCAs specifically allow a corporation to purchase insurance to pay for directors' personal lawsuit and settlement costs, including judgments, settlements, legal fees, and court costs. State statutes normally place no limit on what these policies may cover. Typically, they can cover all kinds of losses, whether or not the losses are eligible for indemnification under the state's BCA.

Commercial insurance companies call director and officer liability policies "D&O liability policies." As with any insurance policy, premium payments vary according to the deductible amount and total liability ceiling selected for the policy. Depending on the policy, insurance companies may make payouts to reimburse a corporation for indemnification it has paid a director, to advance or reimburse legal costs, or to cover settlements or judgments. And, because insurance can cover amounts that can't be indemnified under state law—such as personal liability for a director's breach of duty to the corporation—payouts also can go right to the directors to cover legal costs, settlements, and judgments not indemnified by their corporation.

Of course, D&O policies contain exclusions from coverage—most won't pay if a director knowingly violates the law or commits fraud.

Officers

State BCAs specify the officer positions that a corporation must fill. These are known as the corporation's statutory officers and usually include a president, vice president, secretary, and treasurer. You list the names and addresses of your statutory officers in the annual filing you must make each year with your state corporate filing office. (This filing is a formality, and the fee to file your annual statement is normally small.) Most states allow one person to hold all the required corporate officer positions.

State law normally does not impose specific requirements on what statutory officers must do, except to say that one officer—typically the corporate secretary—must be appointed to keep corporate records, including meeting minutes. Often, the boards of small business corporations fill the statutory officer positions as a formality to comply with state requirements, while the people who supervise and run the corporation day to day are given titles other than those required by law.

EXAMPLE: DD Huge and Max MC form their own rap music publishing and artist representation company, Phat & Phunky Pheatures, Inc. To meet the statutory requirements, DD is appointed as the president and Max as the treasurer of the corporation. No salaries are paid for filling these statutory officer positions. DD is paid a corporate salary for acting as the Chief Rap Rep and Max is paid a salary as Caliph of Phinances. People are paid for what they do, not for their title.

In practice, the title given the top corporate officer is usually Chief Executive Officer (CEO) and the top finance officer is usually called the Chief Financial Officer (CFO). (A COO is a Chief Operating Officer.) Even the title vice president is outdated. Most corporations instead refer to second-tier corporate officers as associates, managers, or directors of a particular corporate department—such as marketing associate, sales director, publicity manager, or director of online operations—rather than using a vice president title.

The statutory officer position of secretary normally has no real-life counterpart in the everyday world of the corporation. In other words, the position of corporate secretary is one created to accommodate state BCA legal requirements, not the entrepreneurial needs of the corporation. However, the person appointed as secretary does have real work to do. As mentioned above, the secretary must keep the legal records of the corporation, preparing minutes of board and shareholder meetings. And banks and other financial institutions often require the signature or certification of the corporate secretary to attest that the board has approved items of business, such as a formal board resolution to approve a bank loan or line of credit. The secretary also normally handles

Answering to a Broader Class of Stakeholders— Do you Need a Socially Sustainable Certification?

Due in part to growing consumer demand, many publicly traded corporations, as well as small businesses, want to show their "stakeholders" (shareholders, employees, suppliers, creditors, and members of the community served or affected by the corporation) that they are socially responsible. Instead of focusing on short-term, profit-focused plans that may have negative financial, social, and environmental impacts, these businesses commit to maintaining a low carbon footprint, fair labor practices, socially responsible investing, and long-range planning strategies. Instituting sound practices and getting certified as a socially responsible company are great ways for corporations to accomplish these goals. (For the names of popular certifications, see "Do-Good LLCs and Corporations," at the beginning of this chapter.)

Whether you're a certified business or just doing business with one that is, understand that some certified corporations won't or can't do business with uncertified companies. That is, certified corporations may be required, as part of their certification, to ensure that all companies in their supply chain (vendors and creditors) are certified as well.

On the accounting front, sustainability standards similar to the Financial Accounting Standards Board (FASB) rules are being developed by the Sustainability Accounting Standards Board (SASB). These rules will enable publicly traded corporations and other commercial enterprises to report their sustainability metrics to the public and government agencies, such as the Securities and Exchange Commission.

If your corporation deals with an SASB reporting company, they may ask you to supply them with information or a report that shows you are also in compliance with the SASB standards. Look up "SASB" online for more information.

---

all requests from the board or shareholders for copies of corporate legal documents—such as corporate articles, bylaws, or minutes of meetings, or records of stock ownership in the corporation. Common practice is to delegate many of the duties of corporate secretary to another salaried officer—commonly the chief corporate financial or administrative officer.

Whatever you call corporate officers—and whatever tasks you delegate to them—keep the following points in mind:

- Officers can bind the corporation legally to a contract or other business relationship unless the party they do business with knows the officer does not have authority to transact the particular business—an exception that rarely occurs.

- Officers, like all corporate employees, are generally not personally liable for their acts while working for the corporation. However, like other employees (as well as directors), they are personally liable for any harm (personal injuries or torts) they cause to another person. (The corporation can be liable, too, if it was negligent in hiring the officer.)

CAUTION

Officers should sign contracts in their corporate capacity. No matter what their title, officers should sign contracts and transact business in the name of the corporation, showing the officer's title next to their signature. If the officer signs a contract without affixing a title after or under the signature, and the corporation defaults on the deal, the officer may be held personally liable for any loss caused by the corporation's default if the other party can show it was reasonable to believe the officer was transacting business on the officer's own behalf.

Shareholders

Shareholders invest in a corporation and elect its board of directors. They are not personally liable for corporate debts or other obligations. A shareholder's basic financial rights in the corporation are:

- participation in corporate dividends, and
- a stake in corporate assets (the shareholders' equity as shown on the corporate balance sheet).

In practice, shareholders of small corporations normally do not receive dividends. Rather, they wait until the corporation's overall value increases, then sell their shares. In a small, closely held corporation, the only market for these shares is another shareholder or the corporation itself. If the corporation has a good chance for success, the shareholder waits until the corporation is sold to another business that cashes out the existing shareholders or converts their shares to marketable shares in the acquiring business. And, of course, the corporation may go public and create a market for its own shares.

State BCAs contain various provisions that regulate and define shareholder responsibilities and rights. In this section, we look at the most common shareholder meeting provisions and stock issuance rules.

Annual Shareholder Meetings

Most state BCAs require shareholders to meet annually to elect (or reelect) the board of directors to a one-year term. Even in a small corporation, shareholders must receive written notice of annual meetings. Typically, this notice must be mailed or delivered within ten to 60 days before the meeting.

At a shareholders' meeting, a quorum must be present before the meeting begins. Most state BCAs require the presence, in person or by written proxy, of at least a majority of all the voting shares. The corporate secretary is normally required to bring an alphabetically ordered list of current voting shareholders and their share interests to the meeting, and to have it available for inspection by anyone who wants to see it.

Once a quorum is counted and the annual meeting begins, the names of directors are placed in nomination by those present, and the shareholder votes are taken. The standard voting rule is that each share gets one vote, and the nominees to the board who receive the highest number of votes (up to the number of directors to be elected) are designated as directors for the next one-year term.

EXAMPLE: Widgetless Web Works, Inc., has a three-person board of directors and ten shareholders who own a total of 50,000 shares. At the annual meeting, five shareholders attend who collectively own 40,000 shares (8,000 each) and vote on four nominees to the board. The results of the voting are as follows:

Nominee	Votes	
Jane	40,000	(all five shareholders voted for her)
George	40,000	(all five shareholders voted for him)
Bill	24,000	(three shareholders voted Bill as their third choice)
Sally	16,000	(two shareholders voted Sally as their third choice)

Jane, George, and Bill are the three new board members.

In addition to standard voting practices, most states allow shareholders to use special cumulative voting procedures to elect directors. Under cumulative voting rules, a shareholder gets a number of votes to cast in an election that equals the number of shares owned multiplied by the number of directors to be elected. This total number of votes can be cumulated and voted for just one director, or split up and voted for more than one nominee.

Cumulative voting procedures vary from state to state. Some statutes say that shareholders can use cumulative voting unless it is prohibited in the articles. Some say that the articles must specifically authorize cumulative voting before it can be used. Even if cumulative voting is authorized by state law or the articles, the normal rule is that a shareholder must specifically request to use it at a shareholder's meeting to elect directors. If so, then all shareholders must cumulatively vote their shares for the election of directors.

EXAMPLE: Building on the previous example but using cumulative voting in place of normal one-vote-per-share voting, each shareholder gets 24,000 votes (8,000 shares times three nominees to be elected). This time, the two shareholders who voted for Sally decide to cumulate and vote 24,000 votes each for Sally. This means the other shareholders have total control over the election of the other board members: The other three shareholders cast 12,000 votes each for Jane, 8,000 for George, and 4,000 for Bill, the cumulative vote tally looks like this:

Nominee	Votes
Jane	36,000
George	24,000
Bill	12,000
Sally	48,000

This time, the Sally shareholders have enough voting clout to get her elected; they let the other directors decide the other two slots with their Jane and George votes, but they didn't allow the others to get Bill on the board. Cumulative voting was designed to allow minority shareholders to achieve exactly this kind of result—namely, getting someone elected to the board even though they own a minority of the total shareholder voting power.

Most small corporations do not need or use cumulative voting. If you are interested in your state's cumulative voting provisions, look for a section called "Cumulative Voting" or "Election of Directors" under the "Shareholders" heading of your BCA. Also look in the "Articles of Incorporation—Required Provisions" section of the BCA to see whether you must place provisions to authorize or prohibit cumulative voting in your articles.

Special Staggered Board Election Rules

Most states allow you to split up your board and elect just a portion of its directors each year. Larger corporations with bigger boards may prefer to elect directors this way, rather than electing a larger board en masse each year. Boards split up in this manner are referred to as "classified boards" or "staggered boards" in state BCAs. This jargon derives from the fact that using this scheme, shareholders elect only one class (or portion) of directors each year. For example, the shareholders of a corporation with a nine-person board can be asked to elect just three board members annually. This means that each group of three directors serves for three years before their time comes for reelection. If you are interested in authorizing the election of your board by shareholders under these staggered board rules, look for a statute titled "Staggered Board of Directors" or "Classified Board of Directors" in the "Directors" section of your state BCA. If you do decide to follow these rules, you will need to add your staggered election board procedure to your bylaws.

Special Shareholder Meetings

The board calls special shareholder meetings during the year whenever it needs shareholder approval for an important item of corporate business. In most states, the board must ask shareholders to approve:

- amendments (changes) to the corporation's articles
- the sale of substantially all corporate assets
- the merger of the corporation with another business, or
- other structural changes that affect existing shareholders.

For example, the board may wish to attract investment capital by creating a new class of preferred shares of stock that provide a liquidation preference to investors—that is, that guarantee the preferred shareholder a return of two times the purchase price of their shares when they are sold back to the corporation or when it liquidates or is merged. (Regular shares do not contain this sort of preference.) State BCAs normally require the approval of at least a majority of all the existing shares of the corporation to create a new class of shares that has preferences not enjoyed by the existing shareholders.

The shareholders themselves can decide to call a special meeting of shareholders to exercise authority granted under the state BCA—for example, to fill a vacancy on the board or replace a director, to amend the articles or bylaws, or even to vote to dissolve the corporation. State law normally sets a low ownership threshold for calling a shareholders' meeting—typically, 10% or less of the corporation's shares.

A standard state corporate law requirement is that only the business described in the notice of a special shareholders' meeting can be approved at a special shareholders' meeting. If new business comes up during the meeting, another special shareholders' meeting must be called and held to take care of it. You can look up your state's rules for the calling of shareholders' meetings in your state BCA.

Capitalization of the Corporation

A corporation needs people and money to get started. The money or dollar value of assets used to set up a corporation is called its capital, and the process of obtaining these start-up funds and property is called capitalizing the corporation. Most states have no minimum capitalization requirements. The District of Columbia is the exception. There a corporation must have at least $1,000 in capital before it begins doing business.

Courts Sometimes Pierce the Corporate Veil

What if you don't follow most of the basic rules for organizing and running your corporation outlined in this chapter? That is, if you don't contribute adequate capital to your corporation, adopt bylaws, appoint officers, issue stock, hold annual shareholders' and directors' meetings, keep corporate records, or generally pay much attention to the director/officer/shareholder distinctions set up by your state's BCA? The answer is that if you end up in a court, a judge may decide that your corporation is not a real legal entity worthy of respect, but simply a bogus legal device you are using to cloak yourself in the mantle of corporate limited liability. If that happens, the court can hold you personally liable for corporate debts or claims. This dire result is called piercing the corporate veil.

Veil piercing is the exception, not the rule. It happens mostly in cases where the corporation's founders have not only ignored all or most corporate formalities, but have also engaged in devious or underhanded business practices. Nonetheless, it's wise to take your corporation seriously to avoid even a remote chance of having your corporation's limited liability protection disregarded by a court. Just follow the standard corporate organizational and operational formalities discussed in this and the following chapters, and you should be safe from legal attack.

While it may be tempting to start a business on a shoestring and earn as you learn, the idea of starting a corporation with little money or assets is usually impractical. Business corporations are in business to make money, and you normally need at least a reasonable amount of cash and assets to begin corporate operations. To give your corporation the best chance of succeeding, we recommend that you fund your corporation with enough money and other assets to begin doing business and to cover short-range expenses, taxes, and debts. Of course, if your business will be based in your home, or otherwise get off to a low-key start, your initial investment or capitalization can be appropriately modest. In short, the important thing is not the amount you contribute, but that your start-up capital is large enough to meet initial business needs.

There are various ways to capitalize a new corporation. Here are the most common:

- **Incorporating an existing business.** The existing owners transfer the assets of an unincorporated business to the corporation in exchange for shares. Each owner of the previous business (who now becomes a corporate shareholder) receives a percentage of stock ownership equal to their ownership percentage in the prior business. This book provides a bill of sale form that unincorporated business owners can use to document the transfer of the assets from their unincorporated business to a new corporation in return for shares. (See "Prepare Receipts for Your Shareholders," in Chapter 4, Step 7, for the form and for a discussion of legal and tax issues that may arise when you incorporate an existing business.)

- **Incorporating a new business.** The founders pay cash and transfer property to the corporation in exchange for shares. If state law allows, some founders receive shares in return for a promise to provide services to the corporation or by promising to pay for the shares later. We discuss the specifics of stock issuance in "Sale and Issuance of Stock," below.

- **Personal loans.** Whether incorporating a new or existing business, some owners may decide to make a personal loan to the corporation in addition to buying shares. The corporation normally repays these loan funds within a few years, often with the corporation making interest-only payments during the loan term and paying off the principal at the end of the loan period.

CAUTION

Keep loan transactions reasonable. If shareholders will lend money to the corporation, it's best not to overdo it. Some tax advisers think it's dicey to have a debt-to-equity ratio of more than 3:1, while some are more aggressive and balk if the ratio gets close to 10:1. Ask your tax adviser for specific advice. During a subsequent corporate tax audit, the IRS may become suspicious of a corporation with a high ratio of debt to equity or with very loose shareholder loan arrangements. The IRS may treat shareholder loans as contributions of capital if (1) all or most shareholders contribute very little equity capital to buy shares and then lend money to their corporation in relative amounts that reflect their share ownership percentages; and/ or (2) the loans are not backed up with written promissory notes, or don't contain a commercially reasonable rate of interest. This means that the corporation cannot deduct interest payments it makes under the loans and that all payouts made by the corporation—both interest and principal repayments—will be taxed to the shareholder as a taxable dividend.

RESOURCE

For promissory notes and other corporate forms. Nolo's *The Corporate Records Handbook*, by Anthony Mancuso, provides several types of shareholder and corporate promissory note forms with instructions, plus many useful corporate minute forms and resolutions for approving and implementing standard items of ongoing corporate business.

Sale and Issuance of Stock

Under state law, several things must happen before your corporation can issue stock to its shareholders:

- Your articles must authorize the number and type of shares you wish to issue.

- Your corporation must actually receive cash or property in exchange for the stock to be received by your corporation—or written shareholder promises to provide services or pay cash if your state allows it.

- Your board must approve the value of non-cash payments for stock. ("Minutes of First Meeting of the Board of Directors," covered in Chapter 4, Step 6 let you do this.) For a copy of this form see Appendixes B and C.

- You must meet the requirements of state and federal securities laws.

How Many Shares Should You Authorize?

Since many states charge an incorporation fee based on the number of shares authorized in the articles of incorporation, many small business incorporators sensibly authorize the maximum number of shares they can for the smallest incorporation fee. In some states, more shares that have a nominal or "par" value can be issued than shares without par value to obtain the smallest filing fee, so this also is a consideration. (For a full explanation of the par value concept, see "Par Value States," below.)

The instructions to your state's online articles of incorporation form will tell you whether your state charges an incorporation fee based on the number of shares authorized in your articles. They will also tell you how many shares you can authorize (with or without par value) for the minimum fee.

In states where your incorporation fee is not based on the number or type of shares authorized in your articles, you can authorize as many shares as you wish, including shares for later issuance to shareholders. In all cases, keep the following points in mind:

- The shares authorized in your articles place an upper limit on the number and type of shares you can sell to your shareholders. If you want to issue more shares than the number authorized in your articles or wish to issue a new type not mentioned in your articles, you must amend the articles and file the amendment with the state corporate filing office prior to issuing the new shares.

- The actual number of shares you authorize in your articles and later issue to your shareholders is arbitrary. It is the relative stock ownership percentages that have real meaning to shareholders when it comes time to pay dividends, buy back shares, or sell your corporation.

EXAMPLE: Bob and Charlie form their own corporation and contribute equal amounts of cash to buy its initial shares. Each should get one-half of the shares issued by the corporation, so that each ends up with half of the total shareholder voting power, each participates equally in any payouts of corporate profits, and each receives equal net sales proceeds when the corporation is sold. To accomplish this, the corporation could issue Bob and Charlie each one share, one million shares, or any number in between, as long as each gets the same number of shares.

- You set the value of your shares when you form a corporation. You can choose whatever price you wish, as long as it is set the same for all of your initial shareholders. If you set a low share price, you issue more shares to each shareholder than you would if you set a higher share price.

EXAMPLE: Let's say Bob and Charlie from the previous example each paid $10,000 into the corporation to buy its initial shares. If you set a share price of $10,000 per share, each is issued one share. If you set a share price of one cent per share, each receives one million shares (1,000,000 x $0.01 = $10,000).

In some states, the maximum number of shares that can be authorized in the articles for the smallest fee is small—perhaps just 100 shares. But this isn't a problem, for the reasons set out above. If you have ten shareholders and issue each five shares (for a total of 50 shares), each gets a one-tenth ownership interest in the corporation, even though each holds only ten shares. And you have 50 shares left to issue to future shareholders.

Par Value States

The instructions to your state's online articles form will tell you if your state uses the concept of par value. Par value is a nominal dollar amount given to corporate shares—it is not their real value, just a stated value that has legal significance under the laws of the some states. These par value states employ the concept of par value to regulate the issuance of corporate shares. In par value states, shares of stock are authorized in the articles with either:

- a statement of their designated monetary par value, such as "100,000 shares with a par value of $1.00 per share," or

• a statement that the shares are without par value, such as "100 shares without par value" (these are referred to as "no-par" shares in some states).

Despite the recognition of par value in some state BCAs, par value is not given much weight in the commercial marketplace. Instead, under modern financial reporting procedures, the value of shares is a floating figure, based on a corporation's current net asset value—that is, the amount by which corporate assets exceed corporate liabilities (also called "stockholders' equity"). In other words, it's outdated to assign a fixed or par value to shares.

Shares within each class must have the same par value or must all be designated "without par value." We assume your corporation will authorize just one class of stock—called common stock—in which each share has the same voting, dividend, and liquidation rights.

The incorporation fee in some par value states is based on the total par value of the shares authorized in the articles; if you authorize shares without par value in these states, the shares are nevertheless assigned an assumed par value per share for purposes of computing the incorporation fee. Generally, if you are given a choice as to whether to issue par or no-par value shares in your state (you can't do both), you will choose no par unless you can issue more par value shares than no-par shares for a lower incorporation fee.

Par value shares must be sold to shareholders for at least their par value. In most cases, par value amounts are set at a low, nominal amount, so typically par value shares are sold for more—usually much more—than their stated par value. In par value states, there is no lower limit on the price for which you can sell shares without par value.

The corporation's capital accounts reflect amounts received by a corporation for the sale of par value shares, as well as the amounts received by the corporation for the sale of shares without par value.

There is another capital account: the earned surplus account. It contains the corporation's retained earnings, and it is from this account that the corporation may pay dividends to shareholders.

RESOURCE

For an excellent discussion of the U.S. corporate capital rules as they have evolved into present-day practice, see the article, "Capital Requirements in United States Corporation Law" by Richard A. Booth (available online—enter this title and author in your browser's search box).

SEE AN EXPERT

Find an accountant who has experience with small corporations. At first encounter, some of this accounting information may appear daunting. Fortunately, the terms are often more complicated than the underlying concepts. If you don't have experience in this area, find an experienced small business accountant who does. A good accountant should make sure your financial record-keeping system is properly designed to accommodate your corporation's capital accounts under the legal and accounting rules that apply in your state.

Issuance of Shares for Notes and Future Services May Be Prohibited

In some states, a corporation cannot issue stock in return for a promise by a shareholder to perform future services for the corporation (a written promise of this sort is normally made in an employment contract) or a promise to pay cash later (a written promise to pay cash later is normally memorialized by a promissory note).

EXAMPLE: Thomas and Richard decide to form a hang gliding tour service. They're sure someone with expertise can modify a standard solo hang glider to accommodate a workable tour seat outfitted with a short-range wireless intercom headset (to listen to scripted commentary on the shifting landscape below) as well as other amenities. In fact, they know someone who might be willing to strap himself in as their pilot: Harold, a local hang gliding enthusiast, who can be seen most weekends soaring above the windswept hills that surround their city. After deciding to join Tom and Dick, Harry agrees to accept one-third of the corporation's shares in return for entering into an employment contract with the enterprise. The three toast the deal and their new corporate name, Go Fly a Kite, Inc. The next day, Tom browses the state BCA and discovers that it does not allow shares to be issued in return for future services. Harold suggests an alternative: The corporation can issue its shares to him in return for a long-term note; he'll be happy to pay for them after he's survived a few test flights in the dual glider. Tom explains that their state's BCA also prohibits the issuance of shares for a promissory note. Harold decides to pay (actually, borrow from the other founders) enough cash to purchase his shares outright.

Today, corporate creditors look at the entire financial picture of the corporation, not simply its stated capital accounts, to decide the corporation's creditworthiness.

Payments for Shares

In all states, a corporation may sell shares for cash and both tangible and intangible property, such as equipment, machinery, computers, patent rights, copyrights, or trademarks. A corporation can also issue stock in return for the cancellation of a debt owed by the corporation to the shareholder. Normally, this occurs when a corporation issues shares as a payback for money owed to a shareholder who helped start the corporation.

Some states also allow you to issue shares in return for the promise to pay for them later (by signing a promissory note) or to work for the corporation later (by entering into an employment contract). Some states specifically forbid the issuance of shares for these types of "future payments." Most new corporations don't issue shares in return for these promises because other shareholders who pay cash don't like it and because the issuance of shares for services is normally taxable—see "Stock Issuance and Taxes," below. If you want to look up your state's rules, see the "Stock Issuance" section of your state BCA.

TIP

Issuing stock certificates. The issuance of stock signifies the formal acceptance of payment for the shares and recording of a shareholder's interest in the corporate records. Technically, you do not have to issue paper stock certificates under most states' laws (recording the transaction on the corporate books is enough). But following tradition, most incorporators do issue certificates. (For more information, see "Payments for Shares," above.)

Stock Issuance and Taxes

Let's look at the basic tax treatment of the most common stock issuance scenarios: stock for cash, stock for services, and stock for property. This is a general guide. For more technical information, consult your tax adviser—and check the small business tax information on the IRS website at www.irs.gov.

CAUTION

State tax law normally follows federal law. The very basic tax rules discussed here come from the federal Internal Revenue Code. Fortunately, state tax rules normally follow these federal rules.

Stock for Cash

The issuance of stock for cash is normally not taxed. The tax consequences of the investment are usually deferred until shareholders sell their shares. At that time, buyers report on their individual income tax return any gain or loss on the sale, paying capital gains tax on any gain. (The capital gains rates are usually lower than the individual income tax rate that would otherwise apply to income earned by the individual if the shares are held for at least one year.)

Stock for Services

The issuance of stock for services is normally taxable. The person who provides the services must pay income tax on the value of the stock received—just as if the corporation paid the person for performing work or promising to perform work for the corporation.

Stock for Property

The issuance of stock for property is normally taxable—the person transferring the property pays taxes on the difference between the value of the shares and the person's income tax basis in the property. The person's basis in the property is normally the amount paid for it, less depreciation and other adjustments to the basis that were or could have been claimed by the person on his or her individual income tax return.

Fortunately, there is one big exception to the rule that the issuance of shares in return for property is taxable. Specifically, Section 351 of the Internal Revenue Code says that a property transfer in exchange for shares is tax-free—just as if you bought corporate shares with cash—if all the shareholders buying shares with cash and property at the same time end up with at least an 80% ownership stake in the corporation. There are two basic ways to use Section 351 to qualify under this tax-free property exchange rule:

- **You transfer property to your corporation for shares.** If you, together with the other shareholders of your new corporation who pay cash and/or property for their shares, will own at least 80% of your corporation's voting shares, each of you qualifies for tax-free treatment for your exchange of shares for property (the cash transfers are already tax free).

- **You and your co-owners incorporate an existing business.** If you and the other co-owners of the unincorporated business will own at least 80% of the voting shares of the new corporation, your transfer of business assets in return for shares will be tax-free under Section 351.

In addition, there are many rules under IRC 351 that cover special situations—such as the purchase of shares by someone who contributes both services and property. We discuss the special IRC 351 rules that apply when incorporating an existing business in "Tax Treatment When Incorporating an Existing Business" in Chapter 3. Again, your tax adviser and the IRS website (www.irs.gov) can help you further understand these technical tax rules.

Stock Issuance and the Securities Laws

A share of stock in your corporation is classified as a security under state and federal securities laws. These laws regulate the offer and sale of stock by small and large corporations alike. Federal securities law is contained in the federal Securities Act. We discuss its basic application to the sale of your initial stock to the founders of your corporation in "Federal Securities Laws," below. First, let's look at how your state regulates the sale of initial shares in your corporation.

State Securities Law

Each state enacts and enforces its own securities law. This law applies to the offer and sale of stock within the state. If you offer or sell shares outside your state, the securities law of the outside state applies to your out-of-state transactions.

Overview

The securities acts in each state are quite different, but they share the following five features:

- voluntary compliance
- disclosure requirements
- registration of nonexempt issues of stock
- agency approval of nonexempt issues of stock, and
- penalties for noncompliance.

Voluntary compliance. State securities agencies do not automatically track private sales of shares by corporations. You are expected to learn the rules and voluntarily comply with state law to protect your corporation and its investors.

Disclosure requirements. The basic rule for sales of stock in each state can be summarized simply: disclose, disclose, disclose. To comply with state law, you have a duty to disclose to investors all material financial and business information concerning the sale of shares. (This is called material disclosure; see "What Does 'Material Disclosure' Mean?" below.) If you don't follow this rule, an investor can sue your corporation—and in some cases, your founders personally—to get their money back. And in some situations, investors may be able to collect punitive damages to punish dishonest sellers of stock for their underhanded business practices. So, the best way to comply with this basic disclosure rule is to honestly, and in advance of any stock sales, discuss the risks inherent in purchasing stock in your corporation, and to provide full financial disclosure to potential investors. Doing this will minimize your chances of being sued later by a disgruntled investor—or, if you do get sued, of losing. In short, if you can show a court that an investor knew the risks of investing in your corporation before buying your corporation's shares, the investor, not your corporation or you, should have to assume any financial losses that result from the investment.

Registration. All states implement a securities registration system, which requires corporations that sell shares—called issuers under the securities laws—to file registration materials with the state prior to a sale of stock, unless the stock issuance is exempt from the registration requirements. Fortunately for new corporations, state securities laws contain exemptions that excuse many incorporators from registering their corporation's initial stock issuance. The idea behind these exemptions is to allow small corporations to obtain modest amounts of capital from well-informed insiders without having to bother with full-blown registration paperwork and fees. Most states provide more than one exemption that may apply to your new corporation. We discuss the most common exemptions in "State Securities Law Exemptions," below.

Agency approval of nonexempt issues of stock. If your stock issuance is not exempt, you must wait for your registration application to be approved by the state securities agency. If it is, your corporation receives a permit from the state to issue its shares. Most states implement a disclosure registration system that requires the issuer to file paperwork with the state containing all the financial, legal, and business details of the stock sale, as well as the risks associated with the investment. Potential buyers of the stock normally must receive a copy of these disclosures in a prospectus provided by the issuer before the sale. You will probably need to hire a lawyer and an accountant to help you prepare both your registration application and your stock prospectus.

Other states implement what is called a "merit" system of registration. In these states, you must provide the state and potential investors with all necessary registration information, just as in a disclosure state. Then, you must satisfy the state securities agency that your sale of stock is fair. Essentially, they scrutinize your registration application, then ask questions. To assure fairness, the office may impose restrictions on the securities offering—for example, it may set a share price or limit the people to whom you may sell shares. The securities agency may place a limit on the sales price for shares, the number and types of shares you may sell, the types of people who may buy your shares, and how much each can invest.

Penalties for noncompliance. If you are required to register your stock issuance and you fail to do so, your corporation and you, personally, can be required to pay noncompliance penalties to the state. In extreme cases, you may face criminal charges authorized under state securities laws; but these are rarely brought to bear unless you really rip off your investors—for example, by depositing their funds in your personal account instead of letting the money work to get your corporation off the ground.

RESOURCE

To read your state's Securities Act and Regulations. In Appendix A, we explain how you can locate your state's security office online. This website provides forms and exemption information, plus links to your state's securities laws.

What Does "Material Disclosure" Mean?

Unfortunately, material disclosure is not specifically defined in securities statutes. Essentially, it means all the information and known risks associated with an investment that an investor would want to consider.

Think of it this way: If someone sells you something but fails to mention a fact that, had you known it, would have made you consider the investment slightly differently, then that fact is material information. If knowing the information would not have mattered in the slightest to you, then it is immaterial information.

Material facts related to an investment usually include all the basic financial information you have on hand on past and expected financial performance: profit and loss statements, cash flow statements, and balance sheets, plus the context and risks of the investment (for example, competing business pressures, how much more work your corporation needs to do to launch a product or service, and the other factors that will affect the success of your enterprise).

Determining Your Securities Law Comfort Level

Before we describe the types of securities act exemptions you are likely to learn about on your state's securities office website, it's important to place this information in the context of forming a small corporation. Once you see the big picture, you can narrow your focus to the details of your state's specific exemption requirements. To do this, we recommend that you assess your securities law comfort level. This means asking yourself two questions:

How eager are you to learn the legal and technical requirements of securities act exemptions? If the whole idea of learning about securities law exemption requirements is unappealing or too technical for your tastes, it makes sense to pay a business lawyer to help you learn the rules.

Are your investors sophisticated businesspeople who are involved in running the corporation? If you're forming a small corporation with a close-knit group of business-savvy people who know each other well and will work together to manage and run the corporation, no one stands in a superior position to any of the others. You all know the risks of the enterprise, and each of you will stay equally informed as you try to make it a success. If things go badly, it is unlikely that one investor will sue the others for damages under the securities laws.

However, if any of your founders are unsophisticated or if you sell shares to outside investors who will not actively manage and run the corporation, the securities laws take on added significance. After all, the laws are designed precisely to protect people who pay money to others with the expectation of making a profit from the business activities of those who get the money. In other words, if your corporation fails, an unsophisticated or outside investor is more likely to ask a lawyer to sue to recover their investment from your corporation and its managers—and that lawyer will, no doubt, look to see if the founders were in full compliance with the securities statutes when they asked for and received the investor's funds. If they weren't, the disgruntled investor may succeed in obtaining a court judgment for full repayment with interest to their clients plus attorney's fees, court costs, and perhaps punitive damages—without having to show that their clients were treated unfairly.

EXAMPLE 1: Barry and Beth incorporate their existing co-owned partnership to insulate themselves from personal liability, take advantage of corporate income tax splitting (see Chapter 4), and set up a stock option plan to motivate their employees. Each will receive one-half of the new corporation's shares in return for a transfer of their one-half interest in the partnership's assets to their new corporation. They both have a very high securities law comfort level: (1) after checking the securities laws, they know an exemption is available for the issuance of their initial shares, and (2) each knows what to expect from the other, and the risks associated with their existing business. Neither is very worried about their investment of partnership assets in the new corporation—both understand that they will have to continue working hard to continue making a profit. With full disclosure of all business prospects and risks, neither is likely to sue the other over securities laws issues.

EXAMPLE 2: After establishing that the securities law provides an applicable exemption, Beth asks her parents if they'd like to invest in Beth and Barry's reorganized business by buying shares in the new corporation. Her parents are fairly familiar with the business, accustomed to receiving a blow-by-blow description of its ups and downs from their daughter in her phone calls home. They say they'd be happy to invest a little to help give Beth's business a corporate facelift. Beth's securities law comfort level is high— she believes her parents, who are reasonably experienced investors, understand the pros and cons of investing in her corporation. But Barry is more cautious. Knowing that Beth's parents may not fully appreciate the difficulties of making money in his and Beth's line of work, he insists on making a full disclosure of all material facts

relating to their investment in a formal way. This consists of giving Beth's parents copies of current and past financial statements prepared for the partnership and a proposed business plan for the corporation's first year of operation. In addition, he insists on sitting down with both of them to explain the risks of their investment to them.

EXAMPLE 3: Beth and Barry decide to use their incorporation as a means to obtain additional capital from unrelated outside investors. They plan on calling a number of their friends and acquaintances to see if any are interested in investing in their new company. This time, since they will be dealing with outside investors who won't know the business intimately, Beth's and Barry's security law comfort level is fairly low. Barry and Beth hire their own business lawyer to help them obtain a securities exemption for their stock issuance. They have browsed the securities laws and know they probably qualify for an exemption, but they want to make sure they dot all the i's and cross all the t's before selling any shares to outsiders. In addition, they recommend in writing that each investor have his or her own personal lawyer review the transaction.

After you consider your own situation and review your exemption choices, you may find that your comfort level is high and decide that you're ready to go ahead and issue your shares. But if the rules that apply to your situation look complex or your comfort level is lower than you'd like for other reasons, ask a business lawyer for help. In all cases, you will probably want to add a "legend" to your stock certificates that indicates they are subject to securities law or resale (see below). A lawyer can help you draft a legend that complies with both state and federal securities laws.

State Securities Law Exemptions

State securities laws contain different types of exemptions:

- **Exempt issuer transactions.** These exemptions apply to your corporation's initial sale of shares. Your corporation is the issuer.

- **Exempt nonissuer transactions.** These apply to sales of shares owned by your shareholders. You need not be concerned about these exemptions now, but your shareholders may want to rely on a nonissuer exemption later when deciding to sell their shares.

- **Exempt securities.** These exemptions apply to special types of securities, whether sold by an issuer or shareholder. State law often exempts securities of banks and other financial institutions, pension plans, stock option shares, and the like. In most cases, these security exemptions do not apply to the average business corporation wishing to sell initial shares to its investors.

If You Want to Make a Modest Public Offering

A common feature of all the exemptions listed above is the requirement that the issuer—your corporation—must offer and sell its shares privately, without advertising to the public. Since the great majority of small corporations are funded by friends and family, this normally causes no problem. But if you want to make an offering to the public, you must usually obtain a registration permit for your shares.

Some states let you make a public offering through a streamlined registration process, promulgated by the North American Securities Administrators Association (NASAA), called the Small Company Offering Registration, or SCOR, process. This standardized procedure allows you to raise up to $1 million from the public in the 45 states that have approved it. It utilizes a simple 50-item question-and-answer prospectus form and is less costly in terms of accounting and legal fees than a full-blown registration. Many states also let you use the SCOR prospectus to "test the waters" and raise $100,000 in capital from the public at the start of the SCOR offering. Some states also allow you to provide your prospectus to potential investors online. State rules for Internet solicitations for the sale of stock vary. Call your state securities office for more information. To learn more about SCOR, go to the NASAA site at www.nasaa.org.

Most state securities acts are arranged in a predictable way. One section of the act lays out the dealer registration requirements and exemptions. Another section contains the issuer registration rules and exemptions. A third section typically contains the nonissuer exemptions. You'll first want to go to the "Issuer" section to look for a law titled "Exemptions" or "Exemptions From Registration." This topic is normally broken down into (a) and (b) sections. The (a) section often contains the exemptions for specific types of securities, and is usually titled "Exempt Securities." The (b) section, usually titled "Exempt Transactions," is the one you are interested in. It should contain a list of specific exemptions from registration that apply to the offer and sale of securities by an issuer, including one or more of the exemptions discussed above.

- **Broker or dealer exemptions.** States not only regulate the sale of securities, but also the people and businesses who sell them. State securities law requires those who sell shares to meet licensing requirements and register as brokers, dealers, and salespeople. Fortunately, since your corporation does not expect to engage in the regular sale of securities as a business, it should qualify for an exemption from registration as a broker, dealer, or salesperson. But to be absolutely sure your state's broker-dealer rules do not apply to your initial issuance of shares, make a quick call to your state's securities office.

The remainder of this section discusses state exemptions from security transactions for issuers. This is the category of state law that helps most smaller corporations offer and sell their initial shares without having to obtain a registration permit from the state securities agency.

Your state's securities act may contain one or more of the following common exemptions in a section on exempt issuer transactions.

Incorporation exemption. Many states provide a straightforward exemption from registration for the initial issuance of shares to ten or fewer shareholders by a newly formed corporation. If your state offers this exemption, it is normally self-executing. This means that you don't have to file a form or pay a fee to take advantage of the exemption.

Small offering exemption. Many states allow a corporation, whether new or existing, to issue shares to a relatively small number of individuals without registration—typically ten to 35—within a 12-month period. Some small offering exemptions require that: (1) you can't issue shares to more than ten in-state people within a 12-month period; and (2) the total number of in- and out-of-state shareholders during the 12-month period, counting all new and existing shareholders, cannot exceed 35. Pay particular attention to how the small offering exemption is worded. It can make a difference in how you count your shareholders. For example, you may not have to include certain shareholders in your count.

Limited offering exemption. Many states allow you to make a limited offering to 35 or fewer investors. Typically, you must offer and sell your shares privately, without advertisement. And you can't pay anyone a commission—a percentage of the stock sale proceeds—for helping to sell the shares. A limit may be placed on the total amount of money the corporation receives for the shares, and a time frame may be specified—for example, you must count all sales made within a 12-month period. Some states require you to file a notice and pay a fee to rely on the state-limited offering exemption.

Most states make this exemption easier to use by saying you do not need to count "accredited investors" against the investor limit. (Spouses and relatives who share the same residence with an accredited investor normally do not need to be counted, either.) Accredited investor is a term borrowed from the federal Regulation D securities rules (see "Federal Securities Laws," below). Such investors often include corporate principals such as directors and executive officers, and sophisticated investors who meet specific net worth or annual income standards. Under most limited offering exemptions, you can sell shares to as many accredited investors as you like, as long as you meet the other exemption requirements.

Regulation D filings. Many states automatically exempt your issuance if you comply with one of the federal Regulation D stock issuance rules (see "Federal Securities Laws," below). Typically, you must file a copy of Form D (originally filed online with the federal Securities and Exchange Commission) with the state and pay a state filing fee.

Summing Up

Although state securities laws are highly technical, most states provide exemptions that small corporations can use easily, efficiently, and safely to offer their initial shares privately to founders and a limited group of family and/or sophisticated investors, without much red tape or fee expense. Appendix A shows you how to go to your state's securities office website where you can learn about your state's securities laws and exemptions and, in most cases, also find a link to your state securities act.

If you don't want to dig into the information provided on your state website, you may decide to hand the task over to a lawyer. And again, let your comfort level be your guide. It is one of the best indicators of how much to do yourself, and how much you may decide to pass along to a lawyer to do for you.

Federal Securities Laws

Federal securities laws apply to the issuance of corporate shares in all states. The reason the feds have a say in your stock issuance is that, one way or another, you will use the telephone, the mail, the Internet, or some other form of interstate commerce to carry out offers and sales of shares. This means that you can't ignore the federal rules when issuing corporate shares.

Federal securities law regulations parallel the state model discussed just above. You must register your initial offering of stock with the federal Securities and Exchange Commission (SEC) unless you qualify for an exemption. Failure to register, if you're required to do so, can result in financial penalties under the act and liability for your corporation and its founders. A disgruntled shareholder can seek rescission of the stock sale and collect interest on the money plus, perhaps, punitive damages. As discussed in the previous section, your best approach is to know your shareholders, make full disclosure to your investors, and pay close attention to your comfort level.

There are several federal exemptions available. Most small corporations that are eligible for a state exemption from securities registration should qualify under at least one of them. We present the most commonly used federal exemptions in the remainder of this section, in their normal order of applicability and usefulness. The first two do not require you to file any forms or pay fees, so look to them first. The third choice—the Regulation D exemption scheme—requires the online filing of a form (but no fees). You probably will find that the initial sale of your new corporation's stock qualifies under more than one of the exemptions listed below. You should pick the one that's most convenient for you to use.

RESOURCE

For more federal exemption information. The SEC website has a small business information page with links to helpful information on each of the federal exemption rules covered here, plus information on streamlined small business registration procedures if you decide someday to make a public offering of shares to obtain higher levels of capital. Go to the SEC website at www.sec.gov and look for the "Small Businesses" link on the home page.

Intrastate Exemption

Section 3(a)(11) of the Securities and Exchange Act contains the intrastate offering exemption for a sale of any share "which is a part of an issue offered and sold only to persons resident within a single State or Territory, where the issuer of such security is a person resident and doing business within . . . such State or Territory." It is available for issuances of shares by a corporation to shareholders who reside in the state where the corporation was formed and where it carries out most of its business. This exemption is self-executing—meaning that there is no form to file or fee to pay, and no limit is placed on the number of shareholders or the amount of money they can pay for their shares.

The intrastate exemption comes in handy for most newly formed, locally based corporations that simply issue their shares privately to a local group of shareholders. If your company owns out-of-state assets or does a substantial amount of business out of state, it may not qualify for the exemption. Federal Rule 147 (see "Intrastate Offering Regulations," below) provides a "safe harbor" set of rules for meeting the generally expressed requirements of the exemption. That

is, it shows one way to be sure you are making a qualified intrastate issuance of shares. In part, it says that your corporation should qualify for the intrastate exemption if your corporation:

- has at least 80% of its assets, and earns 80% of its revenue, in your state
- has its principal office in your state
- makes offers and sales only to people who reside in your state, and
- intends to use 80% of the proceeds for business operations in your state.

You can make reliance on the intrastate offering exemption safer by getting each shareholder to sign a statement affirming that they are a resident of your corporation's state of formation and agreeing not to sell the shares to an out-of-state resident for a period of at least nine months after the initial issuance of the shares by your corporation.

You also make reliance safer if you place language on the face of your stock certificates—this language is called a legend—that says the shares have not been registered with the SEC and that they are subject to restrictions on resale. You also should place a notation in your corporation's stock records that the corporation should not transfer any stock certificates within nine months to out-of-state shareholders.

 RESOURCE

To download Rule 147. Rule 147 is posted on the SEC website at www.sec.gov/about/laws.shtml (select the "Rules and Regulations" link, then "Part 230 – General Rules and Regulations," then "§230.147"). You also can download it from other websites—just run an online search for "Rule 147."

Rule 147 — "Part of an Issue," "Person Resident," and "Doing Business Within" for Purposes of Section 3(a)(11)

Preliminary Notes

1. This rule shall not raise any presumption that the exemption provided by Section 3(a)(11) of the Act is not available for transactions by an issuer which do not satisfy all of the provisions of the rule.

2. Nothing in this rule obviates the need for compliance with any state law relating to the offer and sale of the securities.

3. Section 5 of the Act requires that all securities offered by the use of the mails or by any means or instruments of transportation or communication in interstate commerce be registered with the Commission. Congress, however, provided certain exemptions in the Act from such registration provisions where there was no practical need for registration or where the benefits of registration were too remote. Among those exemptions is that provided by Section 3(a)(11) of the Act for transactions in "any security which is a part of an issue offered and sold only to persons resident within a single State or Territory, where the issuer of such security is a person resident and doing business within . . . such State or Territory." The legislative history of that Section suggests that the exemption was intended to apply only to issues genuinely local in character, which in reality represent local financing by local industries, carried out through local investment. Rule 147 is intended to provide more objective standards upon which responsible local businessmen intending to raise capital from local sources may rely in claiming the Section 3(a)(11) exemption.

All of the terms and conditions of the rule must be satisfied in order for the rule to be available. These are:

i. that the issuer be a resident of and doing business within the state or territory in which all offers and sales are made; and

ii. that no part of the issue be offered or sold to nonresidents within the period of time specified in the rule. For purposes of the rule the definition of "issuer" in Section 2(4) of the Act shall apply.

All offers, offers to sell, offers for sale, and sales which are part of the same issue must meet all of the conditions of Rule 147 for the rule to be available. The determination whether offers, offers to sell, offers for sale, and sales of securities are part of the same issue (i.e., are deemed to be "integrated") will continue to be a question of fact and will depend on the particular circumstances. See Securities Act of 1933 Release No. 4434 (December 6, 1961). Release 33-4434 indicates that in determining whether offers and sales should be regarded as part of the same issue and thus should be integrated any one or more of the following factors may be determinative:

i. Are the offerings part of a single plan of financing;

ii. Do the offerings involve issuance of the same class of securities;

iii. Are the offerings made at or about the same time;

iv. Is the same type of consideration to be received; and

v. Are the offerings made for the same general purpose.

Subparagraph (b)(2) of the rule, however, is designed to provide certainty to the extent feasible by identifying certain types of offers and sales of securities which will be deemed not part of an issue, for purposes of the rule only.

Persons claiming the availability of the rule have the burden of proving that they have satisfied all of its provisions. However, the rule does not establish exclusive standards for complying with the Section 3(a)(11) exemption. The exemption would also be available if the issuer satisfied the standards set forth in relevant administrative and judicial interpretations at the time of the offering but the issuer would have the burden of proving the availability of the exemption. Rule 147 relates to transactions exempted from the registration requirements of Section 5 of the Act by Section 3(a)(11). Neither the rule nor Section 3(a)(11) provides an exemption from the registration requirements of Section 12(g) of the Securities Exchange Act of 1934, the anti-fraud provisions of the federal securities laws, the civil liability provisions of Section 12(2) of the Act, or other provisions of the federal securities laws.

Finally, in view of the objectives of the rule and the purposes and policies underlying the Act, the rule shall not be available to any person with respect to any offering which, although in technical compliance with the rule, is part of a plan or scheme by such person to make interstate offers or sales of securities. In such cases registration pursuant to the Act is required.

4. The rule provides an exemption for offers and sales by the issuer only. It is not available for offers or sales of securities by other persons. Section 3(a)(11) of the Act has been interpreted to permit offers and sales by persons controlling the issuer, if the exemption provided by that Section would have been available to the issuer at the time of the offering. See Securities Act Release No. 4434 (December 6, 1961). Controlling persons who want to offer or sell securities pursuant to Section 3(a)(11) may continue to do so in accordance with applicable judicial and administrative interpretations.

a. Transactions Covered.

Offers, offers to sell, offers for sale, and sales by an issuer of its securities made in accordance with all of the terms and conditions of this rule shall be deemed to be part of an issue offered and sold only to persons resident and doing business within such state or territory, within the meaning of Section 3(a)(11) of the Act.

b. Part of an Issue.

1. For purposes of this rule, all securities of the issuer which are part of an issue shall be offered, offered for sale, or sold in accordance with all of the terms and conditions of this rule.

2. For purposes of this rule only, an issue shall be deemed not to include offers, offers to sell, offers for sale, or sales of securities of the issuer pursuant to the exemptions provided by Section 3 or Section 4(2) of the Act or pursuant to a registration statement filed under the Act, that take place prior to the six-month period immediately preceding or after the six-month period immediately following any offers, offers for sale or sales pursuant to this rule, Provided, That, there are during either of said six-month periods no offers, offers for sale, or sales of securities by or for the issuer of the same or similar class as those offered, offered for sale or sold pursuant to the rule.

Note: In the event that securities of the same or similar class as those offered pursuant to the rule are offered, offered for sale, or sold less than six months prior to or subsequent to any offer, offer for sale or sale pursuant to this rule, see Preliminary Note 3 hereof, as to which offers, offers to sell, offers for sale, or sales are part of an issue.

c. Nature of the Issuer.

The issuer of the securities shall at the time of any offers and the sales be a person resident and doing business within the state or territory in which all of the offers, offers to sell, offers for sale, and sales are made.

1. The issuer shall be deemed to be a resident of the state or territory in which:

  i. it is incorporated or organized, if a corporation, limited partnership, trust, or other form of business organization that is organized under state or territorial law;

  ii. its principal office is located, if a general partnership or other form of business organization that is not organized under any state or territorial law;

  iii. his principal residence is located, if an individual.

2. The issuer shall be deemed to be doing business within a state or territory if:

  i. the issuer derived at least 80 percent of its gross revenues and those of its subsidiaries on a consolidated basis

    A. for its most recent fiscal year, if the first offer of any part of the issue is made during the first six months of the issuer's current fiscal year; or

    B. for the first six months of its current fiscal year or during the twelve-month fiscal period ending with such six-month period, if the first offer of any part of the issue is made during the last six months of the issuer's current fiscal year from the operation of a business or of real property located in or from the rendering of services within such state or territory; provided, however, that this provision does not apply to any issuer which has not had gross revenues in excess of $5,000 from the sale of products or services or other conduct of its business for its most recent twelve-month fiscal period;

ii. the issuer had at the end of its most recent semi-annual fiscal period prior to the first offer of any part of the issue, at least 80 percent of its assets and those of its subsidiaries on a consolidated basis located within such state or territory;

iii. the issuer intends to use and uses at least 80 percent of the proceeds to the issuer from sales made pursuant to this rule in connection with the operation of a business or of real property, the purchase of real property located in, or the rendering of services within such state or territory; and

iv. the principal office of the issuer is located within such state or territory.

d. Offerees and Purchasers; Person Resident.

Offers, offers to sell, offers for sale, and sales of securities that are part of an issue shall be made only to persons resident within the state or territory of which the issuer is a resident. For purposes of determining the residence of offerees and purchasers:

1. A corporation, partnership, trust, or other form of business organization shall be deemed to be a resident of a state or territory if, at the time of the offer and sale to it, it has its principal office within such state or territory.

2. An individual shall be deemed to be a resident of a state or territory if such individual has, at the time of the offer and sale to him, his principal residence in the state or territory.

3. A corporation, partnership, trust, or other form of business organization which is organized for the specific purpose of acquiring part of an issue offered pursuant to this rule shall be deemed not to be a resident of a state or territory unless all of the beneficial owners of such organization are residents of such state or territory.

e. Limitation of Resales.

During the period in which securities that are part of an issue are being offered and sold by the issuer, and for a period of nine months from the date of the last sale by the issuer of such securities, all resales of any part of the issue, by any person, shall be made only to persons resident within such state or territory.

Notes:

1. In the case of convertible securities resales of either the convertible security, or if it is converted, the underlying security, could be made during the period described in paragraph (e) only to persons resident within such state or territory. For purposes of this rule a conversion in reliance on Section 3(a)(9) of the Act does not begin a new period.

2. Dealers must satisfy the requirements of Rule 15c2-11 under the Securities Exchange Act of 1934 prior to publishing any quotation for a security, or submitting any quotation for publication, in any quotation medium.

f. Precautions Against Interstate Offers and Sales.

1. The issuer shall, in connection with any securities sold by it pursuant to this rule:

i. Place a legend on the certificate or other document evidencing the security stating that the securities have not been registered under the Act and setting forth the limitations on resale contained in paragraph (e);

ii. Issue stop transfer instructions to the issuer's transfer agent, if any, with respect to the securities, or, if the issuer transfers its own securities, make a notation in the appropriate records of the issuer; and

iii. Obtain a written representation from each purchaser as to his residence.

2. The issuer shall, in connection with the issuance of new certificates for any of the securities that are part of the same issue that are presented for transfer during the time period specified in paragraph (e), take the steps required by subsections (f)(1)(i) and (ii).

3. The issuer shall, in connection with any offers, offers to sell, offers for sale, or sales by it pursuant to this rule, disclose, in writing, the limitations on resale contained in paragraph (e) and the provisions of subsections (f)(1)(i) and (ii) and subparagraph (f)(2).

Intrastate Offering Regulations

We've just summarized the intrastate offering exemption requirements, above, but above are the actual regulations if you want to look at the details. Be warned that they are full of legalese and not easy to follow. We provide them simply as an additional resource to help you assess your federal securities law comfort level. If you question your corporation's qualification for this exemption, and none of the other federal exemptions seems to apply to your initial stock issuance, you'll probably need a lawyer's help to sift through the regulations and find an applicable exemption.

Private Offering Exemption

Another exemption available under the Securities and Exchange Act is the private offering exemption. (It's actually called the nonpublic offering exemption, but we prefer to characterize it positively.) It is a one-line exemption contained in Section 4(2) of the Act for "transactions by an issuer not involving any public offering." It is a very generally stated exemption. Mostly, it applies to the private issuance of shares by a corporation to a small number of people closely connected with the business of the corporation. These individuals buy shares understanding the risk of their investment and knowing there is no market for the shares—that is, they do not expect to sell the shares to another person. This is another self-executing exemption—there are no forms to file or fees to pay.

The courts have discussed the basic elements that should be present when relying on this exemption (a leading case is *SEC v. Ralston Purina Co.*, 346 U.S. 119 (1953)):

- The purchasers are able to fend for themselves due to their previous financial or business experience, because of their relationship to the issuer (the corporation, or its directors or officers), and/or because they have significant personal net worth.
- The transaction is truly a nonpublic offering involving no general advertising or solicitation.
- The shares are purchased by the shareholders for their own account and not for resale to others.
- The people to whom shares are offered are limited in number.
- The people to whom shares are offered have access to or are given information relevant to the stock transaction in order to evaluate the pros and cons of the investment—for example, financial statements, a business plan, and information about risks.

In order to better understand the factors that should, and should not, be present when relying on the private offering exemption, the SEC issued Release No. 33-4552. This document contains several statements and examples regarding the private offering exemption. (See the text of the release itself, below.) For the most part, the release restates the factors listed above. It does provide additional guidance, however, to make reliance on the private offering exemption more certain. The guidelines are "safe harbor" rules, meant to show you a safe way to issue shares in a qualified private offering. You do not have to follow them, but we suggest you do to increase your chances of qualifying for the exemption.

Here are a few of these additional points (we've paraphrased and lowered the legal content a notch or two to make the material more digestible):

- The sale of stock to promoters who take the initiative in founding or organizing the business falls within the exemption. Sales of shares to people who will constitute the executive level of the corporation —for example, directors and principal executive officers, such as the president, vice president, and chief financial officer— also qualify. However, if stock is sold to uninformed friends, neighbors, and associates with no connection to the inner workings of corporate management, the stock sale doesn't qualify.

- If you go out and ask everyone who will listen to buy shares in your new corporation, you are making a public, not a private, offering, and you do not qualify for this exemption. This is true even if you end up selling shares only to insiders.

- Size matters. If you sell a significant dollar amount of shares—even if you sell them to insiders, privately—you are making a nonqualified public offering. The release

doesn't provide numbers, just this general admonition not to get greedy.

- Don't sell shares to day traders or other high rollers. Selling shares to people with a penchant for stock flipping—buying it one day, selling it the next—will taint your private offering and make it look more like a public sale of stock.

- Your corporation should make an effort to control resales of stock issued under the exemption. The release suggests getting each shareholder to sign a statement that says the shareholder is buying the shares for investment, not for resale. Another suggestion is to place language on each issued stock certificate (called a legend) that says the shares have not been registered under the federal securities laws, have been purchased for investment, and can't be resold by the shareholder unless the resale transaction itself is registered under the federal securities laws or is exempt from these laws.

Federal Private Offering Exemption Regulations

Below is the text of the federal private offering exemptions regulations: Release No. 33-4552. It doesn't make for easy reading, but you can refer to it for more information and to help you assess how comfortable you feel about relying on this private offering exemption.

Nonpublic Offering Exemption—Release No. 33-4552

The Commission today announced the issuance of a statement regarding the availability of the exemption from the registration requirements of section 5 of the Securities Act of 1933 afforded by the second clause of section 4(1)❶ of the Act for "transactions by an issuer not involving any public offering," the so-called "private offering exemption." Traditionally, the second clause of section 4(1)❶ has been regarded as providing an exemption from registration for bank loans, private placements of securities with institutions, and the promotion of a business venture by a few closely related persons. However, an increasing tendency to rely upon the exemption for offerings of speculative issues to unrelated and uninformed persons prompts this statement to point out the limitations on its availability.

Whether a transaction is one not involving any public offering is essentially a question of fact and necessitates a consideration of all surrounding circumstances, including such factors as the relationship between the offerees and the issuer, the nature, scope, size, type and manner of the offering.

The Supreme Court in *S.E.C. v. Ralston Purina Co.*, 346 U.S. 119, 124, 125 (1953), noted that the exemption must be interpreted in the light of the statutory purpose to "protect investors by promoting full disclosure of information thought necessary to informed investment decisions" and held that "the applicability of section 4(1) should turn on whether the particular class of persons affected need the protection of the Act." The court stated that the number of offers is not conclusive as to the availability of the exemption, since the statute seems to apply to an offering "whether to few or many."❷ However, the court indicated that "nothing prevents the Commission, in enforcing the statute, from using some kind of numerical test in deciding when to investigate particular exemption claims." It should be emphasized, therefore, that the number of persons to whom the offering is extended is relevant only to the question whether they have the requisite association with and knowledge of the issuer which make the exemption available.

Consideration must be given not only to the identity of the actual purchasers but also to the offerees. Negotiations or conversations with or general solicitations of an unrestricted and unrelated group of prospective purchasers for the purpose of ascertaining who would be willing to accept an offer of securities is inconsistent with a claim that the transaction does not involve a public offering even though ultimately there may only be a few knowledgeable purchasers.❸

A question frequently arises in the context of an offering to an issuer's employees. Limitation of an offering to certain employees designated as key employees may not be a sufficient showing to qualify for the exemptions. As the Supreme Court stated in the *Ralston Purina* case: "The exemption as we construe it, does not deprive corporate employees, as a class, of the safeguards of the Act. We agree that some employee offerings may come within section 4(a), e.g., one made to executive personnel who because of their position have access to the same kind of information that the Act would make available in the form of a registration statement. Absent such a showing of special circumstances, employees are just as much members of the investing 'public' as any of their neighbors in the community." The Court's concept is that the exemption is necessarily narrow. The exemption does not become available simply because offerees are voluntarily furnished information about the issuer. Such a construction would give each issuer the choice of registering or making its own voluntary disclosures without regard to the standards and sanctions of the Act.

The sale of stock to promoters who take the initiative in founding or organizing the business would come within the exemption. On the other hand, the transaction tends to become public when the promoters begin to bring in a diverse group of uninformed friends, neighbors and associates.

The size of the offering may also raise questions as to the probability that the offering will be completed within the strict confines of the exemption. An offering of millions of dollars to non-institutional and non-affiliated investors or one divided, or convertible, into many units would suggest that a public offering may be involved.

When the services of an investment banker, or other facility through which public distributions are normally effected, are used to place the securities, special care must be taken to avoid a public offering. If the investment banker places the securities with discretionary accounts and other customers without regard to the ability of such customers to meet the tests implicit in the *Ralston Purina* case, the exemption may be lost. Public advertising of the offerings would, of course, be incompatible with a claim of a private offering. Similarly, the use of the facilities of a securities exchange to place the securities necessarily involves an offering to the public.

An important factor to be considered is whether the securities offered have come to rest in the hands of the initial informed group or whether the purchasers are merely conduits for a wider distribution. Persons who act in this capacity, whether or not engaged in the securities business, are deemed to be "underwriters" within the meaning of section 2(11) of the Act. If the purchasers do in fact acquire the securities with a view to public distribution, the seller assumes the risk of possible violation of the registration requirements of the Act and consequent civil liabilities.❹ This has led to the practice whereby the issuer secures from the initial purchasers representations that they have acquired the securities for investment. Sometimes a legend to this effect is placed on the stock certificates and stop-transfer instructions issued to the transfer agent. However, a statement by the initial purchaser, at the time of his acquisition, that the securities are taken for investment and not for distribution is necessarily self-serving and not conclusive as to his actual intent. Mere acceptance at face value of such assurances will not provide a basis for reliance on the exemption when inquiry would suggest to a reasonable person that these assurances are formal rather than real. The additional precautions of placing a legend on the securities and issuing stop-transfer orders have proved in many cases to be an effective means of preventing illegal distributions. Nevertheless, these are only precautions and are not to be regarded as a basis for Federal Private Offering Exemption regulations exemption from registration. The nature of the purchaser's past investment and trading practices or the character and scope of his business may be inconsistent with the purchase of large blocks of securities for investment. In particular, purchases by persons engaged in the business of buying and selling securities require careful scrutiny for the purpose of determining whether such person may be acting as an underwriter for the issuer.

The view is occasionally expressed that, solely by reason of continued holding of a security for the six-month capital-gain period specified in the income-tax laws, or for a year from the date of purchase, the security may be sold without registration. There is no statutory basis for such assumption. Of course, the longer the period of retention, the more persuasive would be the argument that the resale is not at variance with an original investment intent, but the length of time between acquisition and resale is merely one evidentiary fact to be considered. The weight to be accorded this evidentiary fact must, of necessity, vary with the circumstances of each case. Further, a limitation upon resale for a stated period of time or under certain circumstances would tend to raise a question as to original intent even though such limitation might otherwise recommend itself as a policing device. There is no legal justification for the assumption that holding a security in an "investment account" rather than a "trading account," holding for a deferred sale, for a market rise, for sale if the market does not rise, or for a statutory escrow period, without more, establishes a valid basis for an exemption from registration under the Securities Act.❺

An unforeseen change of circumstances since the date of purchase may be a basis for an opinion that the proposed resale is not inconsistent with an investment representation. However, such claim must be considered in the light of all of the relevant facts. Thus, an advance or decline in market price or a change in the issuer's operating results are normal investment risks and do not usually provide an acceptable basis for such claim of changed circumstances. Possible inability of the purchaser to pay off loans incurred in connection with the purchase of the stock would ordinarily not be deemed an unforeseeable change of circumstances. Further, in the case of securities pledged for a loan, the pledgee should not assume that he is free to distribute without registration. The Congressional mandate of disclosure to investors is not to be avoided to permit a public distribution of unregistered securities because the pledgee took the securities from a purchaser, subsequently delinquent.❻

The view is sometimes expressed that investment companies and other institutional investors are not subject to any restrictions regarding disposition of securities stated to be taken for investment and that any securities so acquired may be sold by them whenever the investment decision to sell is made, no matter how brief the holding period. Institutional investors are, however, subject to the same restrictions on sale of securities acquired from an issuer or a person in a control relationship with an issuer insofar as compliance with the registration requirements of the Securities Act is concerned.

Integration of Offerings

A determination whether an offering is public or private would also include a consideration of the question whether it should be regarded as a part of a larger offering made or to be made. The following factors are relevant to such question of integration: whether (1) the different offerings are part of a single plan of financing, (2) the offerings involve issuance of the same class of security, (3) the offerings are made at or about the same time, (4) the same type of consideration is to be received, (5) the offerings are made for the general purpose.

What may appear to be a separate offering to a properly limited group will not be so considered if it is one of a related series of offerings. A person may not separate parts of a series of related transactions, the sum total of which is really one offering, and claim that a particular part is a nonpublic transaction. Thus, in the case of offerings of fractional undivided interests in separate oil or gas properties where the promoters must constantly find new participants for each new venture, it would appear to be appropriate to consider the entire series of offerings to determine the scope of this solicitation.

As has been emphasized in other releases discussing exemptions from the registration and prospectus requirements of the Securities Act, the terms of an exemption are to be strictly construed against the claimant who also has the burden of proving its availability.❼ Moreover, persons receiving advice from the staff of the Commission that no action will be recommended if they proceed without registration in reliance upon the exemption should do so only with full realization that the tests so applied may not be proof against claims by purchasers of the security that registration should have been effected. Finally, sections 12(2) and 17 of the Act, which provide civil liabilities and criminal sanctions for fraud in the sale of a security, are applicable to the transactions notwithstanding the availability of an exemption from registration.

Footnotes

1   Second clause of section 4(1) is now section 4(2), as amended August 20, 1964.

2   See, also, *Gilligan, Will & Co. v. S.E.C.*, 267 F.2d 461, 467 (C.A. 2, 1959), cert. denied, 361 U.S. 896 (1960).

3   Reference is made to the so-called "investment clubs" which have been organized under claim of an exemption from the registration provisions of the Securities Act of 1933 as well as the Investment Company Act of 1940. It should not be assumed that so long as the investment club, which is an investment company within the meaning of the later Act, does not obtain more than 100 members, a public offering of its securities, namely the memberships, will not be involved. An investment company may be exempt from the provisions of the Investment Company Act if its securities are owned by no more than 100 persons and it is not making and does not presently propose to make a public offering of its securities (section 3(c)(1)). Both elements must be considered in determining whether the exemption is available.

4   See Release No. 33-4445.

5   See Release No. 33-3825 re The Crowell-Collier Publishing Company.

6   *S.E.C. v. Guild Films Company, Inc. et al.*, 279 F.2d 485 (C.A. 2, 1960), cert. denied sub nom. *Santa Monica Bank v. S.E.C.*, 364 U.S. 819 (1960).

7   *S.E.C. v. Sunbeam Gold Mining Co.*, 95 F.2d 699, 701 (C.A. 9, 1938); *Gilligan, Will & Co. v. S.E.C.*, 267 F.2d 461, 466 (C.A. 2, 1959); *S.E.C. v. Ralston Purina Co.*, 346 U.S. 119, 126 (1953); *S.E.C. v. Culpepper et al.*, 270 F.2d 241, 246 (C.A. 2, 1959).

RESOURCE

To download Release 33-4552. Release 33-4552 can be downloaded from the Securities and Exchange Commission's website at www.sec.gov/rules/final/33-4552.htm.

Regulation D Exemption Rules

Regulation D of the federal securities laws was enacted to make the sale of stock under the federal exemption rules more certain and to help smaller companies raise private capital. Regulation D contains three rules—504, 505, and 506—each of which is a separate exemption for the issuances of shares. The three rules have similarities, and each requires the online filing of federal Form D with the SEC. There is no filing fee.

The amount of money your corporation may receive for shares, the number of purchasers, and the types of people to whom you can sell shares under each of the Regulation D rules vary. Each of the rules places importance on whether your shareholders are accredited investors. This term includes the directors and executive officers of the corporation, and people with either a $1 million net worth or an annual income of at least $200,000. If you limit sales to accredited investors, you may be able to advertise the availability of your shares, issue shares to more individuals, or have less stringent disclosure requirements. Following is a brief summary of the rules.

Rule 504

Rule 504 exempts offerings up to $1 million worth of shares in a 12-month period. In some cases, you can use Rule 504 to publicly advertise and sell your shares, depending on whether you registered your stock issuance with the state securities agency, delivered a disclosure document to your shareholders under your state's rules, or sell only to accredited investors. Many companies use Rule 504 together with their state's SCOR process (see "If You Want to Make a Modest Public Offering," above) to raise $1million in capital in a limited public offering.

Rule 505

Rule 505 exempts private offerings up to $5 million. Generally there must be no more than 35 nonaccredited investors, no general advertising is permitted, and specific financial and business information must be disclosed to any nonaccredited investors included in the offering. Shareholders receive restricted stock: They must agree not to sell their shares for at least one year without registering the sale. And the stock certificates should contain language stating that the shares are unregistered and

that they may not be resold, unless the resale is registered or exempt from registration under the securities laws.

Rule 506

Rule 506 contains an exemption for the private issuance of shares. Most smaller, closely held corporations turn to Regulation D to obtain their exemption for a private offering of shares if they are not comfortable issuing their shares informally (without a filing with the SEC) under the private offering exemption discussed above.

Unlike Rules 504 and 505, there is no limit on the amount of money you can raise under this rule, though advertising is prohibited. As with Rule 505, you can sell shares to an unlimited number of accredited investors, and to no more than 35 unaccredited people. However, all nonaccredited investors must be sophisticated. This means that they, or their lawyer or other adviser whom they designate to represent them, must have enough knowledge and experience in financial and business matters to make them capable of evaluating the merits and risks of the prospective investment. The corporation must provide specific financial and business disclosures to all nonaccredited investors. You must also give each purchaser the opportunity to ask questions and receive answers concerning the terms and conditions of the offering and to obtain any additional information that the corporation possesses, or can acquire without unreasonable effort or expense, that is necessary to verify the accuracy of information already furnished to the prospective shareholders. Stock issued under this rule is restricted. A legend on the stock certificates should say that future resales must be registered or exempt from registration under the securities law.

SEE AN EXPERT

Doing a Regulation D filing under any of the Regulation D exemption rules requires work and technical expertise. You'll probably need the help of a lawyer who knows the federal securities rules to pick the best rule to use, meet its requirements, and prepare Form D. Lawyers typically charge $3,000 or so to help you with this task.

Strategies for Dealing With the Federal Securities Rules

Please review our discussion of assessing your state securities law comfort level, above. It applies here as well. Then consider these suggestions for approaching the federal exemptions and your initial stock issuance:

- Start by determining whether you clearly fall within the intrastate or private offering exemption. Probably 80% or more of small corporations issue shares in their state to their founders and easily qualify for both.

- If you are fairly sure you qualify for one of the two basic exemptions, but you want to raise your comfort level a little, review Rule 147 and Release 33-4552. Each explains ways to make reliance on each exemption more certain. For example, after reading Rule 147, you may decide to have all shareholders sign a statement that they reside in your state and that they agree not to sell shares to an out-of-state shareholder for nine months. Similarly, Release 33-4552 may motivate you to place a legend on your share certificates indicating that the shares are being purchased for investment and not for resale, and cannot be resold without registration or a determination that an exemption is available.

- If you are not sure whether you qualify for one of the two basic federal exemptions or if you want to use Rule 147 or Release 33-4552 but need help, see a lawyer.

- If you decide that you'd just feel a whole lot better following the specific exemption guidelines of one of the Regulation D rules, see a lawyer to select and meet the requirements of the appropriate rule (most likely Rule 506) and file Form D with the SEC.

Again, let common sense and good business judgment guide you. Whatever you decide, one other point bears repeating: Remember to *disclose, disclose, disclose* all material information to all investors in your new corporation. Finally, we recommend you ask an experienced lawyer to review your proposed stock issuance to ensure compliance with federal and state securities laws. ●

Understanding Corporate Taxes

n this chapter we discuss the principal tax information and concerns associated with starting and operating a business corporation. We also describe the special tax treatment accorded corporate employee equity sharing plans, including stock option and stock purchase plans. These ownership sharing plans are part of the silver lining of the corporate form; they help you increase the profitability of your corporate enterprise by attracting and motivating key employees.

The tax information in this chapter is meant to introduce you to the most important areas of corporate taxation and to provide you with enough background to discuss the issues in greater depth with a tax expert. We focus on the federal rules found in both the Internal Revenue Code (IRC) and the federal income tax regulations, which are enforced by the IRS. Most states adopt and apply the federal rules to business corporations formed or operating in their state, though they apply their own corporate tax rates. Appendix A explains how to locate your state tax office online where you can learn more and download corporate tax publications and forms.

> CAUTION
>
> **Keep up with changing tax laws.** Though we've done our best to provide you with current information, tax laws, regulations, and rates do change. Changes to individual, corporate, dividend, capital gain, and/or estate tax rules and rates occur regularly. To keep up to date, see the most recent IRS and state tax publications, available from your state tax office website and from the IRS at www.irs. gov. Also, consult a tax adviser with small business experience on a regular basis to make sure you understand how to apply the latest tax rules to your corporation.

Federal Corporate Income Tax Treatment

In this section we look at federal corporate income tax rate and compare it to individual income tax rates. We also show you how to enjoy one of the best built-in benefits of forming a corporation: the ability to split income between the corporate and individual income tax brackets to achieve an overall income tax savings for the owners of the business.

Federal Corporate Income Tax Rates

The current federal corporate income tax rate is 21%. This rate is imposed on corporate taxable income—that is, corporate net income computed by subtracting the cost of goods sold, depreciation of business assets, salaries, necessary business expenses, and other allowable credits, exclusions, and deductions from corporate gross income.

Corporations don't have special capital gains tax rates like individuals. In fact, it's more difficult for corporations to generate capital gains than it is for individuals.

Federal Individual Income Tax Rates

The owners of small corporations who work for their corporations, like all other employees, pay individual income tax on salaries and bonuses they receive from the business. The corporation can deduct these employee compensation payouts, so they are taxed just once, at the individual owner-employee level. Even better, some forms of employee fringe benefits paid to the owner-employees are deductible by the corporation and are not taxable to the employee, so no tax is paid. (More on corporate employee fringe benefits in "Tax Treatment of Employee Compensation and Benefits," below.)

Like employee compensation payouts, the payouts of corporate profits directly to the owners of a corporation in the form of dividends are taxed to the owner-employee. However, dividends are not deductible by the corporation. Therefore, owners of small corporations normally do not declare and pay dividends. Instead, to avoid the double tax, they pay out profits to the shareholders who work for the corporation as salaries, bonuses, or employee fringe benefits.

Graduated federal individual tax rates start at 10% and climb to 37%. Individuals pay a 15% or 20% tax on "qualified" dividends (dividends paid on stock in U.S. and certain foreign companies held for a specified holding period). Individuals with lower taxable incomes pay 0%. Check the IRS website at www.irs.gov and with your tax adviser for current dividend tax rules and rates.

Corporate Income and Tax Splitting

A corporation comes with the built-in advantage of allowing owner-employees to split business income between themselves and their corporation. This can result in real tax savings for owners who work for their corporation.

How Income Splitting Works

The way income splitting works is simple: Profits kept in the corporation are taxed at corporate tax rates, while profits paid out to the owners as salaries, bonuses, and other forms of employee compensation are deducted from corporate taxable income and taxed at the owner's individual tax rates. By splitting corporate income between yourself as an owner-employee and your corporation, you can keep corporate and individual income in the lowest possible corporate and individual income tax brackets to achieve an overall income tax savings.

EXAMPLE: Sally and Randolph are married and own their own incorporated lumber supply company, called S&R Wood Supply, Inc. At the close of the third quarter, S&R's CFO reports that they are on course to make $75,000 in profits by the end of the tax year, after paying corporate salaries and other operating expenses. Sally and Randy already receive a generous salary from their corporation, which puts them in one of the higher individual married filing jointly income tax brackets—any additional corporate salary paid to them will get taxed at this marginal individual tax rate. They decide to keep the profits in the business to fund expansion in the following tax year. This $75,000 of retained corporate income is taxed at the 21% corporate tax rate. By comparison, consider what would happen if S&R was a partnership or LLC. All profits would pass through the business, whether or not they were kept in the business bank account to fund expansion or actually paid out to the owners, and would be taxed at their marginal individual tax rate. (Remember, unless a partnership or LLC elects corporate tax treatment, all profits of an unincorporated business are allocated and taxed to the owners each year, whether or not they are actually paid out to them. Sole proprietors can't make this election.)

How Much Money Can You Keep in or Pay Out of Your Corporation?

With all the talk about corporate income splitting, it's natural to wonder just how much flexibility corporate owners have to shift business income between their corporation and themselves to save on income taxes. After all, the IRS knows about corporate income splitting, too, and you can be sure that it doesn't give you a completely free hand to do whatever you wish in an effort to keep business income in the lowest possible corporate and individual income tax brackets.

Be Aware of the Personal Holding Company Penalty

IRC Sections 541 through 547 impose a 20% surtax on the income of personal holding companies (PHCs). Generally, a corporation is a PHC if five or fewer shareholders own 50% or more of the corporation's stock, and if 60% or more of the corporation's gross income for the tax year is from personal service contracts (generally, contracts for personal services that name the person who must perform the services) or from passive sources such as dividends, interest, rents, or royalties. Generally, most small business corporations don't need to worry about being classified as a PHC and having to pay this tax even if they have five or fewer shareholders because: (1) a tax adviser can tell you how to use a corporate services contract that stays clear of being classified as a personal services contract, and (2) most small corporations do not have significant passive income. Also, the PHC rules provide special exceptions for rental income and software royalties (this type of income is not counted to determine if a corporation is a PHC)—two of the categories of passive income most likely to be earned by small corporations. Further, if a corporation is found to be a PHC by the IRS and is assessed a PHC tax, the corporation is normally allowed to avoid the PHC surtax by making dividend payments (direct payments out of current earnings) and profits to shareholders. (Of course, these payouts will get hit with a dividends tax, up to 15% or 20%, on each shareholder's income tax return.) In other words, you are allowed to pay out profits to your shareholders, not to the IRS in the form of a PHC tax.

If the top dividend tax rate is increased, the PHC surtax also will go up (the two are equal).

SEE AN EXPERT

See a tax adviser if your corporation may be classified as a PHC. The PHC rules are too complicated to fully explain here. Just realize that a corporation with five or fewer shareholders that performs services or earns passive income must check with a tax adviser to make sure it avoids the PHC surtax.

Tax advisers suggest the following: (1) Corporate services contracts should allow the corporation, not the client, to designate the person who is to perform the services, and (2) the name of the individual who will be designated to perform the corporate services should not be specified in the contract.

If the IRS had its druthers, it would probably like to see you keep all business income in the corporation, pay corporate taxes on it, and then pay out these after-tax corporate profits to the owners as dividends that will be taxed again—this time on the owners' individual income tax returns. Of course, you're not going to do this; small corporations rarely pay dividends to owners. Instead, as discussed above, they pay out pretax profits to the owners as salaries, bonuses, and employee fringe benefits, which are deducted from corporate income. This is what corporate income splitting is all about: being taxed only once, and at the lowest possible tax rates, on corporate profits. In this section, we discuss the basic rules that affect how far you can go under IRS rules when splitting corporate income.

Retaining Income to Cover Operating Expenses

So, how much income can you keep in your corporation to take advantage of the low corporate income tax rate? The answer is simple: as much income as you need to do business. This is an obvious, practical rule, but the IRS also accepts it. IRS rules say that you can keep income in your corporation—that is, you do not have to pay it out as dividends that are taxable to your shareholders—as long as you have a business reason for retaining the income. Obviously this includes retaining income to meet normal operating expenses, such as rent, utilities, salaries (including the owners' salaries; we discuss this more below), working capital requirements, and other normal business expenses. A corporation can also retain income for nonrecurring costs, such as paying off debt, expanding the business, covering product liability losses, or acquiring a new business.

How Much Working Capital Do You Need?

The courts have adopted a formula that tells you how much working capital is normally necessary for one corporate business cycle. (One cycle includes the manufacture or procurement of inventory, its sale to consumers, and the eventual receipt of payment for the goods by the consumer.) This is called the *Bardahl* formula, because it comes from a case called *Bardahl Mfg. Corp. v. United States* (29 A.F.T.R. 2d 72, 72-1 USTC 9158 (1971)). The IRS automatically signs off on this much working capital retention. The formula is complex, but your tax adviser can show you the math if you're interested in more information.

Retaining Additional Income: The Accumulated Earnings Credit

The basic rule for retaining income is simple enough, but things change when you want to retain income in your corporation that is not absolutely necessary for business. Let's look at an example to understand how.

EXAMPLE: Nicole, who is the sole owner of Nicole's Soles, Inc., a shoe manufacturer, decides it would be nice to save tax dollars by keeping $200,000 in her corporation even though her corporate operating budget only requires $150,000. Here's where specific IRS rules kick in. Under Internal Revenue Code Section 535(c), corporations automatically get what's called an accumulated earnings credit that allows them to keep a certain amount of money in the business whether or not it is needed for business purposes. The credit is $250,000 of earnings and profits (E&P) for most corporations. (Certain professional service corporations, such as health, law, accounting, architectural, engineering, actuarial, and consulting corporations, get a $150,000 credit.)

This credit seems simple enough, too. Nicole doesn't have to worry about keeping a $50,000 over-budget amount in her corporation, because her automatic $250,000 credit covers the entire $200,000 of retained earnings. Of course, little is simple under the IRS rules, and the accumulated earnings credit is no exception. There are two technical points to keep in mind, each having to do with the fact that the automatic credit is a cumulative amount:

- The credit applies to the first $250,000 ($150,000 for certain professional service corporations) of retained corporate earnings, not just to the first $250,000 ($150,000 for certain PSCs) retained for nonbusiness purposes. In other words, if Nicole decides instead to keep $300,000 in her corporation—$150,000 to meet her budget plus $150,000 extra—her retained earnings credit covers the first $250,000—the remaining $50,000 isn't covered by the credit.

- You get one cumulative credit that applies to the ongoing balance in the corporation's earnings and profits account (a corporate financial account). In other words, you don't get a new credit that starts fresh at $0 each year. So, if Nicole starts the current year with a $100,000 balance in her corporation's E&P account, then accumulates $300,000 additional E&P during the current tax year, at year end her corporation's accumulated E&P exceed the automatic earnings credit by $150,000 ($400,000 cumulative E&P minus $250,000).

The upshot of all this is that if your corporation retains income—which it will unless all profits are paid out each year (highly unlikely)—and if the current running balance in the corporation's E&P account is equal to or less than your corporation's earnings and credit amount, you are fine. But if the E&P account exceeds the automatic credit amount, you should be able to show the IRS, if it audits your corporation's tax returns, that the amounts accumulated over the credit amount are for the business needs of your corporation. If you can show a business reason for excess accumulations of income, the IRS will leave you alone. If you can't, under IRC Section 531, the IRS can assess a 20% surtax on excess accumulations. This penalty tax is added to your regular corporate income tax liability for the tax year. In effect, the IRS is saying that you must either pay this money out to your shareholders (who currently pay up to a 15% to 20% qualified dividend tax on the payout), or it will assume that you did and make the corporation pay an additional 20% tax on excess accumulations.

How Much Money Can a Corporation Pay Out?

Now that we've looked at the corporate side of the income splitting equation—namely, how much money a corporation can keep in the business—let's look at the other side. You'll want to understand how much money your corporation can pay out to its owner-employees in deductible salaries, bonuses, and fringe benefits. Fortunately, the answer is very straightforward: as much as it wants, as long as the owners earned it. In other words, a corporation can reduce its taxable income by paying out profits to owners, as long as the owners actually work in the business and are paid reasonably. We talk more about paying reasonable salaries in "Salaries and Bonuses," below.

Tax update. There are a number of definitions, exceptions, and limitations associated with the 20% pass-through deduction. Here are some of the important ones:

- You can deduct 20% of "qualified business income" that is passed through to you from your unincorporated business on your individual federal income tax return. The IRS is expected to issue regulations to indicate what is included and excluded in this type of income, but the most important requirement set forth in the statute is that the income must be "connected with the conduct of the trade of business." The statute excludes certain types of capital gain, dividends, interest passed through the business, and compensation (salary) the business pays to an owner.

- The deduction can be limited or eliminated if the business owner's taxable income exceeds specified threshold amounts (special rules apply to service business owners).

- This isn't a tax credit, just a deduction, so if your effective federal income tax rate is 25%, you can be on course to obtain an effective tax savings of 5% of your passed-through qualifying business income.

The pass-through deduction is scheduled to expire in 2026. As with any tax provision, and particularly with a newly enacted one, it will take time for the IRS to explain all the ins and outs of this deduction. You can take comfort in the fact the IRS should promulgate a form that taxpayers can use to see if they qualify for the deduction. By filling in the form and performing its calculations, the form's bottom line should tell you all you need to know.

Corporate Accounting Period and Tax Year

Under IRS rules, a corporation's accounting period (the period for which it keeps its annual financial records) and its tax year (the period for which it files annual corporate income tax returns) must be the same. You will choose your corporation's tax year and accounting period when you file the first corporate tax return. The ending date of the accounting period for which the first tax return is filed becomes the ending date of the corporation's tax year.

Corporations can choose a calendar tax year ending on December 31—the same tax year used by most individuals. Or a corporation may choose a fiscal year instead, consisting of a 12-month period ending on the last day of any month other than December—for example, from July 1 to June 30. (Personal service corporations are an exception to this rule; see below.) In addition, a corporation may also choose a "52/53-week" year. This is a period that ends on a particular day closest to the end of a month—for example, "the last Friday in March" or "the Friday in March nearest to the end of the month." Most corporations choose either a calendar or a fiscal tax year.

The choice of tax year and accounting period is important. It determines how your books are kept and when corporate financial statements and tax returns must be prepared. Check with your tax adviser before making this decision.

Tax Year Rules for Personal Service Corporations

If your corporation is a personal service corporation as defined by the IRS, you must choose a calendar year for your corporate tax year (and your accounting period) unless the IRS approves your application to use a fiscal year. A personal service corporation is defined in the Internal Revenue Code as "a corporation the principal activity of which is the performance of personal services ... [if] such services are substantially performed by employee-owners." This means that if you are incorporating a service-only business or profession—for example, legal services, architecture, business consulting, or financial planning—you are required to adopt a calendar year as your corporate tax year, unless you qualify to apply for a fiscal tax year under a special IRS exception. If you want to adopt a fiscal tax year for your personal service corporation, your tax adviser can explain the requirements and application procedures.

Tax Treatment of Employee Compensation and Benefits

This section provides an overview of the tax treatment of corporate salaries and basic corporate employee fringe benefits. We'll start with the most basic tax issue: the tax treatment of employee salaries and bonuses.

RESOURCE

For information about equity sharing plans. "Employee Equity Sharing Plans," below, discusses the unique advantages of corporate employee equity sharing plans that allow employees to share a piece of the ownership pie, a particularly bright light in the constellation of corporate employee benefits.

Salaries and Bonuses

A corporation may deduct amounts paid to employees as salaries (including bonuses) for corporate income tax purposes. Salaries and bonuses must be reasonable and must be paid for services actually performed by the employee. If the IRS thinks otherwise, it can disallow the deduction for the amount it decides is excessive. In practice, if your business is profitable enough to compensate its employees handsomely, you should be able to argue that they are worth top dollar, and therefore your salaries are reasonable.

Some payouts of employee compensation are more likely to attract the attention of the IRS, particularly in the context of a small corporation where the owners also manage and work for the corporation. For example, huge salary increases or large discretionary lump-sum bonuses paid to shareholder-employees of small corporations may be questioned by the IRS, because such compensation is sometimes used as a means of paying disguised dividends to the shareholders. That is, the compensation is a return of capital to the shareholder rather than a bona fide payment for services rendered by the employee.

In the unusual event that the IRS claims your salary is unreasonable, it will treat the excess amount as a dividend. This will not have an adverse effect on you as a shareholder-employee, because you have to pay income tax on salaries as well as dividends. (In fact, the current dividend tax of up to 15% to 20% is probably less than your marginal tax rate, so you may save a little in individual tax if income is treated as a dividend.) However, it will prevent your corporation from deducting the disallowed portion of compensation as a business expense.

Don't worry too much about the IRS claiming that your corporation's salaries or bonuses are too high. Compensation should be considered reasonable as long as your corporation remains profitable, and you are paying salaries that are commensurate with what other executives get in similar businesses. As always, ask your tax adviser for guidance if you have doubts. Another strategy is to ask your board of directors to adopt a resolution detailing your abilities, qualifications, and responsibilities and documenting why you are entitled to the wages and benefits that your corporation is paying you. (For board resolutions covering numerous legal and tax matters, including this one, see *The Corporate Records Handbook*, by Anthony Mancuso (Nolo).)

Corporate Retirement Plans

Corporations, like other businesses, may deduct payments made on behalf of employees to qualified retirement plans. Contributions and accumulated earnings under such plans are not taxed to the employee until the employee receives them. As you doubtless know, this is advantageous, because employees generally will be in a lower tax bracket at retirement age, and the funds, while they are held in trust, can be invested and allowed to accumulate with no tax due on investment income or gains prior to their distribution.

If your corporation decides to set up a retirement plan, you will need the help of a retirement plan specialist to establish, administer, and file reports for your plan. (See "How to Set Up a Retirement Plan," below.)

Types of Retirement Plans

There are two basic types of retirement plans: defined contribution and defined benefit plans. (Other plans are hybrids of these two basic types.) A defined contribution plan—the type used by many small corporations—specifies a yearly contribution amount or formula to use to compute contributions on behalf of each employee. A defined benefit plan guarantees a specified benefit on retirement, which can be as large as 100% of an employee's annual pay during the employee's highest-paid years. Defined benefit plans are more expensive to fund and administer, so smaller corporations usually opt for some type of defined contribution plan unless the founders are the only employees—for example, in an incorporated professional practice.

Today, the most common types of retirement plans are defined contribution plans. Here are the most popular:

- **401(k) plan.** Participating employees contribute a portion of their salary (before taxes) to their 401(k) account. The corporation may make contributions to each employee's account as well. The 401(k) plan has become the most widely used type of retirement plan. It is cost-effective for employers and typically allows employees to choose how they want to invest their funds.

- **SIMPLE plan.** A corporation with 100 or fewer employees can adopt this type of plan. The plan can take the form of an IRA established for each participant, or a cash or deferred 401(k) arrangement. The advantage of SIMPLE plans is that they are easier to set up and operate (less paperwork, fewer filing formalities, and simpler rules) than other qualified retirement plans. They also allow top executives to receive a greater level of contributions than those allowed under the nondiscrimination rules that apply to standard retirement plans.

- **SEP (Simplified Employee Pension) IRA.** This is another fairly simple type of retirement plan used by employers. Under a SEP, employers may contribute to their employees' IRAs. The employees maintain their accounts and can personally contribute to their IRAs also. Some SEP plans let employees receive cash payments instead of employer contributions (if so, employees pay tax on the payouts). Under a special type of salary reduction SEP, employees must receive cash payments instead of contributions.

- **Profit-sharing plan.** Unlike other plans, this plan contributes money to an employee's retirement account if the corporation turns a profit. If the corporation is profitable in a given year, a portion of company profits is allocated to each employee retirement account.

- **Money purchase plan.** Under this type of plan, the corporation contributes a percentage of each employee's salary to his or her retirement account.

- **Targeted benefit plan.** This is a hybrid defined contribution/defined benefit plan. Contributions are allocated to each employee's retirement account so that each employee can reach a targeted benefit amount at retirement.

- **Thrift or savings plan.** Employees can set aside a portion of their salary into a savings account. The corporation may make matching contributions.

- **Employee stock ownership plan (ESOP).** The corporation contributes shares of stock to each employee's account.

How to Set Up a Retirement Plan

Fortunately, you don't have to start from scratch with an accountant or tax attorney to adopt a retirement plan that meets your needs.

Retirement plan sponsors, employee benefits firms, and even banks and insurance companies have plans from which you can choose. (These vendors can also provide you with one or more of the other types of employee benefit plans discussed below—such as a medical reimbursement or term life insurance plan.) Because the needs of many, if not most, small incorporated businesses are similar, you'll usually find happiness with a prepackaged plan.

All retirement plans have to be qualified (approved) by the IRS. The standard plans discussed above have already been accepted by the IRS. So what most financial advisers and employee benefits specialists do is let you adopt one of these master or prototype plans and then offer you options within it. To submit a custom plan—that is, a plan outside the established types—to the IRS for qualification takes a long time and costs money in consulting fees. Few smaller corporations think a custom plan is worth all the extra time and money.

When you pick a plan sponsor, keep in mind the difference between custodial and trustee retirement plans. Custodians such as banks and insurance companies often do not have as many options as trustees (who are usually private corporations) when it comes to offering diverse types of investments and flexibility in investment decision making. Thus, though a retirement plan offered by a bank or insurance company is often sufficient and usually inexpensive, be sure that it allows you the freedom you may want to do things like change investments at any time, lend money to participants, allow voluntary contributions, and obtain preretirement death benefits.

RESOURCE

For more information about retirement plans. To learn more about retirement plans, see the following IRS publications, available from the IRS website at www.irs.gov:

Publication 334: *Tax Guide for Small Business*

Publication 560: *Retirement Plans for Small Business*

Publication 575: *Pension and Annuity Income*

Publication 590: *Individual Retirement Arrangements (IRAs).*

Another helpful resource is *IRAs, 401(k)s & Other Retirement Plans*, by John C. Suttle, CPA, and Twila Slesnick, Ph.D. (Nolo).

Medical Benefits

Tax-favored corporate medical benefits include deductible direct reimbursement plans, prepaid accident, health, and disability insurance, and term life insurance. These benefits enjoy a double tax advantage: The corporation can deduct these employee perks from its taxable income, and the employee is not taxed on the benefit, either.

Accident and Health Insurance

A corporation may deduct premiums paid by the corporation for accident and health insurance coverage for employees, their spouses, and their dependents. And these premiums paid by the corporation are not included in the employee's income for tax purposes. In addition, insurance proceeds and benefits are not normally taxable. Coverage need not be part of a group plan. If you prefer, the employee may pick a policy, pay for it, and get reimbursement from the corporation.

Unincorporated business owners also can deduct premiums paid for themselves and their spouses for health insurance.

Medical Expense Reimbursement

A corporation may deduct amounts paid by the corporation to repay the medical expenses of employees, their spouses, and their dependents. These amounts are not included in the employee's income for tax purposes. Typically, a small corporation adopts a reimbursement plan to pay a portion of the medical expenses not covered by a corporate-sponsored health plan—for example, deductible amounts and medical expenses not picked up by the plan.

Term Life Insurance

A corporation can deduct a certain amount of the premiums paid on behalf of employees for group term life insurance, as long as the corporation is not the beneficiary. The employee is not taxed on the value of premium payments assumed by the corporation for up to $50,000 worth of insurance coverage. Death proceeds under such insurance are also generally not included in the employee's income for tax purposes. This corporate tax break is available only if the insurance plan does not discriminate in favor of key employees.

This corporate employee perk is not available to unincorporated business owners and their employees, who do not get to deduct life insurance premiums.

Disability Insurance

Another corporate perk is the ability to provide tax-deductible disability insurance for employees. Premiums paid by a corporation for employee disability insurance coverage are deductible by the corporation and not taxed to the employee. Benefits paid under a disability insurance policy are generally taxable to the employee unless the employee paid the premiums or suffers a permanent injury.

RESOURCE

For more information about the tax treatment of employee benefits. IRS Publication 525, *Taxable and Nontaxable Income,* contains further information on the tax treatment of each of the fringe benefit plans and perks discussed in this section. You can browse or download this and other helpful publications from the IRS website at www.irs.gov.

Employee Equity Sharing Plans

One of the best aspects of the corporate form is its ability to motivate key employees by letting them share in corporate ownership. Giving employees a piece of the ownership pie through the issuance of corporate stock is a unique benefit built into the corporate legal structure and blessed with special tax benefits under the Internal Revenue Code. No other limited liability business form features this ready-made model for capital participation by employees. For example, in a limited partnership or LLC, attempting to give employees an ownership interest is legally complicated and expensive, as well as being uncertain from a tax perspective. The IRS equity sharing rules are meant to apply to corporate stock transactions, and they make an uneasy fit when applied to unincorporated businesses.

TIP

Equity sharing works for start-ups, too. One of the benefits of stock option and other forms of equity sharing plans is that your corporation does not have to be flush with cash or ready to go public to take advantage of them. In fact, equity sharing is one way many cash-challenged corporations provide perks to employees—letting them share in future profits instead of receiving payments from current cash reserves. And even if a small corporation never goes public to create an active trading market for its shares, its stock can be an extremely valuable asset that can be cashed in by employees. For example, once a company becomes profitable, another corporation may buy its shares in a merger or buyout transaction. As part of the merger or sales transaction, the employee stock and option holders get to join the founders of the corporation in cashing in their options and shares.

There are several types of stock participation plans set up by corporations to give employees a stake in corporate ownership. We briefly discuss the most common, below, providing down-to-earth examples to help you appreciate how these plans are used in the real world. Don't let the technicalities put you off; the underlying concepts are not difficult to grasp, and you can master the fine points later. And keep in mind that the main tax benefit all equity sharing plans seek to achieve is a simple one: to change the tax treatment of a person who receives stock for services from that of an employee (who pays individual income taxes on corporate compensation, including stock, when it is paid) into that of an investor (who pays lower capital gains taxes on stock later, when it is sold for a profit).

RESOURCE

How to set up an equity sharing plan. When you are ready to consider implementing an equity sharing plan, ask your tax or legal adviser or an equity plan specialist for help. Many have a standard plan with alternative provisions you can select. If you want to try drafting your own plan to save legal and tax consulting fees, see *Model Equity Compensation Plans*, edited by David R. Johanson (The National Center for Employee Ownership, www.nceo.org). It contains standard ISO, NSO, ESPP, and Phantom Stock plans (discussed below) that you can use as a first draft to customize when you consult a professional.

Stock Option Plans

Stock options come in two flavors: qualified incentive stock option (ISOs) and nonqualified stock option (NSOs). Typically, a corporation sets up a stock option plan that provides for the granting of both ISOs and NSOs to employees. Before discussing the difference between these two types of options, let's look at their similarities:

- Stock options can be granted in privately held or publicly traded corporations.

- Under the tax rules, stock options can be granted to selected employees. The normal employee benefit antidiscrimination rules that apply to retirement and profit-sharing plans do not apply to stock option plans.

- The board of directors or a special employee compensation committee set up by the board decides who gets options each year. The idea is to provide incentives for key employees to keep working for the company.

- An employee first receives a stock option grant, which is a future right to buy shares at a set price (called a strike price). The strike price of options is critical to their value. The options become valuable to an employee only if the value of the stock rises above the option strike price. If the shares stay at or go below the option strike price, the options are valueless to the employee.

- The employee waits until the option vests. This is the time, legally, when the employee can exercise the option and buy the shares specified in the option grant at the specified strike price. Vesting is not required under the tax rules—an option can vest as soon as it's granted—but many companies choose to have options vest over a few years. If an employee stays with the company, the options vest, and the employee can buy the shares. If the employee leaves before they vest, the options disappear and the employee loses the ability to buy shares at a low strike price. Option vesting can be made conditional on corporate performance criteria as well, such as the attainment of corporate profitability thresholds or R&D milestones. (Note that some companies use special reverse-vesting provisions in their option plan that provide for immediate vesting of options, but delayed vesting of the underlying stock. See "ISOs and NSOs in the Real World," below.)

- Once the employee exercises options and buys the underlying shares, the employee can either hold or sell them. In a privately held corporation, there is normally no market for the shares, so the employee waits until a market is created—for example, when the corporation goes public, or when the corporation is sold and the acquiring corporation purchases the shares as part of the buyout.

Now, let's look at the differences between ISOs and NSOs.

Incentive Stock Options (ISOs)

An incentive stock option qualifies for special tax treatment under the Internal Revenue Code. Employees normally pay lower capital gains taxes when they sell shares purchased under an ISO (more on how this works below). To qualify as ISOs, options must meet the rules set out in IRC Section 422 and associated income tax regulations. We don't cover all the requirements, but here are some of the most important:

- ISOs must be issued only to employees of the corporation. Independent contractors and others paid by the corporation for services but not classified as employees don't qualify.

- The ISO strike price—that is, the price at which an employee can exercise an ISO and buy the ISO shares—must be set at no less than the fair market value of the shares at the time the ISO grant is approved by the board.

- If an employee owns more than 10% of the voting stock of the company when the option is granted, the strike price must be set at no less than 110% of the stock's fair market value on the date of the grant.

- The maximum value of ISOs that can vest per employee per year is $100,000.

- Shares bought when an ISO is exercised cannot be sold by the employee until at least two years from the date the option was granted, and at least one year from the date of exercise.

- If any of the ISO rules are not met, the options become nonqualified stock options (NSOs), meaning that they get lesser tax benefits. (See "Nonqualified Stock Options (NSOs)," below.)

Let's now look at the main benefits to employees conferred by the ISO tax rules—and the collateral tax consequences to the corporation.

First, an employee does not pay regular income taxes when an ISO is granted, when it vests, or when the employee exercises the ISO by buying the shares (but see discussion of alternative minimum tax, or AMT, below). Normally, employees are liable for income tax as soon as they have the legal right to receive or ask for a form of compensation. Avoiding this immediate income tax is the major tax benefit of ISOs.

Here's how the basic tax rules work: When an employee exercises an option by buying shares at their strike price, the employee gets an income tax basis in the shares that equals the strike price payment. This basis is used to collect tax from the employee later, when the employee sells the shares.

EXAMPLE: If Veronica exercises a vested ISO to buy 1,000 shares at $1, she pays no tax when she buys the shares for $1,000. Instead, she gets a tax basis of $1,000 in her shares. If the shares go up in value and she sells them two years later for $3,000, she pays tax on the difference between the $3,000 sales price and her $1,000 basis: $2,000. And, she pays tax at capital gains tax rates, which are lower than regular income tax rates if the stock has been held at least one year.

There is one tax wrinkle, however, that applies to ISOs. The employee is subject to paying an alternative minimum tax (AMT) when an ISO is exercised. This is a special federal tax system that imposes tax on special items of tax preference—that is, tax transactions in which taxpayers get a regular income tax break, such as the exercise of an incentive stock option. When an employee exercises an ISO, an AMT tax may be triggered, depending on the employee's total tax picture for the year and the amount of ISOs exercised during the year. Generally, if ISO shares have appreciated significantly since the date they were granted and an employee exercises a large number of ISOs, an AMT tax may be due. And, this AMT tax may be hefty—up to 26% or more of the difference between the current value of the stock and the lower stock purchase price the employee pays to buy the stock under the ISO.

CAUTION

Don't forget the AMT. It is important to investigate any AMT tax consequences before exercising an ISO under an employee stock option plan.

So far, our discussion applies to the way ISOs are taxed under normal rules. But, if an employee does not meet the ISO holding period requirements—that is, if the employee sells shares purchased under an ISO less than two years from the date of the initial grant and less than one year from the ISO exercise date— the ISO becomes an NSO. This means that the employee can't take advantage of the ISO tax rules. Instead, the employee has to pay ordinary income taxes on the difference between the value of the shares on the ISO exercise date and the option strike price. (This is how NSOs are treated; see the discussion and example in "Nonqualified Stock Options (NSOs)," below.)

Sales of ISO stock that violate these holding period requirements are called "disqualifying dispositions." They come up a lot in the ISO world because employees often sell their ISO shares before meeting the holding requirements. *In fact, many ISO holders buy and sell their options on the same date in a cashless exercise.* We talk about these real-world ISO transactions in "ISOs and NSOs in the Real World," below.

Now that you understand how employees do or don't get taxed on ISO transactions, let's look at the corporation itself. The corporation does not get to take an employee compensation deduction when an ISO option is granted, vests, or is exercised by an employee. This is the price the IRC charges a corporation for the tax benefits bestowed on ISO employees. Even though an employee is allowed to buy ISO shares at a strike price that is less than the current value of the shares, the corporation cannot deduct the cost of providing this benefit (the reduced payment for shares) to the employee.

Nonqualified Stock Options (NSOs)

A nonqualified stock option (NSO) is an option that does not meet the ISO rules described above. NSOs can be issued to employees or to nonemployees—such as independent contractors, corporate board members, attorneys, accountants, or even corporate suppliers.

(Of course, outsiders often prefer to be paid hard cash, but the tax law lets a corporation issue NSOs as payment for services to outsiders, whereas ISOs can only go to corporate employees.)

NSOs do not get the same capital gains tax benefit as ISOs; they are subject to ordinary income tax when they are exercised, but this treatment is still better than other forms of employee compensation for two reasons: (1) NSOs are not taxed when they are granted, and (2) an employee pays capital gains rates on appreciation of shares that occurs after the NSO exercise date.

RESOURCE

Where to go for NSO details. We explain the basics of NSO taxation in this section, but you'll find the details in Income Tax Regulation 1.83-7. You can browse this and other federal income tax regulations at www.taxsites.com.

If the options (as distinct from the underlying stock) have a readily ascertainable market value, NSOs are taxed to the employee at the time of the grant—and the corporation gets an equivalent employee compensation deduction. Options have a recognized value if they are publicly traded on an options exchange. Most options are not traded on an options market, so NSOs aren't normally taxed when granted.

NSOs without a marketable option value are not taxed when granted. Instead, they are taxed when the option holder exercises them and buys the underlying shares. At that time, the option holder pays ordinary income tax on the difference between the strike price paid for the shares and their value on the exercise date. The AMT tax does not apply.

EXAMPLE: Veronica exercises a vested NSO option to buy 1,000 shares with a strike price of $1. The shares have a market value of $3,000 on the date that she exercises the option. She owes tax on $2,000: the spread between the stock's $3,000 market value less her $1,000 payment. This is the tax value of the benefit she receives from the NSO grant. Veronica also gets a $3,000 tax basis in her shares (the market value of the shares at the time she purchases them). If she sells the shares later, she pays capital gains taxes on the difference between the selling price and her basis. For instance, if she sells them for $7,000, she pays capital gains taxes on the $4,000 difference.

TIP

NSO rules can apply to ISOs, too. As discussed in "Incentive Stock Options (ISOs)," above, the ISO automatically becomes an NSO if an ISO holder exercises options by buying the shares but sells the shares earlier than two years from the ISO grant date or one year from the stock purchase date, or if the ISO becomes disqualified for any other reason. This means that the seller must pay regular income tax on the difference between the value of the shares on the exercise date and the lower strike price paid for them. (In other words, the seller is taxed just as in the previous example.) The rest of the stock sales proceeds are taxed at capital gains rates.

What are the NSO tax effects to the corporation? When an NSO is exercised, the corporation gets an employee compensation tax deduction equal to the amount that is taxed to the NSO holder (not the tax amount, but the larger amount subject to tax). In the previous example, Veronica's corporation gets to deduct $2,000—this is the amount of the transaction that was taxable to Veronica (the value of the stock she did not have to pay for).

> **CAUTION**
>
> **NSO's are subject to restrictions on valuation and other terms under the Internal Revenue Code (Section 409A).** For example, they can become immediately taxable and subject to an additional 20% tax if they are issued for less than market value. Ask your tax adviser for the latest information on this topic.

ISOs and NSOs in the Real World

Some of the tax rules and consequences associated with options may seem unworkable at first sight. For example, why would a corporation want to grant ISOs if they can't deduct them from corporate taxable income? And how does an employee raise the cash to exercise an option and buy the underlying shares at their strike price? Here are some of the special considerations and workarounds that show how and why stock options are popular with small and large, start-up and established corporations alike. Let's first look at special stock option considerations from the corporation's perspective.

Corporate Considerations

Many fast-growing companies start out spending more than they earn and don't care about the nondeductibility of ISOs as an employee expense. They don't have profits to reduce anyway or, if they do, they want to keep profits on the books to impress investors. They like ISOs because they don't cost the company cash and they help attract key employees who will work hard to raise share value. ISOs are a perfect fit for them.

Moreover, even profitable corporations seeking ways to reduce corporate taxes on income are attracted to ISOs. They provide a strong incentive to employees and don't cost hard cash—except, of course, for the legal and tax help to set up the plan and the administrative costs to implement it. In addition, they know that most employees will not buy shares with their own money or keep them long enough to meet the ISO stock holding period requirements. Instead, they expect employees to make a cashless exercise of their options when the company makes a market for its shares by going public or merging with another company. At that time, the ISOs get converted to NSOs, and the corporation gets an employee compensation deduction to reduce its taxable income.

Here's another real-world option strategy for corporations: Companies that expect to have quickly rising stock prices try to lessen the tax cost of options granted to their employees by letting them exercise their options as soon as possible. This keeps the taxable spread between the market value of the stock and the exercise price small, reducing ISO, AMT, or NSO regular income taxes.

Of course, these companies don't want the employees to walk away from the corporation on the early option exercise date, either; they want their workers to stick around to help increase the corporation's share value. Here's what these companies sometimes do to achieve both goals: (1) they allow options to vest immediately upon their grant date, but (2) the stock itself does not vest until the employee has been with the company for a specified period after the option grant date. (This exercise-before-vesting technique is sometimes called reverse vesting.) The unvested shares can be voted and are eligible to participate in dividends just like other shares of corporate stock, but they do not become the legal property of the shareholder until the end of the stock vesting period set up under the plan. If the employee leaves the company before the shares vest, the company can buy the shares back from the employee at the exercise price paid by the employee.

Note that options plans set up to issue this type of restricted stock work fine if the employee actually buys the shares early on, before the stock appreciates. If the employee waits to buy the shares until after they have appreciated, any AMT or regular income tax savings have been lost.

CAUTION

Employees must file a tax election to avoid restricted stock taxes. The employee must file an IRS 83(b) tax election within 30 days of buying the unvested shares. (We discuss the 83(b) election procedure below.) This election allows unvested shares to be taxed for AMT and regular income taxes on the date of exercise, not later when the shares vest. If the employee gets taxed later when the shares vest, the spread between the market value and exercise price in a successful company will be higher, defeating the purpose of the reverse vesting strategy.

Employee Considerations

Now let's look at how employees use the stock options rules in real life. To start with, employees often don't have to pay cash to exercise their options—or don't really want to risk cash to invest in their corporation, no matter how rosy its balance sheet looks. Here are some strategies employees use to get around paying cash up front to buy option shares:

- Some plans allow employees to borrow cash from the company to buy their ISO or NSO shares.

- If there is a market for the shares, some plans permit employees to make a cashless exercise of some options (see below) to buy the remaining shares.

- Some plans let employees trade their options for the cash value of the stock appreciation rights (SARs) that have accrued on the

underlying shares since the initial grant date. (See the discussion of SARs in "Other Equity Sharing Plans," below.)

CAUTION

Option loans can bite. Employees should think twice before signing a promissory note to exercise options. If the value of the shares goes below the strike price paid for them, the shareholder will walk away with no cash after selling the shares and repaying the loan. Even worse, the employee will have to dip into personal funds to repay the portion of the loan not covered by the sale.

There is one additional strategy often used by stock option employees: ISO and NSO holders often do nothing. They simply hold onto their options until the company makes a move—that is, merges with another company or goes public. At that date, assuming share value has increased over the option strike price, they exercise their options, then immediately sell the shares.

Exercising options, then immediately turning around and selling them, is often accomplished in a cashless exercise. The stockbroker (for publicly traded shares) or acquiring company "lends" the option holder the strike price value of the shares, uses this money to buy the shares from the corporation, sells the shares to the public, or transfers them to the acquiring company and gets repaid the strike price (plus commission if the buyer is a broker). The option holder gets what's left: the value of the shares less the strike price and any commissions paid. Note that a cashless exercise converts all ISOs automatically to NSOs because the one-year holding requirement from date of exercise to sale of stock is not met. Everyone—ISO and NSO holders alike—pays regular income taxes on the net conversion proceeds in a cashless exercise.

Employee Stock Purchase Plans (ESPPs)

Another equity sharing perk with tax advantages is the qualified employee stock purchase plan (ESPP) allowed under Internal Revenue Code (IRC) Section 423. An ESPP is usually adopted as a component of a broad corporate equity plan that also provides for employee stock options. The plan allows a corporate employee to buy additional shares of corporate stock each year, in addition to shares the employee may be able to buy under the corporate ISO and/or NSO plans.

Unlike an option to purchase ISO or NSO shares under a stock option plan, ESPP stock normally must be bought each year by an employee—usually out of the employee's own pocket (employees don't get an option they can exercise in a later year). One of the advantages of an ESPP is that corporations can let employees buy ESPP shares at a discount of up to 15% of the stock's current value. (In comparison, ISOs must be granted at 100% of the value of the underlying shares.)

The Primary Features of an ESPP

Here are the main features of an ESPP:

- An ESPP, like an ISO, can cover only employees, not independent contractors or others not classified as employees.

- Generally, all corporate employees must be included in the ESPP, although some part-time workers, highly compensated employees, and others may be excluded from ESPP coverage; also, employees who own 5% or more of the corporation's voting stock *cannot* be included.

- Under an ESPP, an employee can purchase up to $25,000 worth of corporate stock each year at a price of not less than 85% of the stock's value—this means 85% of its value at the time of the ESPP grant or at time of its exercise, whichever is less. (Since the price of ISO stock must be set at 100% of value at the time of the option grant, the stock discount is one of the advantages of ESPP stock from the employee's point of view.)

- An ESPP may link the purchase of stock to a specified percentage of employee income —for example, employees may be allowed to purchase discounted ESPP stock worth up to 10% of their annual salary, subject to the overall yearly purchase limit of $25,000.

- ESPP shares are subject to the same holding period rules that apply to ISO shares. That is, employees cannot sell ESPP shares within two years from the grant date and one year from the date they purchased their shares.

Tax Treatment of ESPPs

Now let's look at how the IRS treats ESPPs. To start, employees pay no tax when they buy the shares. But assuming the employee sells the ESPP shares at a gain later—and assuming the holding period rules are met—ordinary income tax is due on the difference between the discounted price paid by the employee for the shares and the value of the shares on the date they were granted or purchased, whichever is less. (The corporation gets an employee compensation deduction for same amount.) The rest of an employee's ESPP stock sales profits are subject to capital gains taxes.

EXAMPLE: George buys 100 ESPP shares worth $100 per share at a discounted $85 per share price. He pays no tax when he buys the shares. George sells the shares two years later for a market value of $200 per share. For the year of sale, he pays regular income tax on the $15 per share purchase discount, and capital gains taxes on the remaining $100 per share profit.

If the holding period rules are not met when the employee sells ESPP shares, additional ordinary income tax may be due if the shares appreciate between the date of the ESPP grant and the date the employee buys the shares. In this case, the employee pays income tax on the difference between the value of the shares on the date of purchase, minus the discounted purchase price. (If the holding period rules had been met, the employee could pick the *lesser* of the grant date value and the purchase date value as the measure of how much tax the employee owes.) This tax is due even if the employee sells the shares at a loss.

> EXAMPLE: Bob buys 100 ESPP shares worth $100 each for $85 each. He sells them two months later, owing taxes on the $15 per share discount, even if he sells the shares for $50 each.

Again, there is no need to master these ESPP tax rules. For now, just realize that an ESPP can be a valuable component of a larger employee equity sharing plan—one that lets employees buy discounted shares for favorable tax benefits if the shares go up in value.

Restricted Stock Compensation

Restricted stock is often used to compensate corporate employees. This type of stock, described below, may be issued separately or as part of an employee equity sharing plan. However issued, restricted stock is such a regular and important feature of employee compensation that we want to discuss it here.

To begin with, the basic tax rule is that stock issued to a corporate employee is normally included in the employee's taxable compensation when it is issued, and its full value is subject to ordinary income tax. We have already looked at a few rules that carve out exceptions to this standard rule and bestow favorable income tax deferral and capital gains tax treatment for employee stock issued under ISOs, NSOs, and ESPPs. Here we briefly look at another category of stock that gets special treatment under IRS rules: restricted stock that is eligible for a special tax election under Section 83(b) of the Internal Revenue Code. This sounds more technical than it really is; the basic rules involved are straightforward.

Essentially, restricted stock that qualifies under Section 83(b) doesn't get taxed at the time that it is issued to an employee or other corporate service provider. Instead, the stock is taxed later when the restrictions are removed from the stock. This delayed taxation puts off the payment of tax by an employee—a good thing, because the employee gets to use his or her hard-earned dollars longer. And there's another tax break possible under Section 83(b) if the employee makes a special tax election when the employee gets restricted stock. It lets the employee pay capital gains, not regular income tax at higher rates, on the shares if the employee sells them later for more than the amount the stock was worth when it was issued to the employee. We explain these tax rules in "Tax Treatment of Restricted Shares Under Section 83(b)," below. But first, let's look at what types of stock qualify for special treatment under Section 83(b).

Does Section 83(b) Apply?

Section 83(b) of the Internal Revenue Code applies to restricted stock (or other restricted property) issued by a corporation to a person in exchange for the performance of services, either as an employee or as an independent contractor. Restricted stock is simply stock that has one or more legal limitations associated with it—for example, stock that is subject to being bought back by the corporation if the employee stops working for the corporation.

Other Equity Sharing Plans

In this section, we've discussed the most popular corporate equity sharing plans—ISO, NSO, and ESPP plans—and their general tax treatment. But there are other equity sharing plans in common use by small and large corporations. Here are just a few.

Stock bonus plans. These plans award discretionary shares of restricted stock to key corporate employees. The employee must agree to transfer the shares back to the corporation if the employee does not continue working for the corporation for a specified period, or if specified profit or other corporate performance goals are not met. The employee makes an election under Section 83(b) of the Internal Revenue Code to include the current value of the shares in income. Future appreciation on the shares qualifies for lower capital gains tax treatment when the shares vest and the employer sells the shares. (See "Restricted Stock Compensation," below.)

Stock appreciation rights (SARs). Instead of issuing shares, a corporation may wish to let employees participate in an increase in corporate share value without granting them stock rights, such as the right to vote or participate in dividends or corporate sales proceeds. SARs let an employee receive cash for any increase in value of the corporation's stock that occurs from the vesting of the SAR. SARs are also used in conjunction with stock option plans. For example, under some plans, an employee can turn in a vested option and receive a stock appreciation rights payment equal to the current value of the shares underlying the option, minus the option exercise price. In effect, the SAR pays the option holder the appreciation value that has accrued on the shares underlying the option from the option

grant date. SARs are also a handy way for a privately held corporation to make a market for its own shares: The corporation can cash out the employee option holder instead of waiting for a public market to develop for the shares.

Phantom stock plans. Like SARs, a phantom stock plan gives employees stock rights, but not the stock itself. A phantom stock plan can provide employees with a cash payment that tracks appreciation of the corporation's stock (like SARs) plus other stock-related rights, such as increases to the employee's phantom stock account when dividends are paid to the corporation's shareholders. Again, the employee gets treated like a shareholder without forcing the corporation to dilute the stock ownership percentages of its current shareholders.

Deferred compensation plans. DCPs are not equity plans per se, but because they often include payment in shares of corporate stock we mention them here. Under these plans, a corporation agrees to pay key employees cash or other benefits in the future. The compensation payments are spread out over time, which minimizes the tax bite to the employee—the employee isn't taxed on the payments until they are received. Deferred compensation plans may be tied to corporate profits or may simply specify amounts of stock or sums of money to be paid to an important employee—for example a signing bonus paid to a key exec, which will be paid and taxed in installments.

Tax, legal, and financial advisers who help set up ISO and NSO plans usually handle these additional plans as well. (See "How to set up an equity sharing plan" in "Employee Equity Sharing Plans," above.)

Other Equity Sharing Plans (continued)

CAUTION

Watch out for IRC Section 409A.
The Internal Revenue Code contains a complex set of provisions (buttressed by pages of federal regulations) that apply strict standards to nonqualified deferred compensation plans. Future payments and benefits under deferred compensation plans are subject to immediate income taxation unless the plans are set up in compliance with Section 409A and its associated regulations. If you run afoul of these provisions, you can expect to pay regular income tax, interest, and an additional extra 20% income tax on deferred compensation. And note this important hitch: These rules and penalties also apply to nonqualified stock options, stock appreciation rights, and other forms of nonqualified equity sharing plans. If you do not structure stock options and stock appreciation rights correctly, you can be hit with Section 409A tax liability. The lesson is clear: Check with your tax adviser to make sure that all your equity-sharing and deferred compensation plans pass muster under Section 409A and its associated regulations.

EXAMPLE 1: Bert's Cafe, Inc., has been going gangbusters for well over one year, due to the round-the-clock service provided by Bert's hard-working waiters. Bert rewards his cafe crew by issuing 1,000 shares of common stock to each worker. The stock has the following restriction typed on the back of each share certificate: "If the shareholder stops providing services for Bert's cafe during the one-year period following the stock issuance date, the shareholder agrees to transfer the shares back to Bert's Cafe for no consideration."

Section 83(b) provides tax deferral benefits (discussed below) only for restricted stock with temporary restrictions. If the restrictions will never lapse, Section 83(b) does not apply, and the employee must follow the regular tax rules and pay income tax on the current value of the shares when they are issued. Of course, permanent restrictions of this sort may lower the value of the shares, so less income tax will be due. Here is an example of permanent restrictions to which Section 83(b) does not apply.

EXAMPLE 2: Bert wants his employees to get shares right away for all their hard work without having to wait one year before the shares are fully theirs, so he puts the following statement on the shares instead: "These shares are subject to a right of repurchase by the corporation. If the shareholder wishes to transfer the shares other than to a spouse or to the shareholder's beneficiaries upon the shareholder's death, Bert's Cafe has a right of first refusal to purchase the shares from the shareholder at their book value. For a definition of book value and other provisions associated with this right of first refusal, see the provisions of the Bert's Cafe buy-sell agreement on file with the Secretary of Bert's Cafe at its principal office."

Bert also drafts a buy-sell agreement that each shareholder is required to sign prior to receiving the shares. The agreement specifies the mechanics of how the buyback works and defines book value. (Normally, "book value" is the value of the corporate assets minus liabilities of the corporation divided by the number of shares outstanding.) The main point is that this right of first refusal restriction on the shares is a permanent restriction that never lapses, so Section 83(b) does not apply. Each employee must pay ordinary income taxes on the value of the shares when they are issued.

Of course, the value of shares with a restriction of this sort is probably less than that of the unrestricted common shares that Bert owns, so each shareholder pays lower taxes on these shares than would be the case if each received unrestricted common shares. And, as always, once employees pay ordinary income tax on their shares, future appreciation on the shares that the employees get when they sell them is taxed at capital gains rates if the shares are held for the minimum capital gains holding period. (See Example 5, below.)

Tax Treatment of Restricted Shares Under Section 83(b)

Section 83(b) provides two main tax advantages: The first is a tax deferral benefit, touched on above—namely, the person receiving stock that qualifies as restricted stock under Section 83(b) does not have to pay income tax on the value of the stock when it is issued, only when the temporary stock restrictions lapse. Let's go back to and build on Example 1, above, where Bert's Cafe issues stock with a temporary restriction that qualifies under Section 83(b).

EXAMPLE 3: Assume that Bert's restricted shares are worth $1 each when issued. Bert's staff does not pay income tax on the shares when they are issued, only when the restrictions on the shares lapse one year from the issuance date. At that time they are included in the worker's income (at their current value) and taxed at the worker's regular individual income tax rates. Bert's Cafe gets a corresponding corporate income tax deduction at that time. After regular income taxes are paid on the shares, any future appreciation of the shares that the employee realizes on a sale of the stock is taxed at capital gains rates (assuming the capital gains holding period rules are met; see Example 5, below).

There is a second feature of Section 83(b) that delivers more good news. Here's how it works: Even though Section 83(b) says an employee must normally wait until the stock restrictions lapse to pay income taxes on the stock under 83(b), it allows the employee to change this income tax deferral tax treatment by electing within 30 days of receiving restricted stock to pay regular income taxes on the shares at the time they are issued. This election is made by mailing a simple 83(b) election form to the IRS. (The IRS doesn't provide a ready-made form to use; you or your tax adviser must prepare an election according to the 83(b) requirements.) If the employee makes this election, the employee is taxed right away on the current value of the shares. And future appreciation on the shares is taxed at capital gains tax rates when the shares are sold, as long as the shares are held for the minimum capital gains holding period. (See Example 5, below.)

Why is this election a possible tax benefit in some situations? Let's go back to Example 1 again. The shares that Bert issues to employees contain restrictions that will lapse in one year, so the first rule of Section 83(b) says that the shares will be taxed at that time. This may be fine for shareholders who believe that Bert's Cafe is not on track to earn enough money to increase the value of its shares significantly. These shareholders will prefer to wait to pay income taxes on their shares when the restrictions lapse. But what if a shareholder believes that Bert's Cafe will continue to do well and its shares will be worth twice as much one year down the road? That's where the 83(b) election comes in. It allows a shareholder to pay income taxes on the current value of the shares instead of waiting to pay tax on the value of the shares when the restrictions lapse. If this election is made, the shareholder pays tax on the current $1 share value (from Example 3). If the shares are worth $2 one year later when the restrictions lapse, this increase in value is not taxed to the employee at regular income tax rates. Instead, the employee pays capital gains taxes on this increase in value when the employee sells the shares (assuming the employee holds the shares for the capital gains holding period as explained in Example 5, below). Another example is in order.

EXAMPLE 4: Katherine is Bert's only employee who is concerned about the eventual income tax bite on Bert's Cafe shares when the restrictions lapse. She is the only employee who files an 83(b) election within 30 days of the issuance of the shares. She includes the $1,000 value of her 1,000 shares in her taxable income on her tax return and pays ordinary income tax on them at her current tax rates. One year later the restrictions lapse, and the value has increased to $5 per share. (Bert's Cafe had continued to do well and this is the price Bert charges his nephew Stan to buy shares in the cafe that following year.) Katherine pays no additional income tax when the restrictions lapse, but the other employees do. They must include $5,000 of income on their individual tax returns and pay regular income tax on it. When Katherine sells her shares, any amount she receives that exceeds $1,000 will be taxed at lower capital gains rates (if she owns the shares for the minimum capital gains holding period, discussed in the next example).

A final example will help illustrate the capital gains tax treatment of the shares.

EXAMPLE 5: Picking up where Example 4 left off, assume that Bert makes an offer six months after the restrictions lapse to buy the shares back from employees at $7 per share. If Katherine agrees, she has a capital gain of $6,000 ($7,000 minus the $1,000 value of the shares she paid income tax on when she filed her 83(b) election; this $1,000 is called her "basis" in her shares). Because Katherine filed the 83(b) election, her capital gains holding period started on the date she was issued the shares (this is another advantage of making the election). And because she held her shares for longer than one year, she pays lower capital gains tax on the $6,000. If another employee, Jeff, sells his shares back to Bert, Jeff's capital gain is $2,000 ($7,000 minus their $5,000 basis, the value of the shares Jeff paid tax on when the restrictions lapsed). But Jeff doesn't qualify for long-term capital gains rates yet. Because he didn't make an 83(b) election when the shares were issued, Jeff's capital gains holding period started on the date the share restrictions lapsed. He will probably want to wait until one year from this date to take Bert up on his offer.

The main point of the previous examples is that restricted stock provides tax advantages to an employee. It gives a shareholder flexibility to decide when to pay income tax on the restricted stock.

Other Tax Advantages of Restricted Stock

There are numerous other ways corporations take advantage of the tax flexibility of restricted stock to provide an advantage to corporate employees as well as the corporation. Here are just a few.

Discounted shares. A corporation can allow key employees to buy restricted shares at a low price—for example, one-half the current value of the corporation's regular common stock. These shares can be bought back by the corporation (for the amount paid by the employee) if the employee leaves or the corporation fails to meet performance goals during a specified period. The employee makes an 83(b) election and pays ordinary income tax on the sales price discount—in our example, the one-half of current value the employee did not have to pay—locking in future appreciation of the shares at capital gains rates.

Initial corporate shares issued for services. When a corporation is formed, a shareholder who receives shares of stock for services normally must pay income tax on the value of the shares. (See "Stock Issuance and Taxes" in Chapter 2.) However, if a person receives shares in return for the promise to provide future services and the shares are restricted (reverting to the corporation if the shareholder fails to perform the services), they are not taxed to the shareholder until the restrictions lapse—that is, until the shareholder performs the promised services. In other words, issuing restricted shares to a person who invests personal services in your corporation can delay the tax bite associated with this type of stock issuance transaction. Further, if the shareholder makes an 83(b) election at the time of issuance and pays income tax on the shares at their initial incorporation value, the shareholder does not pay tax when the restrictions lapse, even though the corporation's share value may have increased by then. Instead, the shareholder pays capital gains tax on the shares when sold, just like any other shareholder who invests in your corporation.

NSO plans. If restricted, unvested stock is bought by an employee as part of an NSO plan and the employee files an 83(b) election, the employee pays income tax on the current spread between market value and the exercise price, not the higher spread that may exist when the shares vest. (See the discussion of reverse vesting in "ISOs and NSOs in the Real World," above.)

Estate tax savings. The largest asset in the estate of a deceased business owner may be shares in the owner's corporation. If the shares are restricted—for example, if they are subject to the terms of a buy-sell agreement among the shareholders that requires the purchase of the shares from the estate at a price lower than the value of the shares an outsider might pay for them—the estate tax on the shares can be lowered significantly. If properly crafted as part of a buy-sell agreement, restricted stock conditions can work to dramatically lower the estate tax due on a deceased owner's shares. (For more information on drafting a corporate buy-sell agreement, see *Business Buyout Agreements*, by Anthony Mancuso and Bethany K. Laurence (Nolo).)

Other Equity Sharing Plan Issues

There are nontax issues that need to be considered when you adopt a corporate employee equity sharing plan. In this section, we discuss a few of the most important.

Financial Accounting Treatment

Generally accepted accounting principles (GAAP) are used by accountants and auditors to prepare corporate financial statements. They include special rules to reflect the cost of equity plans on a corporation's balance sheet. The GAAP rules are often different from the tax rules, and they have an enormous effect on how corporate insiders and outsiders judge the financial performance and value of a corporation. For example, even though the IRC may not allow a corporation to deduct the value of an ISO, NSO, ESPP, or other equity plan award to a corporate employee, GAAP may require the corporation to book (include) a portion or all of the employee equity benefit as an expense on the corporation's financial statements. This reduces reported corporate earnings.

Your tax adviser or equity plan specialist can clue you in on the GAAP rules to make sure you consider their impact when adopting an employee equity sharing plan.

ERISA

The federal Employment Retirement Income Security Act (ERISA) is a tangle of constantly changing rules that apply to employee benefit plans. ERISA imposes minimum mandatory vesting, coverage, distribution, and reporting rules. These rules apply to corporate pension and profit sharing plans (discussed in "Corporate Retirement Plans," above), but they can also apply to employee equity plans, unless a plan is specifically exempt from ERISA or is worded carefully to avoid the application of ERISA. In the absence of clear language in an equity plan, even large corporations can be surprised by a court decision that says ERISA requires the corporation to allow all employees and independent contractors to participate in the plan, even though this result was not intended when the plan was prepared.

Many corporations do not want ERISA to apply to their ISO, NSO, ESPP, or stock bonus plan because their plan is meant to motivate key employees whose work has a significant impact on corporate profitability, not to provide a pension or profit-sharing arrangement for the entire corporate workforce. Plan specialists that track the latest ERISA rulings and court decisions can help you make sure that your equity plan covers those workers you intend to cover.

Securities Laws

Equity interests in a corporation, such as options or shares of stock, are securities. They give option holders and other equity plan participants the chance to share in the profit-making potential of your corporation. As such, equity interests are regulated by state and federal securities laws. Fortunately, these laws contain exemptions that allow you to set up and issue equity plan options and stock with a minimum of red tape. Before setting up a plan, you will want to make sure to comply with the exemption rules. For example, you may need to file a notice with your state securities office prior to the award of any options under your corporation's ISO, NSO, or ESPP. The plan specialist or lawyer who helps you set up your equity sharing plan can help you meet these security law requirements.

Tax Concerns When Stock Is Sold

There are numerous tax concerns when selling shares of corporate stock. This section discusses two special provisions that apply to owners of small corporations when their corporation or its shares are sold. (Normally, both occur as part of the same transaction, but one owner may decide to sell shares separately to the corporation, its remaining shareholders, or an outsider.) The first part of this section covers the gloomier situation of an owner selling shares for less than their original purchase price—that is, for less than the amount paid by the owner for the shares when the corporation was founded. The second part is more optimistic, covering the pleasant prospect of selling shares of a small corporation at a profit (as well as the less-pleasant side effect of a profitable sale—paying taxes on the stock profits).

We treat the general rules for these tax perks. If they are of interest to you, make sure to review their requirements in more depth with your tax adviser.

Section 1244 Tax Treatment for Stock Losses

We know you don't plan to sell your corporation or its stock at a loss—that is, for less than you paid for your shares. But if this happens, the sting will be ameliorated to some extent if your stock qualifies for what is called Section 1244 treatment. Although this sounds technical, the concept is simple: Under Section 1244 of the Internal Revenue Code, many corporations can provide shareholders with the benefit of treating losses from the sale, exchange, or worthlessness of their stock as ordinary rather than capital losses on their individual federal tax returns, up to a maximum of $50,000 ($100,000 for a husband and wife filing a joint return) in each tax year. This is an advantage, because ordinary losses are fully deductible against individual income, whereas capital losses are only partially deductible. (Normally they can be used only to offset up to $3,000 of individual income in a given tax year.)

To qualify for Section 1244 stock treatment, your loss on the sale of stock must meet the following requirements:

- You must be the original owner of the shares. For example, if you sell your shares to another shareholder, you give your shares to a family member, or the shares pass according to your will to heirs or living trust to beneficiaries at your death, the transferees, heirs, and beneficiaries are not entitled to claim a Section 1244 loss.

- You must have paid money or property (other than corporate securities) for your shares.

- More than 50% of the corporation's gross receipts during the five tax years preceding the year in which the loss occurred must have been derived from sources other than royalties, dividends, interest, rents, annuities, or gains from sales or exchanges of securities or stock. If the corporation has not been in existence for five tax years, the five-year period is replaced by the number of tax years the corporation existed prior to the loss.

- The total amount of money or the value of property received by the corporation for stock, as a contribution to capital and as paid-in surplus, cannot exceed $1 million.

- At the time of loss, you must submit a timely statement to the IRS electing to take an ordinary loss under Section 1244. There is no special form to use for this purpose; your tax adviser can draft a statement that contains the required information.

Section 1202 Capital Gains Tax Exclusion

People who acquire small business stock (defined later) may be eligible to exclude all of the gain on sales of the shares from federal taxation, subject to a maximum exclusion of $10 million—or ten times the shareholder's basis in the stock. Note that for small business stock acquired before September 28, 2010, only a portion of the capital gains from the sale of the shares may be eligible for exclusion from taxation.

> **EXAMPLE:** Bob and Ken are 50-50 owners of Grass Roots Turf Supplies, Inc. Each founder paid $20,000 for his initial shares (the company was formed after 2010). Six years later, Bob decides to move on to greener pastures and agrees to sell his shares to Ken for $50,000. Bob's capital gain on the sale of his shares is $30,000. If Bob's stock qualifies as small business stock (see below), he can eliminate capital gains tax on the sale.

Stock qualifies as small business stock only if:

- You hold the shares for at least five years. However, if you receive the shares or inherit them during the five-year period, you can add on the amount of time the shares were held by the person who gave or bequeathed them to you. Also, if you've held the shares for six months, you can defer paying taxes on 100% of the gain from a sale if you reinvest the sales proceeds into another small business corporation within 60 days. (The taxes on the gain from the first sale are deferred until you sell the second corporation's shares.)

- You purchased the stock with money or property (other than stock), or you received it as employee compensation.

- The corporation had gross assets of $50 million or less on the date the shares were issued to you.

- The corporation is engaged in the operation of an active business (not making money exclusively from investments, rents, and the like). However, the practice of an incorporated profession, such as a medical, accounting, or engineering practice and

several other types of businesses (like hotels, farming, and mining) do not qualify under this tax provision.

You can use the standard IRS 1040 tax return to report and avoid taxation on Section 1202 stock gains. To learn more about how to do this, see the IRS instructions that accompany Form 1040, and ask your tax adviser for the most current rules and exceptions.

Tax Treatment When Incorporating an Existing Business

In this section, we focus on the tax consequences of incorporating an existing unincorporated business, such as a sole proprietorship, partnership, or LLC. This transaction involves the transfer of the assets (and any liabilities) of the unincorporated business in exchange for shares of your new corporation. The mechanics of this type of transaction are simple: The assets and liabilities of the unincorporated business are transferred together to the new corporation, which issues stock to the prior business owners in proportion to each owner's interest in the unincorporated business. We provide instructions and forms for this in Chapter 4. (See particularly the sample Bill of Sale in Chapter 4, Step 7.)

 SKIP AHEAD

Skip ahead if you are incorporating a new business. If you are not incorporating an existing business, you can skip this section and move on to the next chapter.

The tax rules discussed here are complex. Be sure to talk them over with your tax adviser if they apply to you.

Tax-Free Exchange Treatment Under Section 351

When you incorporate an existing unincorporated business, you transfer its assets and liabilities to the new corporation in return for shares of stock. Under the normal federal income tax rules, this sort of transfer of assets would be a sale. And, as you know, when you sell an asset you normally are liable for the payment of taxes on the profit you make from the transaction. In tax terms, the profit is the difference between the selling price and your *tax basis* in the property. Essentially, your tax basis in the property is the amount you paid for it, minus depreciation, plus capital improvements.

> **EXAMPLE:** Assume that your business purchased a building at a cost of $180,000. In the years since the purchase, the business has taken $90,000 depreciation on the property and made $20,000 in capital improvements to the property. This means the adjusted basis of the property is now $110,000 (cost of $180,000 – $90,000 depreciation + $20,000 improvements). If the property is sold for $210,000, the taxable gain (profit) is $100,000 ($210,000 – $110,000 adjusted basis). To keep things simple, we are ignoring the cost, sales price, and basis of the land on which the building is located (land is not depreciable). We are also ignoring special rules that make you "recapture" and pay ordinary income tax on a portion of the depreciation already claimed on the building.

Naturally, most incorporators of an existing business prefer not to pay taxes on the sale of property to their corporation in return for shares of stock. Fortunately, this is where IRC Section 351 comes to the rescue, allowing incorporators (and others) to transfer property to a corporation in return for stock in a tax-free exchange without recognizing any present gain or loss on the transfer. Instead, payment of tax on the gain is deferred until the shares themselves are sold. To qualify for Section 351 tax-free exchange treatment, you must meet certain rules:

- **The transferors must transfer property to the corporation.** For purposes of Section 351, property includes cash and tangible property, such as tools, equipment, real estate, and the like, as well as intangible property, such as patents, copyrights, or stock in another corporation. The property can come from the assets of an existing business or from separate items of property paid in by shareholders who don't own a stake in the prior unincorporated business. Property does not include services, so stock issued to someone in return for work performed for the corporation does not qualify under Section 351 (more on this below). Also, stock issued in return for the cancellation of corporate indebtedness owed to a shareholder—for example, when a corporation issues shares to a founder instead of repaying money it owes to the founder—doesn't count under Section 351.

- **The transferors, as a group, must own at least 80%** of the total combined voting power of all classes of issued stock entitled to vote (voting stock) after all the transfers are completed.

- **The transferors must also own at least 80%** of any other issued classes of stock of the corporation after the transfers are completed. (Most small corporations start out with just one class of voting stock and do not need to worry about this rule.)

Most small corporations' initial stock issuances will meet these tests and therefore will be eligible for tax-free exchange treatment. This includes those who are incorporating an existing business. After all, in this situation, the same person or small group that owns the unincorporated business normally owns 100% of the new corporation's shares after the business assets are transferred.

> **EXAMPLE 1:** Frank and Francis, the owners of an existing partnership, decide to form a corporation. The corporation's initial stock issuance consists of 400 shares of stock at a price of $100 per share. The corporation has just one class of voting stock. Frank and Francis will receive 200 shares apiece for their equal interests in the assets of their partnership valued at $40,000. The transaction qualifies for Section 351 tax-free exchange treatment because at least 80% (in this case, 100%) of all shares in the corporation will be owned after the transfer by the transferors of money and property.

Section 351 also lets the incorporators of an existing business bring in additional investors when they incorporate.

> **EXAMPLE 2:** Frank and Francis decide to let their friend Harvey invest in the new corporation, too. He'll get 100 shares for the payment of $10,000 cash. The initial stock issuance in this situation is 500 shares: 200 to each of the prior business owners and 100 to Harvey. Cash counts as property under Section 351, so it is still true that 100% of the corporation's shares are issued for property. In fact, even if Harvey bought his shares in return for promising to perform future services for the corporation, the transaction qualifies under Section 351. Frank and Francis own 80% (400 of the 500 shares equals 80% of all voting shares and 80% of all classes, which happen to be the same in this example), and they transferred property that qualifies under Section 351. Harvey will have to pay income tax on his shares because of another tax rule (explained below), but the entire transaction qualifies under Section 351, so Frank and Francis still get their shares tax-free.

Of course, very little is really free under tax statutes and regulations. A tax-free Section 351 exchange simply defers the payment of taxes until you sell your shares or your corporation is sold or liquidated. At that time, your shares will have the same basis as the property you originally transferred to the corporation, plus or minus any adjustments made to your shares while you held them and any adjustments made after you incorporate.

> **EXAMPLE:** You transfer property with a fair market value of $200,000 and an adjusted basis of $100,000 to the corporation in a Section 351 tax-free exchange for shares worth $200,000. Your shares will then have a basis of $100,000. If you sell the shares for $300,000, your taxable gain will be $200,000 ($300,000 selling price – $100,000 basis). Note also that the corporation's basis in the property received in a tax-free exchange will also generally be the same as the adjusted basis of the transferred property. In this example, the corporation's basis in the property will be $100,000.

Even in a tax-free transaction, the shareholders must pay tax on any money or property they receive in addition to stock. For example, if you transfer a truck worth $50,000 in a tax-free exchange to the corporation in return for $40,000 worth of shares and a $10,000 cash payment by the corporation, you will have to report the $10,000 as taxable income.

Potential Problems With Section 351 Tax-Free Exchanges

There are, of course, complexities that may arise when you attempt to exchange property for stock in your corporation under Section 351. Let's look at a few of the most common problem areas. As we do, realize that seemingly simple tax rules can often mask many hidden technicalities and exceptions and that this is particularly true in this area. It follows that if you will be transferring property and possibly services to your new corporation in return for shares of stock (and, possibly, promissory notes or other evidence of debt to be repaid by the corporation), you will need to check with an accountant to ensure favorable tax results under Section 351.

Issuing Shares in Return for the Performance of Services

The performance of services is not considered property for purposes of Section 351. (Remember, stock must be issued in return for cash or property to qualify for tax-free treatment.) What this means is that you cannot count shares issued to shareholders in exchange for services or the promise to perform services when calculating the 80% control requirement under Section 351. Even if you are able to meet the 80% control test (not counting the stock issued for services), keep in mind that any shareholder who receives stock for services will have to report the value of the shares as taxable income.

EXAMPLE: Your corporation plans to issue $50,000 worth of shares on its incorporation to you and the cofounder of your corporation, Fred. You will transfer property previously used in your sole proprietorship—a copyright in software, reasonably worth $35,000—for $35,000 in shares. Fred will receive $15,000 in shares in return for work valued at $15,000 that he has already performed organizing the corporation. The transfer will be taxable to both you and Fred, since the basic 80% postissuance control test of Section 351 is not met. You are the only person who will transfer property that qualifies under Section 351 in return for stock, and you will only own 70% of the shares of the corporation.

If we change the facts in this example so that you receive 80% of the stock in exchange for property—for example if you transfer $40,000 worth of property and Fred contributes $10,000 in services—the transfer will be tax-free under Section 351, but Fred will have to report his $10,000 in shares as taxable income.

TIP

How shareholders who contribute services can receive shares that qualify under Section 351. There are ways to issue shares to a service provider and still have your stock issuance transaction qualify under Section 351. Section 351 says that if a shareholder contributes both services and cash or property, all the shares issued to the shareholder can be counted under the Section 351 requirements, including the shares issued for services, provided the value of the cash and property is not just a token amount compared to the value of the services. (Income Tax Regulation 1.351-1(a)(1)(ii).) Tax advisers generally say that the property contributed by a service provider must be equal to at least 10% of the value of the services to pass muster under this regulation.

Intangible Property Qualifies Under Section 351

Unlike services, intangible property, such as the goodwill of a business or patents and copyrights, is considered property for purposes of Section 351. Thus, if you, as a prior business owner, contribute a valuable copyright, trademark, or patent to a new corporation, it qualifies as property under Section 351, and the shares you are issued can be counted in determining whether your incorporation meets the 80% control requirement of Section 351.

Issuing Nonqualified Preferred Shares

Section 351 tax-free exchange treatment applies only to the issuance of stock in exchange for cash or property. Most corporations issue common stock that gives each shareholder a proportionate right to vote and receive any dividends paid by the corporation, as well as an equal right to receive assets and sales proceeds when the corporation is liquidated or sold. However, corporations do sometimes issue preferred shares of stock that give certain shareholders extra rights—such as the right to convert their shares into a specified number of common shares, a preferential right to receive dividends, or a special right to get paid more for their shares if the corporation is liquidated.

You probably will not issue preferred shares as part of your initial stock issuance but, if you plan to, keep the following point in mind: IRS rules say that certain types of preferred stock do not qualify as stock under Section 351. Preferred shares that have a dividend rate that fluctuates with interest rates, or preferred shares that a shareholder can force the corporation

to buy back (that is, shares redeemable at the option of the shareholder), and other special types of preferred shares are nonqualified under Section 351.

If you receive nonqualified preferred shares in exchange for property you transfer to the corporation, you are treated as though you were paid cash. The entire transaction and the other shareholders may still qualify for Section 351 tax-free exchange treatment, but you will have to pay tax on the value of your nonqualified shares. The lesson is this: If you plan to issue preferred shares as part of your initial stock issuance, see a tax adviser to find out how they affect your eligibility for Section 351 tax treatment.

Issuing Stock and a Promissory Note in Return for the Transfer of Business Assets

Section 351 tax treatment applies to the transfer of property to a corporation in exchange for stock, not corporate promissory notes or other debt instruments. For example, if you transfer $100,000 worth of business assets to your new corporation in return for (1) $75,000 in shares, which represents 80% or more of your corporation's initial shares, and (2) a $25,000 promissory note from your corporation (it promises to pay $25,000 cash plus interest to you over a few years), the transaction still generally qualifies under Section 351. However, you will owe tax on the $25,000 face amount of the note. The IRS treats the note portion of the transaction as though you sold property to the corporation and received cash back equal to the face amount of the note—in other words, just as though you sold a piece of property to your corporation that was not part of Section 351 property for stock swap.

SEE AN EXPERT

Check with your tax adviser. Consult your tax adviser if you plan to incorporate an existing business and wish to receive a promissory note in addition to shares of stock from your corporation.

Agreeing to Pay Liabilities Associated With the Transferred Property

Here is another potential hitch contained in the Section 351 rules: Shareholders may have to pay taxes if the liabilities assumed by the corporation exceed the basis of the business assets transferred to the corporation. These liabilities may be those of a prior business that the corporation agrees to assume, or liabilities attached to a specific item of property, such as a mortgage on real estate transferred to the corporation.

SKIP AHEAD

Skim this material. Again, these Section 351 rules are technical, and you don't need to master them. We provide this information to give you a sense of how the rules and their exceptions may apply to you. If any of the issues discussed here raise a red flag or provide an exception that may affect your incorporation, ask you tax adviser to take a closer look at Section 351.

EXAMPLE 1: If you transfer business assets with a basis of $40,000 to your corporation, but your corporation also assumes $60,000 worth of your unincorporated business's debts, the difference of $20,000 is generally taxable to you. Another consequence is that the full amount of the assumed debt (in this case, $60,000) minus the amount of taxable gain recognized (in this case, $20,000) is subtracted from your basis in the stock you receive. This means you pay more tax when the shares are eventually sold.

(This reduction of stock basis happens in most situations when a shareholder transfers property along with debts to a corporation in return for shares, not just when the debts exceed the value of the assets transferred.)

Fortunately, shareholders who transfer business assets along with liabilities to their new corporation do not owe any immediate tax, even though the liabilities assumed by the corporation exceed the value of the assets transferred to it. This is because the tax law contains an exception for some transactions when a cash-basis taxpayer (one who uses the cash method of accounting) transfers assets and liabilities to a corporation. (IRC § 357(c).) Since the majority of unincorporated businesses use the cash method of accounting—income is reported when received, and expenses are deducted when paid—this exception often applies to the incorporation of a business. Because accounts receivable (money owed to a business—an asset) have a zero basis for a cash method business, and since the assets of a business normally have a low basis due to depreciation taken on them, it's easy for the liabilities of an unincorporated business to exceed the basis of its assets. In other words, this exception can be very useful when an existing business is being incorporated.

EXAMPLE 2: Felicia incorporates her dog-walking service, Canine Companions. Her assets consist of $3,000 cash, a computer system, furniture, phones, and other miscellaneous items that originally cost $20,000 but now have a depreciated basis of $7,000. Her accounts receivable are $30,000, but they have a zero basis since Felicia's sole proprietorship uses the cash method of accounting. The business has accounts payable—money owed to others—of $25,000. The liabilities of the business ($25,000 accounts payable) exceed the basis of the business assets ($3,000 cash plus $7,000 of depreciated assets) by $18,000. Under the standard 351 rules, Felicia would pay tax on this $18,000 taxable "gain" at the time of her incorporation, and her shares would have a basis of $3,000 ($10,000 basis in assets plus the $18,000 taxable gain minus the full amount of liabilities transferred of $25,000). However, because of the special exception for cash method businesses, she can ignore the accounts payable in her calculations, and her basis in assets ($10,000) will exceed liabilities (zero), so there will be no tax due when she incorporates. Further, her basis in her stock will be higher (she pays less tax later when she sells her shares), since she can ignore the accounts payable in her stock basis calculations. Her stock basis is $10,000 (the basis of the assets transferred, with no adjustment for liabilities assumed by the corporation).

Is a Section 351 Tax-Free Exchange Desirable?

As discussed above, most incorporators want to qualify for a Section 351 tax-free exchange. But this isn't always true. Some incorporators may wish to avoid Section 351 exchange treatment and recognize a gain or loss on the transfer of property to a corporation. If this is what you want, you may have to do some advance planning—for example, by making sure that *less* than 80% of your shareholders receive shares for qualified property under Section 351 or by transferring property to your corporation for cash or promissory notes, not stock.

Here are some reasons why an incorporator might wish to avoid tax-free exchange treatment under IRC Section 351:

- Some incorporators may wish to recognize a *gain* on the transfer of business assets. For example, incorporators may already have capital losses for the tax year. If they recognize a capital gain on a transfer of property to their corporation, their capital losses can be used to offset the gain, and they still pay no taxes. Without a capital gain, the amount of capital losses an individual can deduct against taxable income is limited (currently, $3,000 per year).

- Some incorporators wish to avoid Section 351 to increase the corporation's basis in the transferred property. In a tax-free exchange, the corporation gets the transferor's basis in the assets; in a taxable exchange it gets a basis in the property equal to its full market value.

EXAMPLE: Assume that you plan to transfer assets with a fair market value of $50,000 to your corporation. Your basis in these assets is $30,000. If you transfer these assets to the corporation for $50,000 worth of stock in a qualified Section 351 exchange, the corporation's basis in the assets is $30,000 (your preincorporation basis in the assets). But if the exchange is taxable—let's say you sell it to the corporation for cash or in a property-for-stock exchange that does not meet the 351 control requirements—the corporation uses the fair market value of the assets as its basis, or $50,000. You, as the shareholder, have a $20,000 capital gain—the difference between the $50,000 sales price and your $30,000 basis in the property.

- Incorporators might want their corporation to have a higher basis in property because a higher basis allows the corporation to take higher depreciation deductions on the property, which reduces the corporation's taxable income. The corporation also may end up with a higher basis in the property when the property is sold, which means the corporation pays less tax on the sale.

- Some incorporators may wish to recognize a *loss* on the transfer of assets to their corporation, to offset capital gains they have recognized from other property sales during the year. If you transfer assets to your corporation in a qualified Section 351 exchange for stock, you cannot recognize a loss on the transfer—you have to wait until your corporation is sold or liquidated or you sell your shares to take the loss on your individual tax return.

EXAMPLE: You paid $70,000 for a business asset. Your depreciated basis in the asset is $50,000 and its current market value is $40,000. You will need to transfer the asset to the corporation for $40,000 cash or in a property-for-stock exchange that does not qualify under Section 351 in order to recognize a $10,000 loss ($40,000 sales price minus $50,000 basis) for tax purposes.

CAUTION

Major shareholders can't sell property to the corporation at a loss. Even if you can avoid Section 351 exchange treatment, you still may not be able to transfer depreciated property to your corporation and claim a loss on your individual income tax return. The reason is that another section of the Internal Revenue Code, IRC Section 267, does not let a shareholder who owns more than 50% of a corporation's stock sell property to it at a loss. (These restrictions are meant to hinder self-serving tax-avoidance schemes between related people and entities they control.)

Additional Tax Considerations When Incorporating an Existing Business

Let's look at some additional tax and business issues associated with the incorporation of an existing business, starting with the best time to switch from an unincorporated business to a corporation.

When Is the Best Time to Incorporate an Existing Business?

Most incorporators have some wiggle room when deciding when to form a corporation—that is, there are no pressing legal reasons for incorporating at a particular time. But the timing of your incorporation may make a difference in terms of taxes.

EXAMPLE: If you anticipate a loss this year and a healthy profit next year, you may wish to remain unincorporated now and take a loss on your individual tax return. (Remember, profits and losses of unincorporated businesses are reported on owners' personal income tax returns; corporate losses can be taken only on the corporation's income tax return.) Next year you can incorporate and split your business income between yourself and your corporation to reduce your overall tax liability. (See "Corporate Income and Tax Splitting," above, for more on the tax savings that can be achieved by income splitting.)

Should You Transfer All Assets and Liabilities to the New Corporation?

When an existing business is incorporated, all assets and liabilities are usually transferred to the corporation in a tax-free exchange under

Section 351. But this may not always be the case. In special circumstances, incorporators may not wish to transfer all assets or liabilities of the prior business to the corporation.

Retaining Some of the Assets of the Prior Business

In some instances, the prior business owners may not wish to transfer some of the assets of the prior business to their new corporation. Here are a couple of reasons:

- You need to retain sufficient cash in the old business to pay liabilities not assumed by the corporation, such as payroll and other taxes.

- You want to continue to own some of the assets of the prior business. For example, you may wish to continue to own a building in your name and lease it to your corporation. By doing this, you can continue to personally deduct depreciation, mortgage interest payments, and other expenses associated with the property on your individual tax return. And, of course, your corporation can deduct rent payments made under the lease. (A rent comparable to the amount that similar commercial space rents for in your geographical area should pass IRS muster.)

Finally, don't forget that if property is transferred to your corporation and it later appreciates, both your corporation and its shareholders may have to pay tax on the appreciation. Incorporators may decide not to transfer real property to their corporation to avoid this double tax—ask your tax adviser for guidance.

Retaining Some of the Liabilities of the Prior Business

You may not wish to transfer—that is, have your corporation assume—all of the liabilities of the existing business. Here are two reasons for this:

- Assuming the liabilities of the prior business sometimes results in the payment of tax, even in a Section 351 qualified exchange. (Shareholders must pay tax on the amount by which the liabilities exceed the basis of the transferred assets. See "Agreeing to Pay Liabilities Associated With the Transferred Property," above.)

- Payment of expenses by the prior business owners, rather than by the corporation, allows the owners to deduct these expenses on their individual tax returns, which reduces their individual taxable incomes.

Converting a Co-Owned Business to a Corporation

A common type of conversion is the conversion of a partnership or co-owned LLC to a corporation. As explained in this chapter, a conversion of an existing business to a corporation normally is tax free if the prior business owners are in control of 80% or more of the stock of the new corporation (see IRS Publication 542, *Corporations*). But there's more to it, as explained in IRS Revenue Ruling 84-111. This ruling puts partnership-to-corporation conversions into one of three slots (and also applies to LLC-to-corporation conversions because co-owned LLCs are treated like partnerships).

Here are the three conversion categories:

- **"Assets-over" conversion.** The old business transfers its assets and liabilities "over" to the new corporation, the corporation issues its stock to the business, the business transfers the stock to its owners in proportion to their interests in the business, then the old business dissolves.

- **"Assets-up" conversion.** The old business distributes its assets and transfers its liabilities "down" to its owners in proportion to their interests in the business, the business dissolves, and then the owners transfer their individual share of received assets and liabilities "up" to the new corporation in return for a proportionate share of its stock.

- **"Interests-over" conversion.** The owners of the old business transfer their interests in the business "over" to the new corporation in return for a proportionate amount of corporate stock, and then the business dissolves.

Each of these conversion methods can have a different effect on the corporation's tax basis and holding period in the assets it receives. Further, the prior business owners can end up with a different tax basis in their corporate stock, and each can end up with a different immediate tax result depending on the conversion method used. For instance, an owner may have to pay taxes at the time of the conversion.

This is already sufficiently complicated, but there's more to consider. Revenue Ruling 2004-59 explains how the IRS treats an automatic conversion of a co-owned business to a corporation through the filing of a state conversion form. (As mentioned in Chapter 4, the states often streamline the conversion process by allowing existing businesses to convert a business to a new corporation through the filing of a special articles conversion form.) This ruling says that when a co-owned entity treated as a partnership (again, which includes a co-owned LLC) is converted to a corporation through the filing of a state conversion form without an actual transfer of assets or interests, the IRS assumes the following steps occur, in the following order:

1. The partnership contributes all its assets and liabilities to the corporation in exchange for stock in such corporation.

2. The partnership liquidates, distributing the stock of the corporation to its partners.

This assumed sequence of events matches the sequence of events described in the assets-over conversion listed above, which means it's likely that the IRS will consider the conversion of a partnership or co-owned LLC to a corporation through a state conversion form filing to be an assets-over conversion. This leads to further complications that can have significant tax effects.

Here's one: As discussed in this chapter, Section 1244 allows business owners to treat worthless stock as an ordinary loss, which can be deducted against ordinary income on their tax returns. However, one of the requirements of using Section 1244 is that the shareholder claiming the loss must be the original owner of the stock. But if you reread the description of an assets-over conversion, you'll see that the LLC entity, not its owners, is considered to be the original owner of the shares under that conversion scenario, and the corporation's shareholders are considered to be the second set of shareholders (they receive their shares from the dissolving business).

The upshot is that the use of a simple state conversion form to convert a co-owned business to a corporation may eliminate the future ability of the corporation's shareholders to take a large deduction on their individual tax returns. Instead, the shareholders may be limited to claiming only a capital loss if their corporation fails. Since a capital loss can only be used to offset capital gains, the owners may be unable to deduct the loss on their capital investment or may have to wait several years to do so.

Complications and unexpected tax results of this sort are why it's best to check with a tax adviser before making even the simplest type of filing with the state to form a business entity or convert an entity from one form to another.

Liability for the Debts of the Unincorporated Business

Another consideration when incorporating an existing business is whether the owners of the unincorporated business remain personally liable for its debts after it is incorporated. Although this is technically a legal, not a tax, issue, it is closely tied to the transfer of assets and liabilities to the corporation, so we include it here.

These rules normally have little practical significance for most incorporators who, as a matter of course and good-faith business practice, will promptly pay all the debts and liabilities passed on to the new corporation. But, in case a debt is contested or for some other reason you wish to extend the time for payment, here are the basics of legal liability:

- Whether or not the corporation assumes the debts and liabilities of the prior business, the prior owners remain personally liable for these debts and liabilities unless the creditor signs a release that lets the business owners off the hook personally.

- The new corporation is not liable for the debts and liabilities of the prior business unless it specifically agrees to assume them. If it does assume them, both the corporation and the prior owners are liable.

- If a transfer of assets to the corporation is fraudulent (done with the intent to cheat or deceive creditors), the creditors of the prior business can file legal papers to seize the transferred business assets. Similarly, if the corporation does not, in fact, pay the assumed liabilities of the prior business, the creditors of the prior business may be allowed to seize the transferred assets.

- If transferred assets are subject to recorded liens—for example, a mortgage on real estate or a recorded security interest on personal property—these liens will survive the transfer and the assets will continue to be subject to them.

- The former business owners can be personally liable for postincorporation debts if credit is extended to the corporation by creditors who in good faith reasonably think that they are still dealing with the prior business—for example, a creditor who has not been notified of the incorporation. (See "Postincorporation Tasks" in Chapter 5 for the steps to take to notify creditors when you incorporate.)

- In many states, the corporation may be liable for delinquent sales, employment, or other taxes owed by the unincorporated business. (This type of liability is called successor liability, and you may see this term used in materials you receive from your state's business or employment tax department.) ●

Seven Steps to Incorporation

This chapter shows you how to take the steps necessary to form a corporation in your state. Most important, this means preparing and filing your articles of incorporation. After that, you will prepare your corporate bylaws and the minutes of your organizational meeting. Finally, you'll issue your initial shares of corporate stock. You may be surprised how easy all this is—the basic forms are so easy to understand you can often complete them in less than an hour. Although we point out areas where you may wish to take a little more time to customize the forms to suit special needs, in most cases the basic forms will work just fine to start your small corporation.

After you file your articles, your corporation is an official legal entity. The other steps explained in this chapter are necessary for sound practical reasons. The bylaws contain the essential rules needed to operate your corporation. And the first (organizational) meeting of your directors is necessary to transact the initial business of your corporation by issuing shares of stock in return for investors' capital contributions.

All of the forms shown in this chapter are available online or at the back of the book. (See Appendixes B and C.)

Step 1. Choose a Corporate Name

The first step in organizing your corporation is selecting and reserving a corporate name. To do this, there are a number of hurdles and hoops you must jump over and through. We take you through them in order of importance, below. But before we do, here's something to keep in mind: There are many existing businesses names already on file with the secretary of state, associated with existing business products and services, and in use as domain names online.

You will see that your name must be as distinct as possible from these existing names. Plus, you will want to pick a name that you like and that adds the right spark to your corporation's identity. It isn't easy to satisfy these criteria, particularly in a crowded marketplace. Our best advice is to be patient and to choose a few alternate names you're willing to settle for in case your first choices are unavailable; you may need to compromise a bit. If you're willing to do so, you'll avoid future legal squabbles with existing business name owners, and have a workable name you can use throughout the life of your corporation.

Meet State Corporate Name Requirements

Your first task when choosing a corporate name is to make sure you meet your state's corporate name requirements. In most states, the most basic requirement is that you include a corporate designator in your corporate name such as "Corporation," "Incorporated," "Limited," or an abbreviation of one of these words—"Corp.," "Inc.," or "Ltd." (Your state's online articles form will explain the corporate name requirements in your state.) (See Appendix A for information on how to locate your state's filing office online.) Even if not required, most incorporators use one of these designators at the end of their corporate name precisely because they want others to know that their business is incorporated.

The second basic corporate name requirement is that, in most states, a business corporation cannot use words that connote the formation of a certain type of business, such as a bank or insurance company. Therefore, you should normally avoid words like "bank, "trust," or "insurance" in a corporate name unless, of course, you will obtain the additional state or federal permits necessary to operate in one of these fields.

In addition, most states have special corporate name requirements for professional corporations—that is, corporations formed to practice a state-licensed profession in the medical, legal, accounting, engineering, or architectural fields.

Pick a Likeable, Workable Name

It is extremely important to choose a good name for your corporation. First of all, you have to live with it. Second, everyone you do business with, including your customers, clients, other merchants, vendors, independent contractors, lenders, and the business community generally, will identify your business primarily by these few words. And you certainly want to get it right the first time, since making a change later will often mean printing new stationery, changing advertising copy, creating new logos, and ordering new signs. You will also need to amend your corporate articles if you wish to change your original corporate name.

Of course, if you are incorporating an existing business, you'll likely want to use your current name as your corporate name if it has become associated with your products and services. Many businesses do this by simply adding an "Inc." after their old name—for example, Really Good Widgets may incorporate as Really Good Widgets, Inc. Using your old name is not required, however, and if you have been hankering after a new one, this is your chance to claim it.

Here are a few guidelines to help you in your search for the right corporate name.

Make your name memorable. A creative, distinctive name will not only be entitled to a high level of legal protection; it will stick in the minds of your customers. Forgettable names are those of people (like O'Brien Web Design), those that include geographic terms (like Westside Health Foods), and names that literally describe a product or service (like Appliance Sales and Repair, Inc.). Remember, you want to distinguish yourself from your competitors.

Your name should be appealing and easy to use. Choose a name that's easy to spell and pronounce, and that is appealing to both eye and ear. Try to pick a catchy name that people will like to repeat. Make sure that any images or associations it evokes will suit your customer base.

Avoid geographical names. Besides being easy to forget, and difficult to protect under trademark law, a geographical name may no longer fit if your business expands its sales or service area. If you open Berkeley Aquariums & Fish, for instance, will it be a problem if you want to open a second store in San Francisco? Especially if you plan to sell products on the Internet, you should think twice about giving your business a geographic identifier.

Don't limit expanded product lines. Similarly, don't choose a name that might not be representative of future product or service lines. For instance, if you start a business selling and installing canvas awnings using the name Sturdy Canvas Awnings, your name might be a burden if you decide to also start making other products such as canvas signs or vinyl awnings.

Get feedback. Before you settle on a name, get some feedback from potential customers, suppliers, and others in your support network. They may come up with a downside to a potential name or suggest an improvement you haven't thought of.

Check With the State Filing Office to See If Your Proposed Name Is Available

This is the first procedural hurdle on the way to securing a corporate name. When you file your articles of incorporation with the state, you will include your proposed corporate name. The filing office will not accept your corporate name—and will, therefore, reject your articles of incorporation—unless the name is sufficiently different from other corporate names it has already registered. Each state corporate filing office maintains a list of names that are already taken, including existing in-state corporations, out-of-state corporations qualified to do business in the state, names that have been registered with the state by other out-of-state corporations, and names that have been reserved for use by other corporations in the formation stage. If your proposed name is the same as or confusingly similar to any of these, the state will reject it.

We can't give you an exact definition of the phrase "confusingly similar," but for practical purposes, this restriction simply means that the wording of your proposed name cannot be so close to that of a name already on file with the state that it might result in public confusion. Each state has its own guidelines for determining whether a proposed name is sufficiently different from other registered names. (Some state filing offices publish their name comparison rules on their website.)

As a general rule, a state will disregard differences between corporate name endings, common connectives, prepositions, and the like, as well as descriptive terms. For example, if you want to set up a wholesale house for computer equipment under the name "Compusell, Inc.," and a corporation is already on file with the name "Compusel International, Inc.," your name will most likely be rejected as too similar.

There is one big exception to this rule: Most states let you use personal names in a corporate name, even if the resulting corporate name is similar to a name that's already on file with the state. Thus, while there could be only one Greenal Corp., there could be two corporations called Allworth & Green, Inc. However, if you use a personal name, your state will usually insist that you include a corporate designator, even if a corporate designator normally is not required for a corporate name in your state. For example, "Biff Baxter" normally would be considered an invalid corporate name, but "Biff Baxter, Inc.," would be acceptable in most states.

Because your articles of incorporation will be rejected if the name you've chosen is too similar to the name of a corporation already on file with the state filing office, we strongly recommend that you check your proposed name's availability before filing your articles with the state. If it turns out that your name is available and it will take you a few days or more to get your articles on file, we encourage you to reserve the name in advance. (See "Reserve Your Corporate Name," below.)

Many states let you check name availability by visiting the state filing office website and comparing your proposed name with names already entered in the state corporate database. Doing this is a good way to see if someone else is already using your proposed name. If you discover another name that is close to, but not the same as, your proposed name, you should call the state filing office to see if your name is too close to the similar name. The office will search for similar names and tell you whether your proposed name is too close to them.

Whether or not you visit the state's website first, most states let you call and check name availability for one to three proposed names, free of charge. If you want to use this approach, call the main phone number for the state filing office (listed on the state filing office website—see Appendix A) and select the option to check name availability.

If the name you want is unavailable, you need to select a new name for your corporation. We recommend picking a new name, even though it is possible in most states to use an unavailable name if you get the signed consent of the corporation using it. It's normally not practical to do this; the other company either will refuse to consent or will charge you a bundle to use a name that is similar to theirs.

Filing Your Corporate Name With the Secretary of State Does Not Guarantee Your Right to Use It

When you file articles of incorporation, the state corporate filing office formally approves your corporate name after making sure it meets state law requirements and is not the same or very similar to a name already on file. But of course the state filing office list does not contain all business names and trademarks in use everywhere. In many states, the state filing office list just shows corporate names already registered for use in the state, not the names of unincorporated businesses in the state or even registered state trademarks. In other words, having your name approved by the state corporate filing office does not guarantee that you have the absolute right to use it. You must do some additional research to be relatively sure that no one else has a prior claim to your proposed corporate name. In "Perform Your Own Trademark Search," below, we discuss some self-help measures you may wish to take before you decide on a corporate name.

Here's one more point to consider when checking name availability with the state filing office: Most states allow corporations, as well as other types of business, to use an assumed name (called a fictitious business name in some states). For a corporation, an assumed name is defined as a name that is different from the formal corporate name contained in the articles. Assumed or fictitious business names are registered by filing an assumed or fictitious business name statement either at the state level (usually with the corporate filing office) or at the county level (typically with the local county clerk's or recorder's office). Sometimes the filing must be made at both the state and county levels. Your state corporate filing office website should be able to tell you how to register a fictitious or assumed name for your corporation. Many websites even provide a downloadable form for this purpose.

But even though you may be permitted to use an assumed name, it's not wise to latch onto one as a way of skirting name availability problems. For example, assume you want to incorporate your business as Creativity Systems, Inc., but the state filing office already has a Creativity Systems Corp. on file and tells you that your corporate name choice is unavailable. You decide to pick another corporate name that is available for use in your articles, but hope to register and use your preferred name, Creativity Systems, as an assumed corporate name. Is this a good idea? Probably not. First of all, you'll probably get a lawyer letter from Creativity Systems Corp. demanding that you stop using your assumed name. Second, this double-name strategy is too complicated. Most corporations have a hard enough time establishing a sound corporate identity for one name, let alone two. We suggest you do your best to find one available name for your corporation, then use it in your articles and for all business purposes. In short, don't bother picking a second name and registering it as your assumed or fictitious corporate name.

Choose a Name You Can Use as an Internet Domain Name

Now for your next hurdle. Besides picking a name that's available with the state, you should choose a name that is also available for use as an Internet domain name—that is, your corporation's website address or URL (for example, "mycorporatename.com"). Here's why: If your corporation is a success, you will probably want to promote it on the Internet by setting up a corporate website. And in most cases you will want your Internet domain name to be the same as or very close to your corporate name. For example, if your corporate name is Unipode, Inc., no doubt you will want to register and use the domain name unipode.com for your website. Even if you are not itching to launch a corporate website right away, you may want to do so later. So pick a corporate name, if you can, that is available as a domain name, and register your domain name immediately.

You can go to Network Solutions (www. networksolutions.com) to do a domain name search and register your name. If someone else is already using your proposed corporate name as a domain name, we suggest you choose another name for your corporation. Also, we recommend that you register all major variants of your domain name to avoid anyone else grabbing them later. For instance, the founders of Unipode, Inc., should register unipode.com as well as unipode.org, unipode.net, unipode. tv, and unipode.cc. We know this adds expense to your organizational costs (and your annual budget, because you will want to renew your domain registrations every year), but it is worth it to avoid the much more expensive proposition of changing your name later or fighting with someone else who comes along and grabs one of these domain name variants before you do.

CAUTION

Beware of domain name selection tools. If you use a name selection tool to help find an available domain name, do so carefully. These tools find available names by adding words and special characters to the beginning, middle, and end of names—for example, a name finding tool may suggest myunipode.com if unipode.com is already taken. We think this just leads to trouble: You want your domain name to be as close as possible to your corporate name and as far away as possible from other registered domain names. Simply adding extra letters to an unavailable name is not the best way to select a domain name. Again, if your proposed corporate name is already taken as a domain name, try to choose a distinctly different corporate name that is available as a domain name.

Even if you find that your corporate name is available for use as a domain name, we suggest that you do a wider Internet search to make sure someone else is not using a similar name as a domain name or as the name of their business or product linked to a website. Obviously, this is a large chore, and you probably can't discover all Internet-related names. But here are two basic and easy suggestions to help you uncover similar Internet names:

- When you do your domain name search, also search for slightly different names—for example, the incorporators of Unipode can search for unipodecorp.com, unipodeinc. com, and other variants. Domain name registration engines search for exact matches, so you have to spell out all variations for which you want to search.

- Go to google.com or another major search engine to hunt for any links to your proposed corporate name. Type your proposed corporate name in the search box without the ending corporate designator. For example, Unipode's incorporators would type "unipode" and see what links come up for the name. Try all major search engines; this will give you a good idea of all major competing names currently linked to the Internet.

If you discover a business or individual already using your proposed name or one similar to it as a domain name, a business name, or the name of a product or service, we suggest you pick another corporate name rather than risk tangling with the owner of the competing name.

 RESOURCE

For more information about domain names. For information on choosing and registering domain names and avoiding domain name conflicts, see the "Business Name" articles in the Small Business area of www.nolo.com.

Perform Your Own Trademark Search

Here's another hoop we suggest you jump through in your corporate name selection process. It adds work to the task, but we think it is worth it to avoid legal hassles later. As mentioned, acceptance of your name by the corporate filing office simply means that your name does not conflict with that of another corporation already on file—it doesn't necessarily mean that you have the legal right to use your name. That's because another business (corporate or noncorporate) may already be using the same or a similar name as their trade name (the name of their business), or as a federal or state trademark or service mark used to identify their goods or services.

Without providing a long-winded analysis of the intricacies of federal and state trademark and trade name law, the basic rule is that the ultimate right to use a particular trademark or business name is usually decided on the basis of who was first to actually use the name in connection with a particular trade, business activity, service, or product. For example, if the Brake-In Lock Co. has sold padlocks for 50 years, you do not have the legal right to use the same name to sell locks. This remains true even if you have formed a corporation with the name Brake-In Lock, Inc., registered Brake-In Lock as an assumed or fictitious name with the state or county, or registered brakeinlock.com as your domain name on the Internet.

Even if two companies produce different products—let's say there are two companies named Brake-In, Inc., one in Maine, one in Iowa, each producing different products—trademark law can allow the company that used the name first to stop the other company from using Brake-In in its name, if the court decides that use by the second company is diluting the value of the first company's trademark. Although trademark law has traditionally placed importance on the geographical proximity of the two businesses—for example, by looking to see if the two entities named Brake-In, Inc., market their products in the same geographical region—the Internet has pretty much made this consideration moot. With the predominance of the Web as a relatively cheap and easy place for companies to market their products, it's safe to assume you will someday be marketing your company and products to the same world market served by all other Internet-linked companies.

 RESOURCE

For more information about business names and trademark law. Nolo's website offers plenty of free information on business names, trademarks, and other useful legal information for businesses. (See the Small Business and Patent, Copyright & Trademark areas of www.nolo.com.) For more details, you may want to see Nolo's *Trademark: Legal Care for Your Business & Product*

Name, by Stephen Fishman, which provides detailed information about trademarks and business names and instructions on how to search for, pick, and register a trademark.

The upshot of this discussion is that you should do your best to make sure that your proposed corporate name does not conflict with existing names used by other enterprises to identify their business, services, or products. In "Choose a Name You Can Use as an Internet Domain Name," above, we discussed how you can use the Internet to search for other companies that use your desired name in connection with their business. Here are some additional suggestions:

- **Check with your state's trademark registration office.** Ask whether your proposed corporate name is already registered with them for another company's use. (When you file articles or call to ask the filing office to perform a corporate name availability search, most states do not automatically compare your proposed corporate name to registered state trademarks and service marks. You usually need to do this yourself.) The telephone number of the state trademark office should be listed on your state corporate filing office website— look under "related links" or simply email the corporate filing office and ask for the telephone number. Also, you may be able to check state trademark registration online from the state trademark office website.

- **If your state has a centralized fictitious or assumed name office,** call it to ask if your name, without the "Inc." or other corporate designator, is already in use by another business. (Your state's fictitious or assumed business name office, if there is one, should be listed on the corporate filing office website under "related links.") In states where fictitious names are registered at the county level, check with the counties where you plan to do business. Most county clerks require you to come in and check the files yourself— but it takes just a few minutes to do this.

- **Check with the United States Patent and Trademark Office (PTO)** for trademarks and service marks registered at the federal level. You can perform a free search from the PTO website at www.uspto.gov. If your name, or one similar to it, is registered as a federal trademark, you need to think carefully about using your proposed name. In most cases, it's safest simply to pick a new name rather than risk the possibility of getting tangled up in a trademark lawsuit because your corporate name comes too close to a registered trademark.

- **Check other resources.** To search for trade names that have not yet arrived on the Internet, check major metropolitan phone book listings, business and trade directories, and other business listings, such as the Dun & Bradstreet business listing. Larger public libraries have phone directories for many major cities within and outside of your state.

If you want to check further or don't want to do all the work yourself, you can pay a private records search company to check federal and state trademarks and service marks as well as local and statewide business listings. These firms can check your proposed name against the sources we've listed above plus many other sources.

Alternatively, or in conjunction with your own efforts, you can pay a trademark lawyer to oversee or undertake these searches for you. A lawyer will take the responsibility of hiring a private search company. In addition, a lawyer may provide a legal opinion on the relative legal safety of your proposed corporate name. Normally, this opinion isn't necessary, but it can be valuable if your own search discovers several similar, but not identical, names.

Obviously, the amount of checking and consulting you can do is limited only by the amount of effort or money you are willing to devote to the task and by how safe you need to feel about your choice of a corporate name. If your company is growing fast or will compete with many other businesses over the Internet, you may want to do a fair amount of name checking. If your business will be based locally and compete only with others located in your immediate vicinity, then a more modest amount of name searching may make more sense.

TIP

Pick the best level search for you. Use your own business judgment and your individual comfort level to tell you how many of the self-help measures listed above make sense for you, and whether to pay someone else, like a name search service or a trademark lawyer, to do additional name checking for you.

Reserve Your Corporate Name

After you have completed the above steps and feel satisfied that your corporate name is available and safe to use, it normally makes sense to reserve the name with the state corporate filing office. Doing this means that you have the exclusive right to include the name in your articles (which you will prepare and file to form your corporation as part of Step 2, below) for a specified period of time—usually 60 days, though some states give you a longer reservation period.

Reserving your name ensures that your name will not be rejected because someone else has grabbed it between the time you check its availability and the date your articles are actually received by the state. If you cannot file your

articles within the reservation period, most states let you extend the reservation for another period. (A few states say you must wait at least one business day between consecutive reservations to let others jump in and grab the name by submitting their own reservation during this one-day interval.)

In most states, you can download an Application for Reservation of Corporate Name from your state's corporate filing office website. Some states allow you to complete the application form and submit it online. If your state does not provide an online form, rather than call the state office and wait for it to mail you a form, it's speedier simply to prepare and mail the reservation of name letter shown below. (You can find this form in Appendix C.)

If your name is available when your reservation request is received, the state will mail back a reservation certificate or receipt, showing your corporate reservation date and/or number. Keep the certificate or receipt handy. You will need this reservation information when your file your articles. (See Step 2, below.)

TIP

The person who applies for your corporate name reservation should be the same person who prepares and files your corporation's articles. When you file your articles of incorporation, the state filing office will look to make sure the person who submits the articles (the incorporator) is the same person who reserved the name. If not, it will ask you to obtain the written consent of the person who reserved the name before it will accept your articles. Avoid this delay by having the same person—usually one of the corporation's initial directors—perform both tasks. Following is a sample of the corporate name reservation form we provide online and in Appendix C. Again, prepare and mail this form if your state does not provide a ready-to-use Application for Reservation of Corporate Name on its site.

Request for Reservation of Corporate Name

___[date]_____

___[your name]_____
___[your address]_____
___[your telephone number]_____

___[name of state filing office]_____
___[address of state filing office]_____ **❶**

Re: Request for Reservation of Corporate Name

Corporate Filing Office:

Please reserve the first available corporate name from the list below for my use. My proposed corporate names, listed in order of preference, are as follows:

_____

_____

_____ **❷**

I enclose a check for the required reservation fee. **❸**

Sincerely,

___[your signature]_____
___[your typed name]_____

Instructions

❶ Insert the name and address of your state's corporate filing office (see Appendix A for contact information).

❷ Many states let you list alternative names in case your first choice for a corporate name is taken. If you have chosen one or two backup names that you are sure you will wish to use in case your first choice is unavailable, list them here. Don't list more than a total of three names—most states won't look at more than three choices.

❸ The reservation fee typically is modest ($15–$25). Take a quick look at the corporate fee page on your state filing office website to obtain your state's reservation fee.

Step 2. Prepare and File Articles of Incorporation

After you've chosen a name for your corporation, it's time to prepare and file articles of incorporation. (A few states call this form

---

Sample Articles of Incorporation

Pursuant to the _[name of state]_ Business Corporation Act, the undersigned incorporator submits the following Articles of Incorporation:

1. The name of the corporation is _[name of corporation]_ . ❶

2. The corporation is authorized to issue one class of common shares. The total number of such shares it is authorized to issue is _[number]_ shares. ❷

3. The street address of the corporation's initial registered office is _[address of registered office]_ , and the name of its initial registered agent at this address is _[name of agent]_ . ❸

4. The name and address of the incorporator is _[name and address of incorporator, who dates and signs, below]_ . ❹

Date: _____

Signature of Incorporator: _____

---

a certificate of formation, certification of organization or charter.) You will file your articles with the state corporate filing office. When they are accepted, your corporation is a legal entity. Although the content of the articles form varies from state to state, it's similar enough throughout the country that we can sensibly guide you through it here.

Sample Articles Form

To get a better understanding of what articles are—what they contain and what the form looks like—glance at the generic articles form above and read the accompanying instructions. The next section will show you how to obtain and file your state's articles form.

Instructions

❶ Your proposed corporate name must be shown in your articles. If the name is available for your use, your articles will be filed; if it isn't, your articles will be returned to you. As discussed in Step 1, above, it makes sense to check name availability in advance and, if possible, reserve the name you want. If you have reserved your corporate name, the name you specify must exactly match your reserved name.

❷ In "Sale and Issuance of Stock" in Chapter 2, we explain the basic considerations to take into account when deciding how many shares to authorize in your articles. As you probably know, this authorized number of shares is the number that can be issued to shareholders after your articles are filed. The key point here is that you are not required to issue all of your authorized shares. In fact, most incorporators don't; they want to have a reserve in case they want to issue additional shares later. Generally, if your state bases its filing fee on the number of shares you authorize, you will want to authorize the maximum number of shares for the smallest filing fee. However, if you are located in a state where there is no relationship between the amount of the filing fee and the number of shares, you can authorize as many shares as you wish. (The instructions to your state's online articles form should explain how to compute your filing fee, which will allow you to authorize the greatest number of shares for the smallest filing fee.) In some states, you must also specify whether or not your shares will have a dollar or par value amount. As discussed in detail in "Par Value States" in Chapter 2, unless the state charges a smaller fee for par value shares, most incorporators opt for shares without a

specified par value, since the par value concept is a holdover from the 19th century and no longer has practical meaning.

❸ The registered agent is the person authorized under state law to receive legal papers on behalf of your corporation. The agent need not be a corporate director, officer, employee, or shareholder. The registered office is the agent's business address for purposes of receiving legal papers. The registered office must be located within your state. In practice, incorporators typically name an initial director or officer as agent and specify the address of the corporation as the registered office address.

❹ The incorporator (in some states called the organizer) is the person who prepares and files your articles. You need just one. Typically, an initial director of the corporation acts as incorporator. In most states, the incorporator must sign the articles at the bottom of the form. In some states, the incorporator must sign in the presence of a notary, who will notarize the form.

Optional Article Provisions

State-provided articles forms (or our form if your state does not provide one) contain the minimum information and provisions legally required under each state's Business Corporation Act. For example, most simply allow you to authorize one class of common shares—that is, shares that have equal voting power and proportional rights. (A 10% shareholder, for instance, gets 10% of total voting power and has a right to receive 10% of any dividends or corporate assets that remain after the corporation is dissolved.)

However, state law allows you to add other provisions to your articles to implement more involved management and ownership rights and

procedures. Optional provisions vary from state to state, but typically include the following:

- **Delayed effective date for articles.** Many incorporators add a provision that says the articles are effective on a date later than the date the articles are filed. This allows the legal existence of the corporation to start on a day chosen by the incorporator—for example, on the first or last day of a month, rather than on the unknown date the articles will be processed and filed by the state filing office. The BCA of most states allows the articles to contain this sort of delayed effective date provision, as long as the date specified is within a certain period

Optional Article Provisions (continued)

after the actual filing date, most often 90 days. Your state's articles form may include a blank line where you can specify a delayed date; if not, you can add an article in the "Other Provisions" portion of the form that simply says, "The effective date of these Articles is [*insert the delayed date*]." Before adding this extra article, check your state corporate filing office website or call your state filing office to make sure your delayed date falls within the period allowed under your state BCA.

- **Authorizing more than one class of shares.** Some incorporators set up different classes of stock for different types of investors. Establishing different classes or series of stock—for example, one voting class and one nonvoting class, or one common class and one preferred class entitled to a greater proportionate share of corporate assets if the corporation dissolves —is a common addition to basic articles.

- **Election of directors.** Some incorporators wish to give one or more individuals or shareholders special rights to elect one or more directors. For example, a corporation may give a major investor the right to appoint a board member or let a class of preferred shareholders separately elect their own director.

- **Liability of directors.** If appropriate, you can add provisions that immunize directors from personal liability in suits brought against them by the corporation or the shareholders. As explained in "Directors" in Chapter 2, these provisions can help directors in larger, publicly held corporations avoid personal liability to shareholders.

- **Antidilution provisions.** Some incorporators include preemptive rights that allow existing shareholders a right of first refusal to buy stock issued in the future by the corporation. Or, conversely, they include restrictions that prohibit shareholders from having such preemptive rights. Adding preemptive rights to articles can help ensure that current shareholders get a chance to maintain their current percentage of share ownership when new shares are issued.

- **Cumulative voting.** Your articles can include rights of shareholders to cumulate their votes when voting to elect directors. (See "Shareholders" in Chapter 2.) Some state BCAs require the articles to either allow or prohibit cumulative voting. The "Shareholder Voting" or similar section of your state BCA provides your state's default cumulative voting rule and tells you, if applicable, how you can change it in your articles. Most smaller corporations will not be concerned with cumulative voting procedures nor want to change the state's default cumulative voting rule in their articles. Cumulative voting is helpful mostly in larger corporations to let minority shareholders seat one or more board members.

If you want to customize your articles, browse your state BCA (see Appendix A for information on how to locate your state's BCA online). Look for a section in the BCA titled "Contents of Articles—Optional Provisions." If any catch your eye, you can add them to your articles. If you need help drafting a provision, ask a business lawyer for help. (See Chapter 6.)

Get and Prepare Your State's Articles

The first step to completing your articles is to find the form for your state's articles of incorporation online at your state's filing office website (see Appendix A for information on how to find your state's website). Once you have the articles form, you will find specific instructions on completing the form included with the form or provided in a separate document.

In some states, an additional form must be filed with the articles (such as a Consent to Appointment as Registered Agent). Any additional form can also be downloaded from the site.

CAUTION

Note for Iowa and Nebraska incorporators. At the time of this edition, Iowa and Nebraska do not have any sample articles form for incorporators. Therefore, we provide a ready-to-use articles form with instructions for Iowa and Nebraska. (See Appendixes B and C.) Before using either of these forms, check the state's website or call the state office to see if an articles form has been made available. If not, use the form we provide.

CAUTION

Note for professional corporations. If you are forming a professional corporation to provide services in the fields of health, law, accounting, engineering, architecture, and the like (see "Kinds of Corporations" in Chapter 2), look for special articles for professional corporations. (The state filing office website should list the licensed professions that must use special professional articles to incorporate.)

In some states, you can prepare and submit your articles online and, in some cases, you must file online. Other states offer more limited or no online services. What choices you have for preparing and submitting your articles will depend on what state you are in, but here are some of the options you may have:

- Some states let you fill in *and file* your articles online, either paying online via credit card or making telephone arrangements to pay your filing fee. This is the easiest and fastest way to form a corporation if it is available.

- Some states let you upload and file an articles form you've prepared yourself.

- Other states provide a "fillable" PDF version of the articles that you can complete on your computer. You must have Adobe Acrobat *Reader* (available for free at www. adobe.com) or a compatible PDF reader program. After filling in the form, you must print it from your browser, then mail it with the required fee to the state filing office as explained in the instructions that accompany the form. (See "Prepare Your Articles Cover Letter," below.)

- Some states provide a regular PDF form that you print out and then fill in by hand (using a black pen). In some cases, the articles are also available in alternate word processing file formats, such as Microsoft *Word*, which you can fill in prior to printing if you have the associated word processor installed on your computer.

All states that provide an articles form also provide instructions for filling it out and filing it, together with the filing fee information.

If you are converting an existing business to a corporation, you should check whether your state has an articles conversion form. Many states provide a simple entity conversion form to convert one type of entity to another. You just check the appropriate boxes on the conversion form, add some simple boilerplate as explained in the instructions to the form, file the form, and you're done. Normally, the advantage of using a state's articles conversion form is that the assets of the preexisting business are transferred to the new corporation and the prior business (for example, a partnership or an LLC) is dissolved automatically when the conversion form is filed. However, there can be tax consequences to using a state's conversion form, as explained in Chapter 3. Check with a lawyer and tax adviser to determine if you should or must use a state's conversion form to convert an existing business into a corporation.

Prepare Your Articles Cover Letter

Most incorporators file their articles by mailing them to the state corporate filing office—unless their state provides an online filing service or the filing office is located close by so the incorporators can easily file their articles in person. (See "Filing your articles in person," below.) If you will file your articles by mail, you should include a cover letter like the one that follows. (We provide this letter in Appendix C and online.) Check your state's filing website to see if they provide a cover letter—some do. If you find one, use it instead of the one provided here.

Instructions

❶ Insert the number of copies (in addition to the original) you are including, according to your state's articles instructions. Some states require just the original—in this case, insert "0" in the blank. Many states require the original and just one copy. In most states, you can simply photocopy the signed original of the articles when making copies; in a few others, the incorporator must manually sign each copy. In most states, after the filing office approves your articles, one copy will be file-stamped and/or certified (stamped with a seal or statement that the copy has been compared to the original) for no charge. But in a few states, you must pay to have a copy certified.

TIP

Don't pay for what you don't need. You will want to receive at least one file-stamped copy of your articles for your records. Then you can make additional copies yourself, without paying the state for them. There is no need to include extra payment for a certified copy unless this is required by your state—a file stamp is enough proof that your articles are valid and have been accepted by the state.

❷ Insert the name of the corporate organizational document. In most states, it is "Articles of Incorporation." But some states use other names, such as "Certificate of Incorporation," "Articles of Organization," "Certificate of Formation," or "Charter." Check your state rules for the proper terminology.

❸ If you have any special instructions for the state filing office, include them at the end of the first paragraph. For example, if you are paying extra for expedited filing, insert an appropriate reference to this. If you added a delayed effective date provision to your articles (see "Optional Article Provisions" in "Sample Articles Form," above), it's a good idea to flag it here in your cover letter. Just add a sentence that says: "Note that the Articles request a delayed effective date of [*insert delayed date*]."

❹ If you reserved your corporate name (see "Reserve Your Corporate Name" in Step 1, above), fill in the blank with the date of your name reservation. This date should be stamped on the application or request for name reservation you received from the state filing office. If the reservation was assigned a number by the office, include that number in this blank as well. If you did not reserve your corporate name prior to filing your articles, just insert "N/A" in the blank. Remember that the person who signs your articles and this cover letter should be the same person who reserved the name. (See "Reserve Your Corporate Name," above.)

Sample Cover Letter for Filing Articles

_____[date]_____

_____[your name]_____
_____[your address]_____
_____[your telephone number]_____

_____[name of state filing office]_____
_____[address of state filing office]_____

Corporate Filing Office:

I enclose an original and _[number]_ ❶ copy/copies of the _[insert name of document: in most states, "Articles of Incorporation"]_ ❷ of _[name of corporation]_ . Please file the original document and return any file-stamped copies to me, at the above address.❸

This corporate name was reserved by the undersigned incorporator on _[date of reservation and reservation number, if applicable]_ . ❹

I enclose payment of required filing fees. ❺

Sincerely,

_____[incorporator's signature]_____ ❻
      [incorporator's typed name]

 TIP

Include a copy of your name reservation. If you received a written name reservation form or receipt, include a copy with your cover letter and articles.

❺ Include the required filing fee.

❻ Your incorporator—the same person who signed your articles—should sign your cover letter. Type the incorporator's name under the signature line.

File Your Articles

Filing your articles is a formality. The corporate filing office will accept your papers if they conform to law and you pay the proper fees. The time it takes to have your articles processed and filed varies from state to state and depends on the office's current workload. In most states you can expect to receive your file-stamped copy or copies back from the office in one or two weeks, but in some states at busy times of the year, it can take longer. (In some "budget-challenged" states, such as California, it can take up to three months for mailed articles to be filed.) To avoid this delay, you may wish to send your articles to the state filing office by Express Mail. (Make sure you send them to the street address specified on your state filing office website for express mailings; it may be different from the main mailing address.) In many states, to get even quicker service, you can pay extra for expedited filing. This usually ensures that your articles will be processed within one or two days of receipt by the office. Again, expedited filing procedures, if available, and related fees are posted on your state's corporate filing office website.

> **TIP**
>
> **Filing your articles online.** Some states let you prepare and file articles online. This is the quick and easy way to do it, and we recommend you file online if your state lets you. Uploading Forms: If your state requires you to upload a PDF version of your articles, you can open your non-PDF form in Google docs, then save it as a PDF form.

> **TIP**
>
> **Filing your articles in person.** If you want to file your articles immediately and you are located reasonably close to a corporate filing office, you may usually file them in person, though you may be charged an additional handling fee for this. Check your state corporate filing office website for guidelines for over-the-counter filing.

Step 3. Set Up a Corporate Records Book

Establishing a corporate records book is an essential part of forming your corporation. Your records book will help you keep important corporate papers in good order, including your articles, bylaws, minutes of your first board

meeting and ongoing director and shareholder meetings, stock certificates, and stock certificate stubs. Keep your corporate records book at the principal office of your corporation.

Create a Records Book or Order a Corporate Kit

You can set up a perfectly effective corporate records book in any three-ring binder. Or if you prefer, you can order a special corporate records kit through a corporate kit supplier that will look a bit nicer in your bookcase.

Corporate Seals

A corporate seal is a metal or rubber stamp that embosses (with raised letters) or prints the corporate name on documents. A corporation is not legally required to have or use a corporate seal, but many find it handy to do so. A corporate seal is a formal way of indicating that a given document is the duly authorized act of the corporation. It is not normally used on everyday business papers (invoices, purchase orders, and the like) but is commonly employed for more formal documents such as stock certificates, leases, deeds of trust, and certifications of board resolutions. Embossed and stamped seals are also available separately through legal stationers. Most seals are circular in form and contain the name of the corporation, the state, and the year of incorporation. A corporate seal is available as an option when ordering the corporate kits advertised at the back of this book.

Stock Certificates

This book provides you with ten black-and-white certificates printed on book-quality paper in Appendix C. A stock certificate form is also available online in PDF format.

If You Create Your Own Articles or Attachment Pages

Most states allow you to prepare and submit your own articles form, even if the state provides an official form, as long as your form contains the minimum information required under your state's BCA. (In Iowa and Nebraska you must create your own form, since the state does not provide an official version; this book provides a form for articles in these states.) Most states will not accept fully hand-printed articles. States do allow you to fill in blanks on a computer-generated form, as long as you print legibly. If you prepare your own articles form, we assume you will generate them with a computer.

Even if you use a state-provided articles form (as will most incorporators), you may need to prepare an attachment page to the state form if the space on the official articles form cannot accommodate a response—for example, if you need to list five initial directors and your state form only provides space for three. Again, don't hand-print the attachment: Use a computer.

If you do create your own articles or include an attachment page with the official state form, make sure to follow any requirements noted on your state's filing office website. Even if not required, we suggest any articles or attachment pages you create conform to the following guidelines. These are standard format rules preferred by most corporate filing offices unless otherwise noted in your state sheet:

- the printout must be legible, with good contrast
- use black ink
- use letter-size paper (8½" × 11")
- print on only one side of the page
- use at least one-inch top and side margins, and
- place the title of your document—for example, "Articles of Incorporation" or "Certificate of Organization"—at the top of any attachment pages, and note the article number associated with any text on the page. For example, if you include an attachment page in response to Article III, title the text "Continuation to Article III." If the attachment page contains additional articles that pick up where the articles on the state-provided form stop, simply list the article number before any text—for instance, "Article 10. [*your text*]," "Article 11. [*your text*]."

(See Appendix B.) Just like a homemade corporate records binder, these are perfectly legal. (These certificates may, however, require modifications, such as adding stock transfer restrictions to comply with securities laws. See "Stock Issuance and the Securities Laws" in Chapter 2 and also Step 7, below.) By contrast, corporate kits may contain 20 lithographed green certificates with your corporate name and state of incorporation preprinted on each. If you think you will need more, you can order additional certificates at the time you order a corporate kit, or later, as a separate order.

TIP

Wait before ordering stock certificates or a seal. We suggest you wait until you have received file-stamped articles from the corporate filing office before you order a corporate kit, printed certificates, or a seal. This way, you'll be sure that you really have set up a corporation before you pay for these materials. However, if you are committed to forming your corporation and you have already reserved your corporate name, it's probably safe to order these corporate materials before you file your articles.

Step 4. Prepare Your Bylaws

After you have received file-stamped articles from the corporate filing office and set up your records book, your next incorporation task is to prepare bylaws. Bylaws are an internal corporate document that sets out the basic ground rules for operating your corporation. They are not filed with the state. We provide a bylaws form that you can use. (See Appendixes B and C.)

The Importance of Bylaws

Bylaws are a basic corporate management document that should always be prepared as part of the incorporation process. This is true even though in most states no law specifically requires you to adopt bylaws. Bylaws are important because they let directors, officers, and shareholders know when and how meetings can be held, or, in the absence of meetings, how decisions can be reached and recorded by mutual written consent. In addition, they cover many other essential operating rules, such as notice, quorum, and voting requirements for meetings; the basic titles and responsibilities of corporate officers; rights of directors and shareholders to inspect corporate records; and the requirements for providing annual financial information to shareholders.

Adopting bylaws also shows that your corporation takes its corporate identity seriously. It's a simple fact that shareholders, other businesses, banks, creditors, the IRS, and a court (should your corporation become involved in a lawsuit) will expect your corporation to have bylaws. It's fairly common for a bank, a creditor, or the IRS to ask to see a copy. Even the smallest one-person corporation absolutely needs to adopt bylaws, if for no other reason than to look legitimate to the outside world.

Having said all of this, we should not overstate the legal significance of your bylaws. While they provide many key details for day-to-day corporate housekeeping, the real source of legal authority—and the place you should look whenever you want to make sure your corporation is acting lawfully—is your state's Business Corporation Act. (See Appendix A for information on how to locate your BCA online.)

EXAMPLE: Let's say that your corporation decides to amend its previously filed articles to authorize a new class of preferred shares to investors. The first thing to do is look at your bylaws to see if it tells you the required procedures for amending your articles. Your bylaws cover the process generally, but you want to make sure you have the latest, most complete rules before you approve this important amendment. You go online to your state's BCA and find a section called "Amendment of Articles." You see that the amendment must be approved by directors and by a majority of all the outstanding shareholders (your bylaws got this right). You also see that the notice of the meetings held to approve the amendment must state the purpose of the meeting—that is, the meeting notice must state that the purpose of the meeting is to amend the articles to add a new class of shares (your bylaws didn't mention this requirement). You also double-check your bylaw meeting provisions against the BCA meeting rules to make sure your rules for calling and providing notice of, and quorum rules for, directors' and shareholders' meetings are completely current, too.

Many corporations, particularly those formed with the help of a lawyer, adopt lengthy bylaws that go on for pages repeating the provisions of the state BCA. Having loads of statutory rules repeated in the bylaws may look impressive, but it's counterproductive: Your state BCA will change frequently, meaning the more of it you restate in your bylaws, the more often you'll need to update them or pay a lawyer to do it.

The bylaws included in this book are designed to sensibly accommodate the need to provide procedural specifics without unnecessarily restating areas of the law that can just as easily be found in your BCA. Our bylaws provide commonsense procedures (valid in all states) for holding director and shareholder meetings. For example, the bylaws provide for an annual shareholders' meeting, and this procedure works in all states. But our bylaws do not specifically list the rules for calling special meetings during the year, because each state has different rules for doing this. Instead, the bylaws simply authorize the people who are allowed under your state's BCA to call a special meeting to do so. When you wish to call a special meeting, this bylaw provision alerts you to check your state BCA (it only takes a few minutes when you follow the procedure explained below) to find out who can call a special meeting under your state's BCA rules. This method makes sure you follow the current law.

We also provide bylaws that deal with other areas of interest to corporate directors, officers, and shareholders, such as the rights of directors and shareholders to inspect corporate records, corporate indemnification and insurance, executive committees of the board, and the

like. Again, we either provide a bylaw provision that should work in every state, or we use language that makes reference to your state's specific statutory requirements so you can look them up and follow the latest rule when the need arises.

It is also possible to customize your bylaws by adding your own provisions to our standard form. Below, we explain common items you may wish to cover in your bylaws, and how to find your state's specific rule to implement them. But recognize that in our complicated world there are always additional things you can add. For small business corporations, the most common addition is what are called buy-sell provisions that spell out what happens if one co-owner decides to sell shares or leave the corporation. (See "Adopt a Shareholder's Buy-Sell Agreement" in Chapter 5.) These provisions are complex and require a great deal of thought, so we cover them in detail in another book, *Business Buyout Agreements*, by Anthony Mancuso and Bethany K. Laurence (Nolo).

How to Prepare Your Bylaws

Preparing your bylaws is as simple as filling in a few blanks. Use the bylaws in Appendix C or the electronic file as you follow the sample below. We include bracketed instructions within the sample to help you fill in the blanks and understand the purpose and effect of our bylaw provisions.

Bylaws
of
[Name of Corporation]

ARTICLE 1. OFFICES

SECTION 1. PRINCIPAL OFFICE

The location of the principal office of the corporation will be within the state of   [insert the name of your state]   at an address fixed by the board of directors. The secretary of this corporation will keep a copy of the corporation's Articles of Incorporation (or similar incorporating document), these bylaws, minutes of directors' and shareholders' meetings, stock certificates and stubs, a register of the names and interests of the corporation's shareholders, and other corporate records and documents at the principal office. [**State law allows a corporation to have offices both within and outside the state. But since most smaller corporations also designate the principal office as their corporation's registered office (this designation usually is made in the articles) and that the office must be in the state, the bylaws specify that the principal office will be within the state.**]

SECTION 2. OTHER OFFICES

The corporation may have offices at other locations as decided by its board of directors or as its business may require.

ARTICLE 2. SHAREHOLDERS' MEETINGS

SECTION 1. PLACE OF MEETINGS

Meetings of shareholders shall be held at the principal office of the corporation or at other locations as may be decided by the board of directors.

SECTION 2. ANNUAL MEETINGS

The annual meeting of the shareholders will be held each year on and at the following date and time: [insert the time and date of your annual shareholders' meeting] . At the annual shareholders' meeting, shareholders will elect a board of directors and transact any other proper business. If this date falls on a legal holiday, then the meeting shall be held on the following business day at the same time. [**Most states require an annual meeting for the election of directors unless the corporation elects a staggered board. (See "Corporate People" in Chapter 2.) Staggered boards are normally only of interest to larger corporations, and we assume you will wish to elect directors annually.**]

SECTION 3. SPECIAL MEETINGS

Special meetings of the shareholders may be called by the individuals authorized to do so under the state's corporation statutes. [**Special meetings are infrequently called between annual meetings to seek shareholder approval of special business, such as amending the corporate articles or bylaws. (See the "Shareholder Meeting" section of your state's BCA to find out who may call a special shareholders' meeting in your state.)**]

SECTION 4. NOTICES OF MEETINGS

Notices of meetings, annual or special, must be given in writing to shareholders entitled to vote at the meeting by the secretary or an assistant secretary or, if there is no such officer, by any director or shareholder. [**Written notice of both annual and special shareholder meetings is normally required under state law.**]

Notices of shareholders' meetings must be given either personally or by first-class mail or other means of written communication, addressed to the shareholder at the address of the shareholder appearing on the stock register of the corporation or given by the shareholder to the corporation for the purpose of notice. Notice of a shareholders' meeting must be given to each shareholder no less than 30 days prior to the meeting. [**Most state BCAs require notice to be mailed no fewer than ten days nor more than 60 days before the meeting. In practice, 30 days' notice of a shareholder's meeting works fine for smaller corporations.**]

This notice will state the place, date, and hour of the meeting and the general nature of the business to be transacted. The notice of an annual meeting and any special meeting at which directors are to be elected will include the names of the nominees that, at the time of the notice, the board of directors intends to present for election. [**Under most state BCAs, the notice of a special meeting must describe, in general terms, the purpose of the meeting, and only matters included in the notice can be decided at the special meeting. In contrast, most states don't require similar specificity in the notice of annual shareholder meetings—by law, directors can be elected at an annual meeting and any other business can be considered at them without prior notice to shareholders. We think this is a poor idea, so our bylaws require that shareholders be told what to expect at both annual and special meetings.**]

SECTION 5. WAIVER OF NOTICE

The transactions of any meeting of shareholders, however called and noticed, and wherever held, are as valid as though undertaken at a meeting duly held after regular call and notice, if a quorum is present, whether in person or by proxy, and if, either before or after the meeting, each of the persons entitled to vote, not present in person or by proxy, signs a written waiver of notice or a consent to the holding of the meeting or an approval of the minutes thereof. If the waiver does not include an approval of the minutes of the meeting, it must state the general nature of the business of the meeting. All such waivers, consents, and approvals will be filed with the corporate records or made a part of the minutes of the meeting. [**Most states specifically allow shareholders who do not attend a meeting to waive notice before as well as after a shareholders' meeting. This is necessary when you call a quick meeting to deal with an emergency and don't have time to notify everyone 30 or more days in advance, as required by these bylaws. In some states, the waiver need not include a description of the nature of the business brought up at the meeting except for special decisions. However, for obvious reasons, we believe the waiver should contain such a description, unless a shareholder approves minutes of the meeting that set forth the decisions reached at the meeting. That's why our language, above, requires this.**]

SECTION 6. LIST OF SHAREHOLDERS

Prior to any meeting of shareholders, the secretary of the corporation will prepare an alphabetical list of shareholders entitled to vote at the meeting that shows the address of each shareholder and number of shares entitled to vote at the meeting. This list will be available for inspection at the principal office of the corporation by any shareholder within a reasonable period prior to each meeting and be made available for inspection at the meeting on request of any shareholder at the meeting. [**Most states require the corporation to maintain an alphabetical list of shareholders and have it available for inspection at the meeting. Some states require the list to be available for inspection a specified number of days prior to the meeting. Our bylaws include a "reasonable period" premeeting inspection requirement that should suffice. If you wish to read the exact language of your state's shareholder list inspection rule, see the "List of Shareholders" statute (or a similarly titled section) under the "Shareholder Meeting" heading in your state BCA.**]

SECTION 7. QUORUM AND VOTING

Every shareholder entitled to vote is entitled to one vote for each share held, except as otherwise provided by law. A shareholder entitled to vote may vote part of his or her shares in favor of a proposal and refrain from voting the remaining shares or vote them against the proposal. If a shareholder fails to specify the number of shares he or she is affirmatively voting, it will be conclusively presumed that the shareholder's approving vote is with respect to all shares the shareholder is entitled to vote. [**One-vote-per-voting-share is the normal shareholder voting rule under state BCAs. Some states allow shareholders to receive fractional shares (for example, 1.5 shares) with fractional voting power (say 1.5 votes), but we assume you will not wish to issue shares of this sort nor issue special shares that have disproportionate voting power, such as two votes per share.**]

A majority of the shares entitled to vote, represented in person or by proxy, will constitute a quorum at a meeting of shareholders. If a quorum is present, the affirmative vote of the majority of shareholders represented at the meeting and entitled to vote on any matter will be the act of the shareholders, unless the vote of a greater number is required by law. [**This section restates the standard shareholder meeting quorum and voting rules found in most state BCAs. (See Chapter 2 for a discussion of the issue.) If you wish to change either of these rules, check the language of your state's shareholder quorum and voting rules, contained in the "Shareholder Meeting" section of your state's BCA. This section of the bylaws recognizes that state law may require a greater vote requirement in special cases—for example, the approval of a majority of all shares, not just those present at a meeting, may be required to amend your articles or change stock rights. Again, it's best to check your state BCA before taking major shareholder action of this sort.**]

The shareholders present at a duly called or held meeting at which a quorum is present may continue to transact business until adjournment notwithstanding the withdrawal of enough shareholders to leave less than a quorum, if any action is approved by at least a majority of the shares required to constitute a quorum. [**This is a standard state BCA rule enacted to defeat "quorum busting" tactics at shareholder meetings. It lets the remaining shareholders vote even if one or more shareholders leaves the meeting and the remaining number of shareholder votes is less than a quorum.**]

Notwithstanding other provisions of this section of the bylaws, if permitted by law and not prohibited by provision of the corporation's Articles of Incorporation (or similar incorporating document), shareholders may cumulate votes for the election of directors as provided in this paragraph. If permitted to cumulate votes in an election, a shareholder must state his or her intention to cumulate votes after the candidates' names have been placed in nomination at the meeting and before the commencement of voting for the election of directors. Once a shareholder has stated his or her intention to cumulate votes, all shareholders entitled to vote must cumulate their votes in the election for directors. A shareholder cumulates votes by giving one candidate a number of votes equal to the number of directors to be elected multiplied by the number of his or her shares or by distributing these votes on the same principle among any number of candidates as he or she decides. The candidates receiving the highest number of votes, up to the number of directors to be elected, are elected. Votes cast against a candidate or which are withheld will have no effect in the cumulative voting results. [**We explain how cumulative voting works in Chapter 2. Cumulative voting is not normally used in smaller corporations, only in larger companies with a significant number of shareholders. This bylaw provision is included just in case you want to use cumulative voting in your elections for directors and (1) state law automatically allows it, or (2) you specifically completed a provision in your articles to allow cumulative voting (the official articles form in a few states allows you to do so). If cumulative voting is allowed under law or in your articles, this bylaw lets your shareholders cumulate their votes if at least one shareholder asks to cumulate votes after names have been placed in nomination and before the voting starts at a meeting held to elect directors.**]

In any election for directors at a shareholders' meeting, on the request of any shareholder made before the voting begins, the election of directors will be by ballot rather than by voice vote. [**This is a sensible provision; state BCAs either specifically provide for this or are silent on the subject. Note that this and the preceding paragraph are the only two rules we provide on shareholder election of directors. Many state BCAs cover other election procedures, such as appointing neutral inspectors who oversee the nomination and mailing of notices to shareholders of an upcoming election of directors, or creating special proxy solicitation and candidate nomination rules. We don't think smaller corporations, which commonly have ten or fewer shareholders, benefit from these extra provisions, so we don't include them in these bylaws. Of course, you are free to follow any election procedures allowed under state law, even though they are not included in your bylaws. If you want to learn about additional options you can use when electing your board, scan your state BCA for statutes that deal with technical provisions for the election of directors.**]

SECTION 8. PROXIES

Every person entitled to vote shares may authorize another person or persons to act by proxy with respect to those shares by filing a proxy with the secretary of the corporation. For purposes of these bylaws, a "proxy" is a written authorization signed by a shareholder or the shareholder's attorney-in-fact giving another person or persons power to vote with respect to the shares of the shareholder. Every proxy continues in full force and effect until the expiration of any period specified in the proxy or until revoked by the person executing it, except as otherwise provided by law. [**As discussed in Chapter 2, state law allows shareholders to appoint another person as a proxy to vote shares at a meeting. Typically, state law** limits the effectiveness of a proxy to specified period—11 months is common—unless it specifically says it will last longer. To find your state's proxy rule, look for a statute titled "Proxies" in the "Shareholder Meeting" section of your state BCA.]

SECTION 9. ACTION WITHOUT MEETING

Any action that may be taken at any annual or special meeting of shareholders, except for the election of directors, may be taken without a meeting and without prior notice if a consent, in writing, setting forth the action so taken, is signed by all the holders of outstanding shares entitled to vote on the action. [**This provision lets shareholders reach a decision by signing a written consent instead of voting at a meeting. Notice that we exclude the election of directors from those actions that may be approved by unanimous written shareholder consent. Many states don't allow election of directors by written consent. We also think shareholders should meet to elect directors to allow the candidates to be discussed and so that names not previously presented by management can be placed in nomination by the shareholders. And we believe a unanimous written consent rule is wisest. If one or more shareholders disagrees with a decision, its best to air these differences at a face-to-face shareholders' meeting. Your state BCA may be more lenient. (See "Action by Written Consent" or a similarly titled section in the "Shareholder Meeting" part of your state BCA.)]**

ARTICLE 3. DIRECTORS

SECTION 1. POWERS

The business and affairs of the corporation will be managed by, or under the direction of, its board of directors.

SECTION 2. NUMBER

The authorized number of directors is ___[number]___ . [**All states allow a corporation to have one or more directors, but a few states have a restriction on appointing fewer than three directors. For example, some states say the following: A corporation can have one director only if it has just one shareholder; if the corporation has two shareholders, it must have at least two directors; and if the corporation has three or more shareholders, it must have at least three directors. (See "One Person Can Wear Several Corporate Hats" in Chapter 2.) Many states let you set up a variable board—that is, one that has a certain minimum or maximum number of directors (within the allowable lower limits in the states just mentioned). Most smaller corporations prefer to set up a fixed board, so we do not allow for establishing a variable board in these bylaws. If you want to authorize a variable board, read the relevant rules in your state's BCA. (Look for the "Board of Directors" or "Variable Board" statute.)]**

SECTION 3. ELECTION AND TENURE OF OFFICE

The directors are elected at the annual meeting of the shareholders and hold office until the next annual meeting and until their successors have been elected and qualified. [**Most states specify a one-year term for directors and require their election (or reelection) by shareholders each year. Even if your state allows a longer term, we think annual elections make sense to confirm management by the current directors or the election of new directors if the shareholders desire a change. Most states allow you to set up a staggered system of director election (see "Corporate People" in Chapter 2) that appoints a portion of the board each year, which obviously also means that each director serves for more than one year. Most small corporations with modest-sized boards do not need to stagger elections. But if you are interested in adopting a staggered board system to replace this bylaw provision, see the "Staggered Board of Directors" or "Classified Board of Directors" (a "classified" board is the legal term used in some states to describe a staggered board) statute in your state BCA.]**

SECTION 4. RESIGNATION AND VACANCIES

Any director may resign, effective on giving written notice to the chairperson of the board of directors, the president, the secretary, or the board of directors, unless the notice specifies a later time for the effectiveness of the resignation. If the resignation is effective at a later time, a successor may be elected to take office when the resignation becomes effective. [**This provision simply lets a director resign at any time. There is no point in trying to be more restrictive, since you really can't stop a person from leaving if he or she wishes to do so.**]

A vacancy on the board of directors exists in the case of death, resignation, or removal of any director or in case the authorized number of directors is increased, or in case the shareholders fail to elect the full authorized number of directors at any annual or special meeting of the shareholders at which directors are elected. The board of directors may declare vacant the office of a director who has been declared of unsound mind by an order of court or who has been convicted of a felony. [**State law may contain special requirements for approving an increase in the authorized number of directors or the removal of a director by other directors or shareholders. In the highly unlikely event you'll ever need to remove a director, check your state BCA prior to taking action. This bylaw simply notes that these and other acts result in the creation of a vacancy on the board.**]

Vacancies on the board may be filled by the remaining board members unless a vacancy is required by law to be filled by approval of the shareholders. Each director approved to fill a vacancy on the board holds that office until the next annual meeting of the shareholders and until his or her successor has been elected and qualified. [**This provision refers you to your state BCA before filling a vacancy. In most cases, state law will let the directors (even if less than a quorum) appoint a temporary director to a board seat until the next annual election of directors by shareholders. State law may require that a vacancy caused by the removal of a director be filled by the shareholders, and may give shareholders the right to fill any vacancy on the board not filled by the remaining directors.**]

SECTION 5. PLACE OF MEETINGS

Meetings of the board of directors may be held at any place, within or without the state, that has been designated in the notice of the meeting or, if not stated in the notice or if there is no notice, at the principal office of the corporation or as may be designated from time to time by resolution of the board of directors. Meetings of the board may be held through use of conference telephone, computer, electronic video screen communication, or other communications equipment, so long as all of the following apply:

(a) Each member participating in the meeting can communicate with all members concurrently.

(b) Each member is provided the means of participating in all matters before the board, including the capacity to propose, or to interpose, an objection to a specific action to be taken by the corporation.

(c) The corporation adopts and implements some means of verifying both of the following:

(1) A person communicating by telephone, computer, electronic video screen, or other communications equipment is a director entitled to participate in the board meeting.

(2) All statements, questions, actions, or votes were made by that director and not by another person.

[**This section recognizes that directors of corporations may not always be able to meet in person, and sometimes may need or prefer to hold a meeting through a conference call, computer chat on the corporation's intranet, or in a video-conference-call. Some technology-savvy states specifically mention virtual meetings of this sort in their statutes; the few that do make provisions similar to those above to require some means of ensuring that the directors can simultaneously "talk" to one another and that the corporation is able to verify that each person involved in the discussion is, in fact, who they claim to be.**]

SECTION 6. ANNUAL AND REGULAR MEETINGS

An annual meeting of the board of directors will be held immediately after and at the same place as the annual meeting of the shareholders. [**This provision reflects the standard practice of holding the annual meeting of directors on the same date and just after the annual shareholders' meeting. The newly elected or reelected board members accept their election to the board, then discuss and approve any items of business specified in the notice of the annual board meeting. You can change this provision to schedule the annual directors' meeting on whatever date you decide best meets the needs of your corporation and its directors.**]

Other regular meetings of the board of directors will be held at the times and places fixed from time to time by the board of directors. [**This provision simply lets the board decide when to hold other regular meetings—that is, meetings held at regular times throughout the year in addition to the annual meeting scheduled in the previous paragraph. If you know when you will hold regular board meetings, you can specify their dates in this provision. Often, bylaws make it unnecessary to notify directors of annual and regular board meetings. Since we think it's a good idea to remind directors of every meeting, our bylaws require all director meetings to be noticed. (See Section 8 of this article, below.)**]

SECTION 7. SPECIAL MEETINGS

Special meetings of the directors may be called by the individuals authorized to do so under the state's corporation statutes. [**Directors may want to call special meetings during the year to discuss management issues, to review corporate goals and performance, to set up and hear from special committees of the board, and to transact special corporate business such as authorizing the signing of a lease or bank loan. (See "Corporate People" in Chapter 2.) The "Director Meeting" section of your state's BCA shows who may call a special directors' meeting.**]

SECTION 8. NOTICES OF MEETINGS

Notices of directors' meetings, whether annual, regular, or special, will be given in writing to directors by the secretary or an assistant secretary or, if there be no such officer, by any director. [**Notice of both annual and regular directors' meetings is normally not required under state law but, as we say above, we think you should give notice to make sure each director knows to attend. State BCAs normally require notice of special directors' meetings and, of course, we require that, too. (To see your state's requirements for notice of directors meetings, see the "Director Meeting" section in your state's BCA.) Remember that, if you are pressed for time, an alternative to holding a special meeting is to obtain the written consent of directors to an action. (See Section 11 of this Article, below.)**]

Notices of directors' meetings will be given either personally or by first-class mail or other means of written communication, addressed to the director at the address of the director appearing on the records of the corporation or given by the director to the corporation for the purpose of notice. Notice of a directors' meeting will be given to each director at least two weeks prior to the meeting, unless a greater period is required under the state corporation statutes for giving notice of a meeting. [**Most states require notice of special directors' meetings to be given a specified number of days before the meeting. Two days is typical; some states require more, sometimes up to ten days. Again, no notice is normally required for other director meetings. We think two weeks' prior notice is appropriate for all meetings. Our notice rule applies unless your state BCA requires more. (See the "Director Meeting" section in your state's BCA for the minimum notice rules in your state.)**]

This notice will state the place, date, and hour of the meeting, and the general nature of the business to be transacted. [**Under most state statutes, the notice of a directors' meeting does not need to describe the purpose of the meeting. However, we think it makes good sense to state the purpose of a meeting, so our bylaws require it.**]

SECTION 9. WAIVER OF NOTICE

The transactions of any meeting of the board, however called and noticed or wherever held, are as valid as though undertaken at a meeting duly held after regular call and notice if a quorum is present and if, either before or after the meeting, each of the directors not present signs a written waiver of notice, a consent to holding the meeting, or an approval of the minutes of that meeting. If the waiver does not include an approval of the minutes of the meeting, it will state the general nature of the business of the meeting. All such waivers, consents, and approvals will be filed with the corporate records or made a part of the minutes of the meeting. [**As noted just above, most states specifically allow directors who do not attend a meeting to waive notice before as well as after a directors' meeting (those who attend obviously received notice of the meeting). Having nonattending directors sign a written waiver makes sense when you need to act quickly and don't have time to formally call or notice a directors' meeting as required under your bylaws. In many states, the waiver need not include a description of the nature of the business brought up at the meeting, except for special decisions. However, we think waivers should contain this sort of description, unless a director is** approving minutes of the meeting that describe decisions reached at the meeting. Our bylaws specify this. (For a written waiver form you can use at both shareholder and director meetings, see *The Corporate Records Handbook*, by Anthony Mancuso (Nolo).)]

SECTION 10. QUORUM AND VOTING

A quorum for all meetings of the board of directors consists of a majority of the authorized number of directors. [**This is the standard rule in most states. Within limits, you can change this quorum requirement if you wish. In most states, you can't lower your quorum far below a majority of the full board. But you can usually raise it to whatever level you wish. (To find your state's director meeting quorum rules, see the "Director Meeting" section of your state's BCA.)**]

Except as otherwise required under state corporate statutes, every act or decision done or made by a majority of the directors present at a meeting duly held at which a quorum is present is the act of the board. [**This is the standard vote approval rule under state BCA statutes. (For more information on how directors vote at meetings, see "Corporate People" in Chapter 2.) Your state's law is contained in the "Director Meeting" section of your state sheet. Your state BCA may have special director voting rules for certain types of decisions, such as the approval of business that personally benefits one or more directors. You must follow the state rules if they are different from the basic majority-vote rule stated here. That's why we always suggest checking your BCA before taking major corporate action.**]

SECTION 11. ACTION WITHOUT MEETING

Any action required or permitted to be taken by the board may be taken without a meeting, if all members of the board individually or collectively consent in writing to that action. Such written consents will be filed with the minutes of the proceedings of the board. Such action by written consent has the same force and effect as a unanimous vote of the directors. [**This provision lets directors approve a decision by unanimous written action or consent. The written document should describe the transaction or matter to be approved, and it should be signed by all directors. This requirement of unanimous signed approval of directors is found in most states. (If you want to look up the rule in your state, look for "Action Without Meeting" or "Written Consent by Directors" under the "Director Meeting" heading in your state BCA.)**]

SECTION 12. COMPENSATION

No salary will be paid directors, as such, for their services but, by resolution, the board of directors may allow a reasonable fixed sum and expenses to be paid for attendance at regular or special meetings. Nothing contained in these bylaws prevents a director from serving the corporation in any other capacity and receiving compensation for it. Members of special or standing committees may also be allowed compensation for attendance at meetings. [**This provision states the generally accepted practice of not paying salaries to directors, but permitting directors to be compensated per diem, per meeting, and/or for travel expenses and other costs associated with attending a meeting. It also makes it clear that directors may be paid for working for the corporation in a nondirector capacity. (This is the normal practice in small corporations where owner-directors also work as officers or in other salaried supervisory capacities.)**]

ARTICLE 4. OFFICERS

SECTION 1. OFFICERS

The officers of the corporation include a president, a secretary, and a treasurer, or officers with different titles that perform the duties of these offices as described in Sections 2 though 4 of this Article. Except as otherwise provided under state corporate statutes, any number of these offices may be held by the same person. The corporation may also appoint other officers with such titles and duties as determined by the board of directors. [**Your state's officer rules are contained in the "Officers" section of your state's BCA. (For a summary, see "One Person Can Wear Several Corporate Hats" in Chapter 2.) Most states allow one or more (or all) of any required officer positions to be held by the same person. Notice that the first sentence of this bylaw has been worded to allow you to call your president, secretary, and** treasurer whatever you want, as long as someone is appointed to perform the duties associated with these positions, which we list in Sections 2 through 4 of this Article. This means that, if you prefer, you can call your president the Chief Executive Officer (CEO) and your treasurer the Chief Financial Officer (CFO). There is no common alternative title for corporate secretary, but you are free to make one up (Chief Information Officer or CIO, perhaps).]

SECTION 2. PRESIDENT

The president (or chief executive officer or alternately titled chief corporate officer designated by the board of directors) has general supervision, direction, and control of the day-to-day business and affairs of the corporation, subject to the direction and control of the board of directors. He or she presides at all meetings of the shareholders and directors and is an ex officio member of all the standing committees, including any executive committee of the board, and has the general powers and duties of management usually vested in the office of president or chief executive officer of a corporation and other powers and duties as may from time to time be prescribed by the board of directors or these bylaws. [**State law normally does not specify what a president must do. This bylaw tries to fill in the gaps in a general way. It lists the generally accepted duties of a corporate president, and it indicates that the president chairs all director and shareholder meetings and is a member of all board committees. This is standard corporate procedure. Also, the president generally runs the corporation as its chief officer on a day-to-day basis. But because state law is silent in this area, you can change or add any provisions you wish when defining the role of your CEO. We believe, however, that this is normally unnecessary, since a general statement of the sort provided here is sufficient to allow you maximum flexibility to define the role of CEO without being hemmed in by a more specific bylaw provision.**]

SECTION 3. SECRETARY

The corporate secretary (or other corporate officer designated by the board of directors to maintain and keep corporate records) will keep, or cause to be kept, at the principal office of the corporation, a book of minutes of all meetings of directors and shareholders. The minutes will state the time and place of holding of all meetings; whether regular or special, and if special, how called or authorized; the notice given or the waivers of notice received; the names of those present at directors' meetings; the number of shares present or represented at shareholders' meetings; and an account of the proceedings.

He or she will keep, or cause to be kept, at the principal office of the corporation, or at the office of the corporation's transfer agent, a share register, showing the names of the shareholders and their addresses, the number and classes of shares held by each, the number and date of certificates issued for shares, and the number and date of cancellation of every certificate surrendered for cancellation.

He or she will keep, or cause to be kept, at the principal office of the corporation, the original or a copy of the bylaws of the corporation, as amended or otherwise altered to date, certified by him or her.

He or she will give, or cause to be given, notice of all meetings of shareholders and directors required to be given by law or by the provisions of these bylaws. He or she will prepare, or cause to be prepared, an alphabetical listing of shareholders for inspection prior to and at meetings of shareholders as required by Article 2, Section 6, of these bylaws.

He or she has charge of the seal of the corporation and has such other powers and may perform such other duties as may from time to time be prescribed by the board or these bylaws. [**A corporation may delegate the duties of the corporate secretary to another officer or high-level corporate employee, such as the corporate treasurer or CFO, who is paid primarily for performing other more active corporate duties.**]

SECTION 4. TREASURER

The treasurer (or other officer designated by the board of directors to serve as chief financial officer of the corporation) will keep and maintain, or cause to be kept and maintained, adequate and correct books and records of accounts of the properties and business transactions of the corporation.

He or she will deposit monies and other valuables in the name and to the credit of the corporation with the depositories designated by the board of directors. He or she will disburse the funds of the corporation in payment of the just demands against the corporation; will render to the president and directors, whenever they request it, an account of all his or her transactions as chief financial officer and of the financial condition of the corporation; and will have such other powers and perform such other duties as may from time to time be prescribed by the board of directors. [**Your corporation, of course, needs a chief financial officer. The duties listed here are general and comprise the basic responsibilities of this office. You can add to the list of duties and responsibilities if you wish, but there is normally no need to do so.**]

SECTION 5. APPOINTMENT, REMOVAL, AND RESIGNATION

All officers of the corporation will be approved by, and serve at the pleasure of, the board of directors. An officer may be removed at any time, either with or without cause, by written notification of removal by the board. An officer may resign at any time on written notice to the corporation given to the board, the president, or the secretary of the corporation. Any resignation takes effect at the date of receipt of the notice or at any other time specified in it. The removal or resignation of an officer is without prejudice to the rights, if any, of the officer or the corporation under any contract of employment to which the officer is a party. [**This provision recognizes that the board approves officers and can decide to dismiss and replace them, subject, of course, to the general precepts of employment law and any employment contract officers may have with the corporation. Officers, too, must abide by the terms of any contract when deciding to leave the corporation—for example, by providing sufficient notice to the board and abiding by the terms of any noncompete provisions in their contract.**]

ARTICLE 5. EXECUTIVE COMMITTEES

SECTION 1. REGULAR AND EXECUTIVE COMMITTEES OF THE BOARD

The board may designate one or more regular committees to report to the board on any area of corporate operation and performance.

To the extent allowed under state corporate statutes, the board also may designate and delegate specific decision-making authority to one or more executive committees, each consisting of two or more directors, that will have the authority of the board to approve corporate decisions in the specific areas designated by the board. [**This provision allows the board to set up regular committees that report to the board. For example, corporations with larger boards may want to set up finance, personnel, and perhaps other committees. In addition, this section allows the board to establish one or more executive committees, consisting of at least two directors, that can take over decision-making authority on specific matters delegated to them by the full board. (For a discussion of regular and executive committees of the board, see "Corporate People" in Chapter 2.) Most state statutes allow you to establish executive committees of this sort, but do not allow the committees to approve a few types of major corporate decisions such as distributions to shareholders, and the amendment of articles or bylaws. In practice, most small business corporations with relatively small boards made up of owners who participate in the business will not set up decision-making committees, preferring instead to reserve management power to the full board. To find your state's executive committee requirements, look for a section in your state BCA titled "Executive Committees of the Board" under the "Directors" heading of your BCA.**]

ARTICLE 6. CORPORATE RECORDS AND REPORTS

SECTION 1. INSPECTION BY SHAREHOLDERS AND DIRECTORS

The corporate secretary will make available within a reasonable period after a request for inspection or copying made by a director or shareholder or a director's or shareholder's legal representative the Articles of Incorporation (or similar organizing document) as amended to date; these bylaws as amended to date; minutes of proceedings of the shareholders and the board and committees of the board; the share register of the corporation, and its accounting books and records; and any other corporate records and reports. The requested records will be made available for inspection and copying at the principal office of the corporation within business hours. Any copying costs incurred by the corporation necessary to comply with a request for copies of records may be collected by the secretary from a requesting shareholder; the corporation assumes the cost of copies made for a requesting director. [**This general and permissive provision allows directors and shareholders complete access to all corporate records within a reasonable time after a request is made. Copying costs may be charged to a shareholder, but directors always get free copies—after all, they volunteer their time and make requests for inspection and copying to carry out their official director duties. Your state BCA may not require such generous inspection and copying rights—for example, it may only require inspection and copying by shareholders for a purpose reasonably related to a shareholder's interest in the corporation, or it may allow the corporation an extended period to comply with an inspection request. (Directors are normally given complete access to all corporate records under state BCA rules.) We don't think most corporations should worry about the reasons for requests or decide to limit access to any corporate records. However, if you wish to give shareholders only the specific inspection and copying rights mandated by your state BCA, look for a section titled "Inspection of Records" under the "Records and Reports" heading toward the end of the BCA. You can use your state's language to craft a more limited provision in place of ours.**]

SECTION 2. ANNUAL REPORTS TO SHAREHOLDERS

The secretary will mail a copy of any annual financial or other report to shareholders on the secretary's own initiative or on request made by one or more shareholders as may be required by state corporate statutes. [**This is a general section that reminds the corporate secretary to comply with any annual financial disclosure requirements contained in your state BCA—see the "Financial Statement" or another similar section under the "Records and Reports" section of your state BCA. If you wish, you can substitute your state's specific disclosure requirements in this provision.**]

ARTICLE 7. INDEMNIFICATION AND INSURANCE OF DIRECTORS AND OFFICERS

SECTION 1. INDEMNIFICATION

The directors and officers of the corporation will be indemnified by the corporation to the fullest extent permitted under law. [**This provision means that the corporation will reimburse the directors and officers for any legal expenses, settlements, fines, and judgments permitted under the state's BCA indemnification statute. (See "Corporate People" in Chapter 2 for a discussion of corporate indemnification.) If you want to learn your state's specific indemnification rules, look for a section in your state BCA titled "Indemnification." Most states require indemnification of legal expenses for a director or officer who is successful in a lawsuit or proceeding. In other situations, indemnification of expenses and other amounts may be allowed if the director or officer is found by the corporation to have acted in good faith and in the best interests of the corporation. If you want to be certain that your directors and officers get as much indemnification as possible under your state's law, see a lawyer to find out whether it's possible to create a separate agreement that will be signed by each director and officer of the corporation. Another more protective approach is to purchase a directors' and officers' liability insurance policy. (See the next section below.)**]

SECTION 2. INSURANCE

The corporation has the power to purchase and maintain insurance on behalf of any director or officer against any liability asserted against or incurred by the agent in that capacity or arising out of the agent's status as such, whether or not the corporation has the power to indemnify the agent against that liability under law. [**This is an enabling provision that lets the corporation purchase director and officer liability (D&O) insurance on behalf of directors and officers. (For information on this type of insurance, see "Corporate People" in Chapter 2.)**]

ARTICLE 8. SHARES

SECTION 1. CERTIFICATES

The corporation will issue certificates for its shares when fully paid. Certificates of stock will be issued in numerical order, and will state the name of the record holder of the shares represented by each certificate; the number, designation, if any, and class or series of shares represented by the certificate; and other information, including any statement or summary required by any applicable provision of state corporate statutes. Each certificate will be signed by the corporate officers empowered under state law to sign the certificates, and may be sealed with the seal of the corporation. [**Although issuing stock certificates to each shareholder is not specifically required under most state BCAs, we assume you will want to follow this traditional practice. (See "Corporate Documents" in Chapter 2.) This bylaw lists the general contents of each certificate and also requires any additional information required by state law to be placed on the certificate. For a list of the specific requirements for stock certificates imposed by your state BCA, see the "Share Issuance" section of your state's BCA. The state BCA also indicates who is required to sign stock certificates in your state. (It is common to have certificates signed by the corporate president and secretary.) Note that state law also requires you to place additional language—called a legend—on stock certificates that summarizes or states in full any special restrictions and rights associated with classes of shares. Since we assume you will issue just one class of common shares, your certificates normally will not require a legend. But realize that you must place a legend of this sort on any special class of shares you issue in the future. Also, if, as is common, you impose special transfer restrictions on your shares, should an owner die or want to sell out, you will need to mention these restrictions in a legend on your certificates. To see the specific types of legends that must be added to stock certificates in your state, look for a section titled "Contents of Stock Certificates" or "Restrictions on Stock Certificates" under the "Shares of Stock" heading of your BCA.**]

SECTION 2. TRANSFER OF SHARES

On surrender to the secretary or transfer agent of the corporation of a certificate for shares duly endorsed or accompanied by proper evidence of succession, assignment, or authority to transfer, it is the duty of the secretary of the corporation to issue a new certificate to the person entitled to it, to cancel the old certificate, and to record the transaction on the share register of the corporation. [**This basic provision is self-explanatory. Typically, the transferring shareholder completes the transfer section of the certificate (usually on the reverse side), then gives the certificate to the secretary. The secretary then cancels the old certificate and issues a new one to the person to whom the shares are transferred, being sure to record the transaction in the corporation's share register.**]

SECTION 3. RECORD DATE

The board of directors may fix a time in the future as a record date for the determination of the shareholders entitled to notice of and to vote at any meeting of shareholders or entitled to receive payment of any dividend or distribution, or any allotment of rights, or to exercise rights in respect to any other lawful action. The record date so fixed will conform to the requirements of state law. When a record date is so fixed, only shareholders of record on that date are entitled to notice of and to vote at the meeting, or to receive the dividend, distribution, or allotment of rights, or to exercise their rights, notwithstanding any transfer of any shares on the books of the corporation after the record date. [**This record date provision is simply a reminder that the board of directors may establish a date for determining who is a shareholder of record on the corporation's books for purposes of notice of shareholders' meetings, shareholder voting, and payment of dividends and other distributions to shareholders. In a small corporation, the board normally does not set record dates, since shares rarely change hands. Similarly, in the somewhat rare event that the corporation declares a dividend (for tax reasons, it is more common to hand out profits in other ways), the shareholders of record on the dividend declaration date are presumed to be the shareholders entitled to receive the dividend. These practices are generally in line with state BCAs. To see your state's rules for declaring a record date and for determining shareholders of record when no date has been set by the board, go to the "Shareholders" section of your BCA, then look for a "Record Date for Shareholders" statute. In many states, any record date set by the board must be no more than 60 nor less than ten days before the upcoming meeting or transaction to which the record date applies.**]

ARTICLE 9. AMENDMENT OF BYLAWS

SECTION 1. BY SHAREHOLDERS

Except as otherwise provided by law, these bylaws may be adopted, amended, or repealed by the affirmative vote at a meeting of holders of a majority of the outstanding shares of the corporation entitled to vote. [**This bylaw allows a majority of the outstanding voting shares (not just a majority in attendance at a meeting) to amend bylaws, except where the state BCA requires a greater vote. In many states, a lesser vote may be allowed—such as a majority of shareholders present at a meeting—but we think our stricter voting requirement makes sense to ensure sufficient shareholder consensus to a bylaw change. State BCAs sometimes limit the right to amend certain bylaws, such as the ability to lower the quorum requirements for meetings below a certain threshold. To find your state's rules for amending bylaws, look for a "Bylaws" or "Amendment of Bylaws" statute in your BCA.]**

SECTION 2. BY DIRECTORS

Except as otherwise provided by law, the directors may adopt, amend, or repeal these bylaws. [**This provision also allows the directors to amend the bylaws. They can do so under normal director voting rules—that is, by a majority of the directors in attendance at a meeting. This is standard practice under most state BCAs. But it is important to understand that state law may limit the ability of directors to change certain bylaws. For example, directors may not be allowed to lower the authorized number of directors below a certain point without also obtaining shareholder approval. Look for a "Bylaws" or "Amendment of Bylaws" statute in your BCA to see any special rules that apply in your state.]**

CERTIFICATE

This certifies that the foregoing is a true and correct copy of the bylaws of the corporation named in the title, and that these bylaws were duly adopted by the board of directors of the corporation on the date set forth below. [**After you prepare the minutes of your first board meeting, your corporate secretary should date and sign below. (See Step 6.)]**

Dated: _____

Signature: _____, Secretary

Incorporator's Statement

The undersigned, the incorporator of _[name of corporation]_ , who signed and filed its
Articles of Incorporation or similar organizing document with the state, appoints the following
individuals to serve as the initial directors of the corporation, who will serve as directors until
the first meeting of shareholders for the election of directors and until their successors are
elected and agree to serve on the board: ❶

_____

_____

_____

_____

_____

Date: _____

Signature: _____, Incorporator ❷

Step 5. Appoint Initial Corporate Directors

SKIP AHEAD

If you named initial directors in your articles of incorporation. If your initial board is listed in your articles, as is required in some states, you have already completed this step. Skip ahead to Step 6.

Your next step is to have your incorporator appoint initial corporate directors if they are not all named in your articles. This is an extremely simple step. The incorporator—the person who signed your articles—fills in an "Incorporator's Statement" to show the names and addresses of the initial directors who will serve on the board until the first annual meeting of shareholders (when the board members who will serve for the next term are elected by the shareholders). The

incorporator signs the statement and places a copy in the corporate records book.

To complete this step, have your incorporator complete the Incorporator's Statement included above and in Appendix C or provided in electronic form online, following the sample form and instructions below.

Instructions

❶ Article 3, Section 2, of your bylaws (prepared in Step 4, above) shows the full number of members on your board. The incorporator should appoint this number of board members if possible. If you must leave a seat open because you have not yet found all the right people to serve on your board, that's okay. Just make sure that you appoint enough directors to meet your bylaws' quorum requirement. Article 3, Section 10, defines a quorum as a majority of the authorized number of directors. So, if your bylaws authorize a four-person board but you only appoint three initial directors, all three of your initial directors must attend board meetings. If less than three attend, you don't have a quorum and the meeting can't be held.

❷ Have the incorporator date and sign the form, then place a copy in the corporate records book.

Step 6. Prepare Minutes of the First Board Meeting

Now that you've filed articles, prepared bylaws, and appointed your initial board of directors, it's time to transact the first important business of your new corporation: You must prepare minutes for your first meeting of the board. This book provides a simple minutes form for you to fill in. Your incorporator or any of the initial directors can prepare the document then ask all the directors to sign it, as explained in the instructions below. Although in theory your board is expected to discuss and complete the minutes together, this is often impractical, since it may take two or more weeks to conclude all the business reflected in the document—such

as ordering stock certificates, selecting an accounting period, selecting a corporate bank, settling on the details of your initial stock issuance, and other matters. In other words, it usually works better to prepare your minutes over a period of a couple of weeks, then pass the minutes around to all directors for their approval once the document is complete.

Fill In the Minutes Form

The purpose of your minutes is to document essential organizational actions approved by your initial board of directors, including:

- specifying the street location of the corporation's principal office
- adopting the bylaws
- electing officers
- selecting the corporation's accounting period
- choosing a bank for corporate accounts
- authorizing the issuance of the initial shares of stock of the corporation, and
- making initial tax elections and decisions.

Complete the minutes form we provide online or in Appendix C, following the sample form and instructions below.

Waiver of Notice and Consent to Hold
First Meeting of Board of Directors

We, the undersigned, being all the directors of *[name of corporation]* , hereby waive notice of the first meeting of the board of directors of the corporation and consent to the holding of the meeting at *[street address of corporation's principal office]* on *[date of meeting; this can be any date after the preparation of your bylaws and on or before the same date shown below (the date the waiver is signed)]* at *[time of meeting]* and consent to the transaction of any and all business at the meeting including, without limitation, the adoption of bylaws, the election of officers, the selection of the corporation's accounting period, the designation of the location of the principal office of the corporation, the selection of the place where the corporation's bank accounts will be maintained, and the authorization of the sale and issuance of the initial shares of stock of the corporation.

Date: _____ **❶**

Signatures:

_____ , Director **⓲**

_____ , Director

_____ , Director

_____ , Director

_____ , Director

Minutes of First Meeting of the Board of Directors

The board of directors of ___*[name of corporation]*___ held its first meeting at ___*[street address of corporation's principal office]*___ on ___*[date of meeting]*___, at ___*[time of meeting]*___. ❷

The following directors, marked as present next to their names, were in attendance at the meeting and constituted a quorum of the board: ❸

___*[name of director]*___   [ ] Present [ ] Absent

___*[name of director]*___   [ ] Present [ ] Absent

___*[name of director]*___   [ ] Present [ ] Absent

___*[name of director]*___   [ ] Present [ ] Absent

___*[name of director]*___   [ ] Present [ ] Absent

On motion and by unanimous vote, ___*[name of director]*___ was appointed chairperson and then presided over the meeting. ___*[name of director]*___ was elected secretary of the meeting. ❹

The meeting was held pursuant to written waiver of notice and consent to holding of the meeting signed by each of the directors. On a motion duly made, seconded, and unanimously carried, it was resolved that the written waiver of notice and consent to holding of the meeting be made a part of and constitute the first page of the minutes of this meeting.

ARTICLES OF INCORPORATION

The chairperson announced that the Articles of Incorporation or similar organizing document of the corporation were filed with the state corporate filing office on ___*[insert the date that the articles were file-stamped or the date shown on your filing receipt (if you requested a delayed effective date for your articles, show the delayed date instead)]*___. The corporate secretary was asked to place a file-stamped copy of the articles or filing receipt showing this filing in the corporation's records book. ❺

BYLAWS

A proposed set of bylaws of the corporation was presented for adoption. On motion duly made and seconded, it was unanimously:

RESOLVED, that the bylaws presented to this meeting are adopted as the bylaws of this corporation;

RESOLVED FURTHER, that the secretary of this corporation is asked to execute a Certificate of Adoption of the bylaws, and to place the bylaws as so certified with the corporation's records at its principal office. ❻

PRINCIPAL EXECUTIVE OFFICE

On motion duly made and seconded, it was:

RESOLVED, that the principal office of this corporation be located at ___*[insert the street address of the principal corporation office, including city, state, and zip code]*___ . ❼

APPOINTMENT OF OFFICERS

On motion, the following persons were unanimously appointed to the following offices: ❽

President (CEO): _____*[name of officer]*_____

Treasurer (CFO): _____*[name of officer]*_____

Secretary: _____*[name of officer]*_____

CORPORATE SEAL

On motion duly made and seconded, it was:

RESOLVED, that the corporate seal impressed directly below this resolution is adopted as the corporate seal of this corporation. The secretary of the corporation is directed to place the seal with the corporate records at the principal office of the corporation, and to use the seal on corporate stock certificates and other appropriate corporate documents as the secretary sees fit. ❾

STOCK CERTIFICATE

On motion duly made and seconded, it was:

RESOLVED, that the form of stock certificate attached to these minutes is adopted for use by this corporation for the issuance of its initial shares. ❿

CORPORATE BANK ACCOUNTS

On motion duly made and seconded, it was

RESOLVED, that the funds of this corporation be deposited with the following bank at the following branch office: ___*[name of bank and branch name or number]*___ located at ___*[address]*___ . ⓫

RESOLVED FURTHER, that the treasurer of this corporation is authorized and asked to establish one or more accounts with this bank and to deposit the funds of this corporation in these accounts.

RESOLVED FURTHER, that any officer, employee, or agent of this corporation is authorized to endorse checks, drafts, or other evidences of indebtedness made payable to this corporation, but only for the purpose of deposit.

RESOLVED FURTHER, that all checks, drafts, and other instruments obligating this corporation to pay money be signed on behalf of this corporation by any ___*[number]*___ of the following: ⓬

___*[name and title of person authorized to sign checks]*___

___*[name and title of person authorized to sign checks]*___

___*[name and title of person authorized to sign checks]*___

RESOLVED FURTHER, that the bank is hereby authorized to honor and pay any and all checks and drafts of this corporation signed in this manner.

RESOLVED FURTHER, that the authority hereby conferred remain in force until revoked by the board of directors of this corporation and until written notice of revocation has been received by the bank.

RESOLVED FURTHER, that the secretary of this corporation is authorized to certify as to the continuing authority of these resolutions and to complete on behalf of the corporation the bank's standard form of resolution, provided that the form does not vary materially from the terms of the foregoing resolutions.

ACCOUNTING PERIOD

After discussion and on motion duly made and seconded, it was:

RESOLVED, that the accounting period of this corporation ends on ___*[ending date of the accounting period of the corporation]*___ of each year. ⓭

PAYMENT, DEDUCTION, AND AMORTIZATION OF
START-UP AND ORGANIZATIONAL EXPENSES

On motion duly made, seconded, and unanimously approved, it was:

RESOLVED, that the treasurer of this corporation is authorized and empowered to pay all reasonable and proper expenses incurred in connection with the start-up and organization of the corporation, including, among others, expenses prior to the start of business necessary to investigate and create the business, as well as organization costs necessary to form the corporation and to reimburse any persons making such disbursements for the corporation.

RESOLVED FURTHER, that the treasurer is authorized to elect to deduct and amortize appropriate start-up and organization expenditures pursuant to and as permitted under Sections 195 and 248 of the Internal Revenue Code and as permitted under similar state tax provisions. ⓮

AUTHORIZATION OF ISSUANCE OF SHARES

On motion duly made and seconded, it was unanimously:

RESOLVED, that the corporation sell and issue the following number of its authorized common shares to the following persons, in the amounts and for the consideration set forth next to their names, below. The board also determined that the fair value to the corporation of any consideration for such shares issued other than for money is as stated below: ❶❺

Name	Number of Shares	Consideration
_____	_____	_____
_____	_____	_____
_____	_____	_____
_____	_____	_____
_____	_____	_____

RESOLVED FURTHER, that the amount of consideration received by the corporation for each and any of the above shares issued without par value that is to be allocated to capital surplus is $_____. ❶❻

RESOLVED FURTHER, that the appropriate officers of this corporation are hereby authorized and directed to take such actions and execute such documents as they deem necessary or appropriate to effectuate the sale and issuance of shares for the consideration listed above.

Since there was no further business to come before the meeting, on motion duly made and seconded, the meeting was adjourned.

_____, Secretary **❶⓱**

Instructions

Waiver of Notice

❶ The waiver of notice form dispenses with formal notice requirements that apply to board meetings under our bylaws. Insert the name and street address of the corporation (its principal office location). Date the form at the bottom of the page and obtain each director's signature after you finish preparing the minutes. (See Instruction 18, below.) This form is effective only if all directors sign it.

Title Page—Minutes of First Meeting of the Board of Directors

❷ The next page of the minutes contains the title of the document. The first paragraph repeats the name of your corporation and the address, date, and time of the meeting given on the waiver of notice.

❸ List the names of each initial director, and check the box that indicates whether each director is present or absent. Normally, you will show each director as present, since we assume that each initial director will approve and sign the minutes. However, if you hold a real meeting for which required notices have been sent and a director does not attend, check the box indicating that the director is absent.

❹ Insert the name of any director as chairperson of this first meeting, and one as secretary (you have not yet appointed officers to serve in these capacities for the coming year). You can insert the name of one director in both blanks if you have only one director.

Articles of Incorporation Resolution

❺ Insert the date your articles (or other organizing document) were filed with the state. If you asked for a delayed effective date in your articles, insert the delayed date instead. Include a file-stamped copy of the articles or the filing receipt returned to you by the state with your completed minutes.

Bylaws Resolution

❻ This resolution shows the formal adoption of your bylaws (prepared in Step 4, above) by the directors. As explained below, after you prepare these minutes, the corporate secretary will fill out the "Certificate" section at the end of the bylaws, which certifies that they have been formally adopted by your board of directors. Our bylaws (and state law) require you to keep copies of minutes and your bylaws at the principal office of the corporation. The best way to do this is to place all your corporate paperwork in a corporate records book, and keep this book at the principal office. (See Step 3, above.)

Principal Office Resolution

❼ Insert the official address of your corporation, which normally is the same as your main place of business. It is also normally the same as your corporation's registered office, as stated in your articles, which is the location where legal papers can be served on your corporation.

Appointment of Officers Resolution

❽ Here you formally appoint the officers whose positions are listed in your bylaws. (See Article 4, Section 1, of the bylaws.) These three positions are normally the minimum required under state law, as well as those that you will need to operate your corporation. As discussed earlier, you can change the titles of the officers listed in this resolution to reflect any alternate titles you will give your CEO, CFO, or secretary. Remember, in most states, you can appoint the same person to fill more than one or all of these three basic officer positions.

Corporate Seal Resolution

❾ Use of a corporate seal is optional in all states. (See Step 3, above.) If you ordered one, impress the seal in the space provided below the resolution. (You can make this impression after you prepare the minutes if you have not yet received your seal.) If you did not order a seal, leave the space blank. The secretary should keep the seal with the corporate records at the principal corporate office.

Stock Certificate Resolution

❿ Here you formally adopt the type of stock certificate you will use. Normally this is the bare-bones certificate included in Appendix C of this book or the fancier certificates that you have purchased on your own. Attach a copy of your approved stock certificate, marked "SAMPLE" across its face, to the minutes of your meeting.

Bank Account Resolution

⓫ This resolution authorizes the opening of one or more accounts with a specified bank. Fill in the blanks to show the bank name and branch office name (or number) and the address where the accounts will be located.

⓬ Specify how many signatures will be required on corporate checks, then list the names and titles of individuals authorized to sign these checks. Generally, you will list the name of one or more officers or key employees (such as your salaried in-house bookkeeper) as individuals authorized to sign checks. You may wish to change this provision to say that one person can sign checks up to a certain amount, but that two signatures must be obtained for checks exceeding the stated amount.

EXAMPLE: The following language can be substituted for our standard check-writing resolution: "RESOLVED FURTHER, that all checks, drafts, and other instruments obligating this corporation to pay money in an amount less than $ _[specify threshold amount]_ be signed on behalf of this corporation by any one of the following; that all checks, drafts, and other instruments obligating this corporation to pay money in an amount greater than the amount just stated be signed on behalf of this corporation by any two of the following:
[specify at least two names with titles] ."

Typically, to open a corporate account, the treasurer must fill out, and impress the corporate seal on, a separate bank account authorization form provided by your bank. But before opening an account, your bank will require your corporation to have a federal Employer Identification Number (EIN). This number is obtained by filing form SS-4 with the IRS or obtaining an EIN online from the IRS website at www.irs.gov. All corporations will also need to register as an employer with the state and make deposits of state and federal withholding and employment taxes with an authorized bank. All of this is explained more fully in Chapter 5.

Accounting Period Resolution

⓭ This resolution reminds you to check with your tax adviser to select an accounting period for your corporation. (For general information on corporate accounting periods and tax years, see Chapter 5.) Insert the expected ending date of the accounting period in the blank—for example, "December 31" or "June 30." Realize that this resolution simply reflects your intention to adopt this accounting period. Your accounting period, which must match your corporate tax year, is officially determined when you file your first corporate income tax returns and specify your tax year. Pay attention to this decision. You must occasionally seek IRS approval if you wish to change your tax year (and accounting period) after you file your first tax returns. If you meet certain conditions, your corporation can change its tax year once every ten years without seeking IRS approval.

Payment, Deduction, and Amortization of Start-Up and Organizational Expenses Resolution

⓮ Subject to specific monetary limits, federal tax law (the Internal Revenue Code) allows a corporation to deduct organizational and start-up expenses in the first corporate tax year. You can amortize and deduct remaining start-up and organizational expenses over the next 15 years. (Ask your tax adviser for more information.) Start-up costs are those incurred before the start of business to investigate or create the business, such as market surveys and analysis, advertisements related to opening the business, and other necessary preopening costs such as travel and employee training. Organizational costs are those paid to actually form the corporation, such as state filing fees, lawyer and tax adviser fees, and the cost of this book.

This resolution authorizes the treasurer to reimburse incorporators for out-of-pocket payments of start-up and organizational costs. It also authorizes the treasurer to make the appropriate elections on the corporation's income tax returns (under IRC Sections 195 and 248 and, if applicable, state corporate income tax law provisions) to deduct and amortize start-up and organizational expenses. The approval of this resolution does not result in the making of these elections. It simply reminds you to cover this matter later—by consulting your tax adviser and having your adviser prepare and include the election statements and necessary information with your first and subsequent income tax returns. Check with your tax adviser for help in deciding whether to use this resolution and for help in preparing your tax returns and statements to send to the IRS to make sure you deduct and amortize these expenses properly.

Authorization of Issuance of Shares Resolution

⓯ Here you authorize your corporation to issue its initial shares to your shareholders after the meeting of your board. Throughout the book, we refer to this resolution as your "stock issuance resolution." This resolution does not result in the actual issuance of shares—it simply authorizes the appropriate corporate officers to issue shares to the shareholders after the meeting. You will issue shares as part of Step 7, below.

Insert the name of each shareholder, the number of shares the shareholder will receive, and the shareholder's payment for shares. For any noncash payment, such as property, state the fair value of the property as a dollar amount. You may need more than one line per shareholder to describe property or services paid as consideration, but be as brief as possible. Before you fill in your resolution, make sure to review the stock issuance considerations discussed in "Sale and Issuance of Stock" in Chapter 2.

Stock Issuance Examples

Here are some examples to help you fill in the blanks on your stock issuance resolution.

Issuance of shares for cash. If shareholders will pay cash for shares, simply state the dollar amount followed by "cash" in the consideration column—for example, "Sarah Bennet—100— $1,000 cash."

Issuance of shares for specific items of property. If a shareholder will purchase shares by transferring specific items of property to the corporation (we are referring to discrete items of property, such as a computer system, a truck, a patent, or copyright; not the complete assets of a business—the latter situation is covered by the next example), be as specific as you can when entering the consideration. Show the fair market value of the property as its dollar value—for example, "$9,000, [year and model], Vehicle ID# VIN555-555-5555."

Issuing Shares: A Quick Review

We discussed stock issuance rules in "Sale and Issuance of Stock" in Chapter 2. Here's a recap:

- Make sure that the total number of shares that you will issue to all shareholders is not greater than the number of shares authorized in your articles of incorporation. (The authorized number of shares stated in your articles places an upper limit on the number of shares that you can actually issue; see "Sale and Issuance of Stock" in Chapter 2, and "Sample Articles Form" in Step 2, above.) Also, you cannot issue a class of shares other than those authorized in your articles. We assume you will authorize and issue only common shares with equal voting and liquidation rights, so our stock issuance resolution refers to common shares.

- If your articles authorize par value shares, most states require each shareholder to pay at least the par value amount for her shares. (See "Par Value States" in Chapter 2.) In most cases, par value is set at a low or nominal amount in the articles, and shareholders pay much more than the par value to buy their shares from the corporation.

- In some states, you cannot issue shares in return for the promise to perform future services by a shareholder or for promissory notes—that is, a promise by the shareholder to pay for the shares later. (See "Payments for Shares" in Chapter 2.)

- As a matter of common sense, and to avoid charges of unfairness or fraud, you should charge the same price per share for all the shares you issue to initial shareholders. Place a fair value on the assets or property received in return for the shares. Be realistic in your determination of fair value of all noncash payments for shares, particularly if you will be issuing shares in return for speculative or intangible property such as the goodwill of a business, copyrights, patents, and the like. You don't want to "shortchange" other shareholders who have put up cash or tangible property of easily determined value. Tax advisers are a good source of information on how to place a fair value on business assets.

- We assume you will issue shares in compliance with state and federal securities laws. In most cases, this means making sure you qualify for both a state and a federal securities law exemption before you issue your shares. (See "Stock Issuance and the Securities Laws" in Chapter 2.)

TIP

It's okay for a shareholder to pay different types of property for shares. A shareholder may pay for shares by contributing two or more types of property for shares—for example, $10,000 in tangible property and $5,000 in cash, for $15,000 worth of shares. If so, show the total number of shares the shareholder is buying in the "number of shares" column, then combine the different payments in the value column—for instance, the description may read "$5,000 cash; $10,000 _[description of property]_."

Issuance of shares for assets of a prior business. If you are incorporating an existing business, and one or more shareholders will transfer their part, or full, interest in it to the corporation in return for shares, describe the interest in the prior business that will be transferred by each owner.

EXAMPLE: If two business owners incorporate their preexisting partnership, Just Bagels, the following simple description in the payment blank would be appropriate for each shareholder (each prior business owner), assuming the entire business was worth $100,000: "$50,000, one-half interest in assets of the partnership 'Just Bagels,' as more fully described in a bill of sale to be prepared and attached to these minutes." (See below for more information about preparing the bill of sale.)

Issuance of shares for a shareholder's cancellation of indebtedness owed by the corporation. This type of transaction is unusual, since a newly formed corporation will not normally owe shareholders any amounts except, perhaps, by way of small advances made to help meet organizational costs that will be directly reimbursed by the corporation. (See "Payment, Deduction, and Amortization of Start-Up and Organizational Expenses Resolution," above.) But if shares will be issued for the cancellation of a debt owed by the corporation

to a shareholder, a description of the debt should be given as the consideration for the shares—for example, "cancellation of $4,500 owed on promissory note dated March 31, 20xx." The dollar value of the payment to be made by this shareholder is the dollar amount of the remaining unpaid principal amount due on the debt, plus any unpaid accrued interest. If possible, attach a copy of the note or other written evidence of the debt to the minutes, marked as "canceled on _[date]_, _[signature of shareholder]_."

Issuance of shares for past services. If you will issue shares to a shareholder in return for past services performed for the corporation (perhaps organizational work for which the person will receive shares), indicate the period of performance of the services and their fair value—for example, "$5,000 in services performed by Bob Beamer, January 5 to February 15, 20xx." A bill from the shareholder to the corporation showing the amount due for these services should be attached to your minutes, particularly if you have other shareholders—the bill helps document the amount and value of the services.

Issuance of shares for future services. If you will issue shares in return for a promise by a shareholder to perform future services (if allowed by your state BCA), describe the nature of the work to be performed, the period for performance, and the cash value of the services. Alternatively, you can prepare a simple contract for the performance of the services and refer to it in your resolution. (We provide a contract you can use for this purpose in Step 7, below.) If you do prepare a contract, you can fill out the description of consideration as follows: "$_____ in services to be performed as described in a contract for future services dated _____, attached to these minutes."

CAUTION

State and federal law can complicate or prevent the issuance of shares for services. Before issuing shares in exchange for services, check to see that your state permits it. (See "Payments for Shares" in Chapter 2, and the "Share Issuance" section of your state's BCA for the types of payment that can be made for shares in your state.) Also, remember that a shareholder who receives shares for services normally must pay income tax on the value of the shares received (which are worth the value of the services paid for them). Finally, if you will issue a significant amount of shares for services, you may cause the entire stock issuance transaction—not just the shares for services portion—to be taxable. Check "Potential Problems With Section 351 Tax-Free Exchanges" in Chapter 3 to be sure you avoid this unfavorable result.

Issuance of shares for promissory notes. If your state allows you to issue shares for promissory notes (again, see "Payments for Shares" in Chapter 2, and the "Share Issuance" section of your state BCA for the types of payment that can be made for shares in your state), you may decide to let a shareholder sign a note agreeing to pay for the shares later. If so, prepare the promissory note (we explain how to prepare one in Step 7, below), and refer to it in the consideration column—for example: "$10,000 promissory note, plus interest, payable on the terms described in the promissory note dated September 15, 20xx, attached to these Minutes."

⓰ If you are in a par value state and your initial stock issuance consists of "shares without par value" or "no-par shares," you may want to allocate some, or even, most of the payments you receive for the shares to capital surplus. Check with your tax adviser to see if this allocation applies to your corporation and if so, how much to allocate. If it doesn't apply, insert "N/A" in the blank and go on to prepare the next Minutes resolution.

Signature of Secretary

⓱ Have your corporate secretary sign at the bottom of the last page of the minutes.

Signatures of Directors

⓲ After you fill in the minutes, present them to each of your initial directors for approval. Have each director sign at the bottom of the waiver of notice.

Consolidate Your Minutes

After preparing and printing your minutes of the first directors' meeting, make sure to do the following before going on to Step 7, below:

1. Have the corporate secretary date and sign the certificate section at the end of your bylaws.

2. Set up a corporate records book containing at least the following four sections (see Step 3, above):

   - articles of incorporation
   - bylaws
   - minutes of meetings, and
   - stock certificates.

3. Place your minutes and attachments (file-stamped articles, bylaws, a sample stock certificate, and any other papers referred to in your minutes resolutions) in your corporate records book.

4. Keep your corporate records book at the corporation's principal office.

Remember that it's important to properly keep your corporate records. Be sure to document future corporate transactions by preparing standard minutes of annual and special director and shareholder meetings and placing copies of the minutes and other documents in your corporate records book. (Nolo publishes *The Corporate Records Handbook,* by Anthony Mancuso, which explains in more detail how to prepare minutes of future meetings; see "Ongoing Corporate Meetings" in Chapter 5.)

You have now completed the minutes of your first meeting. Next, we explain how to accomplish your last major organizational task: the issuance of stock to your initial shareholders. Stay with us, you're just a step away from completing your incorporation.

Step 7. Issue Shares of Stock

The final step in your incorporation process is issuing stock to your initial shareholders and recording your actions in the corporate records. Before you do this, however, glance at "Issuing Shares: A Quick Review," above. And remember: You must issue shares in compliance with state and federal securities laws. In most cases, this means making sure you qualify for a state and federal securities law exemption. (See "Stock Issuance and the Securities Laws" in Chapter 2.)

Fill Out Your Stock Certificates

Ten blank stock certificates are included in Appendix C at the back of this book. Or you can order more professional looking ones, as explained in Step 3, above. In either case, fill in the blanks on the stock certificates contained in Appendix C (or on the fancier ones you may have ordered), following the sample stock certificate and instructions below.

Each stock certificate should represent the total number of shares the corporation is issuing to a particular individual—or two people, such as spouses, if they are buying the shares together.

Instructions

❶ Complete the left and right portions of the stub as indicated on the sample. The date of issuance and shareholder signature lines on the stubs will be filled out when you actually distribute your stock certificates. (See "Distribute Your Stock Certificates," below.)

Number each certificate and its associated stub. (If you've ordered a corporate kit, these stub pages are already numbered.) Each shareholder gets one certificate no matter how many shares the shareholder purchases (joint owners of shares, too, get just one certificate for their jointly owned shares). The stock certificates issued by the corporation should be consecutively numbered and issued in order. This is important, since it helps the corporation to keep track of who owns its shares.

Certificate Number ❶ _____
for _____ [number of shares]
Issued to:
[name of shareholder]
[address of shareholder]
Dated _____ [date of issuance], 20 ____

No. Original Shares	No. Original Certificate	No. of Shares Transferred

From Whom Transferred ❽ _____
_____ Shares
Dated _____ , 20 ____

Received Certificate Number ❶ _____
for _____ [number of shares] Shares
This _____ [date of issuance] _____ Day of, 20 ____
_____ [signature of shareholder]
SIGNATURE

Number ❶ _____ _____ Shares ❷

❾

[Name of Corporation]

Incorporated Under the Laws of _____ **[State of Formation]**

[include capitalization statement if required under state BCA] ❸

This certifies that _____ [name of shareholder] ❹ is the owner of _____ [number of shares] ❺ fully paid and assessable _____ [class and par value designation of shares] ❻ of the above Corporation transferable only on the books of the Corporation by the holder in person or by duly authorized Attorney on surrender of this Certificate, properly endorsed.

In witness whereof, the Corporation has caused this certificate to be signed by its duly authorized officers and to be sealed with the Seal of the Corporation.

Dated: *[date of issuance]* ❼

[signature of officer] _____ , [title] _____ , [signature of officer] _____ , [title] ❼

EXAMPLE: Let's say you establish the price of your shares at $50 per share. If you plan to issue stock to four people (no matter how many shares each person will receive), you should first number the certificates 1 through 4. Then, if Jack pays $10,000, Sam $5,000, and Julie $2,500, and Ted transfers a computer with a fair market value of $1,000, Jack receives a certificate for 200 shares, Sam receives one for 100 shares, Julie gets one for 50 shares, and Ted gets a certificate for 20 shares.

Remember, as discussed in "How Many Shares Should You Authorize?" in Chapter 2, fixing your share price is arbitrary. In the above example, it would be just as easy and sensible to establish a share price of $25, with each shareholder receiving a stock certificate representing twice as many shares. But you obviously want to choose a value that avoids a shareholder receiving fractional shares. For example, you wouldn't want to set a share price of $30 per share in the previous example, since the result would be that your shareholders would get fractional shares. Jack, who pays $10,000, would be entitled to 333⅓ shares. (Actually, for the math-minded reader, Jack is entitled to receive an irrational number of shares with an infinitely trailing sequence of 333s to the right of the decimal: 333.3333333 … and so on. This is not very workable in real life or in the mathematical domain.)

❷ Type in the number of shares that each certificate represents. The number of shares each person is entitled to receive is indicated in the stock issuance resolution of your organization minutes. (See Step 6, above.)

❸ In the first blank of the stock certificate heading, enter the name of the corporation exactly as it appears in your articles of incorporation. Then enter the state where you formed your corporation in the second blank. (Both of these items will be preprinted in any specially ordered certificates.) Adding text on the third line of the heading is optional. The old-fashioned practice is to specify the total capitalization of your corporation on this line—that is, the total number and type of authorized shares specified in your articles (for example: "Authorized Shares: 300,000 Common Shares Without Par Value"). We suggest, as is common today, that you omit this item, since authorized capital information isn't really useful to shareholders. After all, if you amend your articles to authorize a second class of shares or to increase the authorized number of your original class of shares, any information you provide on this line of your certificate will be out of date. Besides, most shareholders just want to know how many shares they are getting, not what your articles say.

❹ Type the name of the shareholder. If the stock certificate will be held by two people, such as spouses, include both names and the form of co-ownership here—for example, "Carolyn Kimura and Sally Sullivan, as joint tenants" or "Mai Chang and Lee Chang, as community property." (For more information, see "How to Take Title (Ownership) to Stock," below.)

❺ Enter the same number that you indicated in Instruction ❷, above.

❻ State BCAs normally require stock certificates to show the name of the class of shares being issued and, in par value states, the stated par value of the shares or a statement that they

How to Take Title (Ownership) to Stock

Taking title to stock, essentially, means putting the owner's name on the ownership line of the stock certificate. For purposes of this book and state corporate statutes, the name or names you put on the ownership line of your stock certificate are important because they specify the record holder of the shares. These are the people who, under state BCAs:

- are entitled to notice of shareholder meetings
- get to vote at these meetings, and
- are entitled to any distributions made by the corporation, such as dividends and distributions of assets when the corporation liquidates.

Many married shareholders take title to stock jointly—that is, in the names of both spouses—to show that they own shares together. Doing this does not make much difference for corporate purposes. Each share still has one vote attached to it and the same proportionate interest in corporate distributions. But joint ownership can make a difference for other legal purposes and for

tax reasons. For example, if married people take title to shares in joint tenancy—a common form of co-ownership—the shares normally do not go through state probate if one of the co-owners dies.

In a community property state—Alaska (by written agreement between the spouses), Arizona, California, Idaho, Louisiana, Nevada, New Mexico, Texas, Washington, and Wisconsin —spouses can take title to property as community property and sometimes achieve a better tax result when one of the spouses dies.

Since it's impractical for this book to deal with all the estate and tax planning issues surrounding the different forms of co-ownership of shares, we recommend that you check to make sure you take title to your shares in a way that provides the best overall legal and tax implications for you. Ask a financial or tax adviser, or check out one of Nolo's helpful resources, including *8 Ways to Avoid Probate*, by Mary Randolph, and *Plan Your Estate*, by Denis Clifford.

---

are without par value. See the "Share Certificate" section of your state's stock certificate rules. Place the required information in this blank on your certificate. Here's an easy way to fill in this blank in all states.

Start by entering "Common Shares" in this blank. We assume you specified only one class of shares in your articles that were either (1) called "common shares" or (2) did not have a name associated with them—for example, you simply authorized "100,000 shares." For many incorporators, that's all you need to do. But

if your articles also say (1) that the shares you are issuing have a par value or (2) are "no-par" shares or shares "without par value," you must also add this description in this blank. Here are a few examples.

EXAMPLE 1: Your articles authorize 100,000 shares of common stock. In this line, describe your shares simply as "Common Shares." (By the way, capitalization does not matter, but most people use title case—that is, first-letter capitalization—to describe the type of shares being issued.)

EXAMPLE 2: Your articles authorize 1,000 shares with par value of $1 per share. Describe your shares as "Common Shares, par value $1.00."

EXAMPLE 3: Your articles authorize 1,000 common shares without par value. Describe your shares as "Common Shares without par value."

EXAMPLE 4: Your articles authorize 1,000 common no-par shares. Fill in this blank to read "Common Shares without par value." In these last two examples, you could say "Common Shares, no-par" instead.

CAUTION

If you will issue more than one class of stock. Very few small corporations issue more than one class of stock. But there are sometimes good reasons to do this—for example, to authorize different voting rights or liquidation preferences. If you authorized more than one class of shares in your articles, you must type the name of the class you are issuing to your shareholders on this line of your stock certificate—for instance, "Class A Preferred Shares."

❼ Enter the date of issuance of the shares, and obtain the signature of your corporate officers when you distribute your certificate as explained in "Distribute Your Stock Certificates," below.

❽ Do not fill in the transfer sections on the stub or on the back of each certificate. These sections should be used only if and when the original shareholders later transfer the stock certificates. If you've ordered a corporate kit, this applies to the transfer sections on the separate stub pages and on the back of the printed stock certificates. The kit should also contain instructions on preparing the transfer information if the stock is resold.

If you have a corporate seal, you should impress it on each certificate. The stock is valid without it, but many private corporations formalize their certificates by impressing them with their corporate seal.

After filling out the stock certificates and stubs, place the completed stubs in consecutive order in the stock certificate section of your corporate records book. (If you use the certificates in this book, you'll need to neatly cut the stub away from the top of the stock certificate along the dotted line. It's easier to do this if you first remove the entire page.) These stubs represent your corporation's share register.

❾ As discussed in Chapter 2, "Stock Issuance and the Securities Laws," you may decide to add a transfer restriction legend on the face or back of your certificate to comply with state or federal securities laws.

Prepare Receipts for Your Shareholders

After filling out your stock certificates, you may wish to issue receipts to your shareholders for the cash or property they paid for their shares. Similarly, if you are incorporating a prior business, you may also want to prepare a bill of sale for your shareholders. You are not legally required to prepare these forms, but we think it's a sensible precaution that will avoid confusion about who paid what for stock in your corporation. This paperwork allows both the corporation and its shareholders to have written statements of the details of each shareholder's stock issuance transaction.

A bill of sale and separate receipt forms are provided in electronic form and at the back of this book. (See Appendixes B and C.) Make copies of the appropriate forms and prepare them according to the sample forms and instructions below.

Preparing a Bill of Sale for the Assets of a Prior Business

If you are transferring the assets of an unincorporated business to your corporation in return for the issuance of shares to the prior owners, here is information on how to prepare a bill of sale. Below is a sample of the bill of sale form. (As mentioned, you can find the blank form in Appendixes B and C.) Fill out the form, following the instructions below.

Important. Check with your tax adviser before using this bill of sale form. There are several ways to transfer prior business interests and assets to a new corporation, each with different tax consequences. (See "Tax Treatment When Incorporating an Existing Business" in Chapter 3.) Your tax adviser can also help you prepare the balance sheet to attach to the bill of sale, as explained in the instructions that follow.

Extra Steps Are Required to Transfer Real Estate or Leases to the Corporation

Real estate transfers. Prepare any new corporate ownership papers, such as deeds and mortgages, and record them with the county recorder or similar local office. If the property being transferred is mortgaged, then you will most likely need the permission of the lender to transfer the property. If your real estate promissory note contains a "due on sale or transfer" clause (which means that if the underlying property is sold or transferred, the entire principal amount of the note becomes due), you may even be required to refinance your deed of trust (mortgage) if rates have gone up substantially since the existing deed of trust was executed. This, of course, may be so undesirable that you decide not to transfer the real estate to the corporation, preferring to keep it in the name of the original owner and lease it to the corporation.

Also, don't forget that the transfer of real estate to your corporation may not be the best way to go for tax purposes. Remember that appreciation on real estate probably will be taxed to the corporation and to the shareholders (a double tax) when the corporation liquidates. (See "The Corporation" in Chapter 1.) Also, remember to check the tax consequences of incorporating a prior business with your tax adviser.

Transfers of leases. If you are transferring a lease from a prior business to your new corporation, you should talk to the landlord about having a new lease prepared showing the corporation as the new tenant. An alternative is to have the prior tenants assign the lease to the corporation; however, read your lease carefully before trying to do this, as many leases are not assignable without the landlord's permission. You should prepare and sign new lease documents before you give the prior leaseholders their shares.

Sample Bill of Sale for Assets of a Business

This is an agreement between:

  [name of prior business owner]

  [name of prior business owner]

  [name of prior business owner] ,❶

herein called "transferor(s)," and _[name of corporation)]_ ,❷ a corporation, herein called "the corporation."

In return for the issuance of _[number of shares]_ ❸ shares of stock of the corporation, transferor(s) hereby sell(s), assign(s), and transfer(s) to the corporation all right, title, and interest in the following property:

All the tangible assets listed on the balance sheet attached to this Bill of Sale and all stock in trade, goodwill, leasehold interests, trade names, and other intangible assets [except _[list any nontransferred assets here]_] ❹ of _[name of unincorporated business]_ ❺, located at _[address of unincorporated business]_ .❻

In return for the transfer of the above property to it, the corporation hereby agrees to assume, pay, and discharge all debts, duties, and obligations listed on the balance sheet attached to this Bill of Sale [except _[list any unassumed liabilities here]_].❼ The corporation agrees to indemnify and hold the transferor(s) of this business and their property free from any liability for any such debt, duty, or obligation and from any suits, actions, or legal proceedings brought to enforce or collect any such debt, duty, or obligation.

The transferor(s) hereby appoint(s) the corporation as representative to demand, receive, and collect for itself any and all debts and obligations now owing to _[name of unincorporated business]_ . The transferor(s) further authorize(s) the corporation to do all things allowed by law to recover and collect any debts and obligations and to use the transferor's(s') name(s) as it considers necessary for the collection and recovery of these debts and obligations, provided, however, without cost, expense, or damage to the transferor(s). ❽

Date: _____

  [signature of unincorporated business owner] , Transferor

  [signature of unincorporated business owner] , Transferor

  [signature of unincorporated business owner] , Transferor

Date: _____

  [name of corporation] , Corporation ❾

By:

  [signature of president or CEO] , President

  [signature of treasurer or CFO] , Treasurer

Instructions

❶ Insert the names of the unincorporated business owners.

❷ Insert the name of your corporation.

❸ Enter the total number of shares to be issued to all unincorporated owners of the business in return for the transfer of the business to the corporation.

> EXAMPLE: If Patricia and Kathleen will each receive 2,000 shares in return for their respective half-interests in their preexisting partnership (which they are now incorporating), they would indicate 4,000 shares here.

❹ Use this line to show any assets of the prior business that are not being transferred to the corporation. For example, you may wish to continue to personally own real property associated with your business and lease it to your new corporation. If you will transfer all prior business assets to the corporation, insert "No Exceptions" here. As indicated in this (and the next) paragraph of the bill of sale, attach a current balance sheet showing the assets and liabilities of the business transferred to the corporation.

❺ Indicate the name of the unincorporated business being transferred to the corporation. For sole proprietorships and partnerships not operating under a fictitious business name, the name(s) of the prior owners may simply be given here—for example, "Heather Langsley and Chester Dodd."

❻ Show the address of the prior business.

❼ This paragraph says that your corporation will assume the liabilities of the prior business that appear on the balance sheet discussed above. Here, list any liabilities of the prior business that will not be assumed by the corporation. If your corporation will assume all liabilities of the prior business, indicate "No Exceptions" here.

❽ This paragraph is included in the bill of sale form to indicate that your corporation is appointed to collect for itself any debts and obligations (accounts receivable) owed to the prior business which are being transferred to the corporation.

❾ Type the name of the corporation on the line indicated. Don't fill out the date and signature lines yet. You will do this when you distribute the stock certificates to the prior business owners, as explained in "Distribute Your Stock Certificates," below.

Preparing Receipts

You may wish to prepare one or more receipts for your shareholders. You can find receipt forms online by following the instructions in Appendix B, and at the back of this book in Appendix C. These forms allow you to document the following types of payment made by a shareholder:

- cash
- specific items of property
- past and future services
- promissory notes, and
- cancellation of a debt.

Let's look at each of these transactions and the relevant receipt form below. If you'll need several of a certain type of receipt—for example, separate receipts for three shareholders who contribute cash—make copies.

CAUTION

Don't sign receipts until you receive payment and distribute stock certificates. Don't fill in the date or signature lines on your receipts until you successfully distribute your stock certificates in return for the payments made by each of your shareholders. (See "Distribute Your Stock Certificates," below.)

(To prepare a bill of sale for the assets of a prior business, see the previous section.)

Receipts for Joint Shareholders and Joint Payments

If you will issue shares to joint owners, it's best to show the names of both joint owners on the receipt. Of course, if two shareholders jointly contribute an item of property but prefer to receive two separate blocks of individually owned shares, you should prepare a separate receipt for each shareholder.

> EXAMPLE 1: Teresa and Vernon Miller will pay $1,000 for 1,000 shares that they will own jointly. You make out a receipt in the name of both shareholders.

> EXAMPLE 2: Mike and his brother, Burt, transfer a jointly owned lathe with a value of $5,000. Each will receive 250 shares in exchange for his half-interest in the lathe. You make out a separate receipt for each brother, showing the transfer of a one-half interest in the lathe in return for the issuance of 250 shares.

Receipt for Cash Payment

If your corporation issues shares for cash, the shareholder normally pays by check and the shareholder's canceled check serves as additional proof of payment. Below is a sample of the cash receipt form.

Instructions

❶ and ❷ After receiving payment from the shareholder (see "Distribute Your Stock Certificates," below), your treasurer should date and sign the receipt.

Receipt for Specific Items of Property

If a shareholder is transferring specific items of property to the corporation (other than the assets of an existing business; in which case see "Preparing a Bill of Sale for the Assets of a Prior Business," above), you may wish to prepare a receipt (bill of sale) for the property to the shareholder. Make sure that the property has first been delivered to the corporation and that any ownership document—such as the title slip for a vehicle—has been signed over to the corporation. If you are transferring real estate interests to your corporation, see "Extra Steps Are Required to Transfer Real Estate or Leases to the Corporation," above.

A sample of the bill of sale for property follows.

Sample Receipt for Cash Payment

Receipt of $ *[amount of cash payment]* from *[name of shareholder]* representing payment in full for *[number of shares]* shares of the stock of this corporation is hereby acknowledged.

Dated: *[date of payment]* ❷

Name of Corporation: *[name of corporation]*

By: _____ *[signature of treasurer]* , Treasurer ❶

Sample Bill of Sale for Items of Property

In consideration of the issuance of _[number of shares]_ shares of stock in and by _[name of corporation],_   _[name of shareholder]_ hereby sells, assigns, conveys, transfers, and delivers to the corporation all right, title, and interest in and to the following property:

[description of property] _____ ❶

Date: _____ ❷

_[signature of shareholder]_____

Instructions

❶ Provide a short description of the property that the shareholder is transferring to the corporation. This description should be brief but specific—for example, the make, model, and serial numbers of property, or vehicle identification number for vehicles.

❷ Complete this date line and have the shareholder sign the bill of sale when you distribute your shares.

Receipt for Past Services

If you are transferring shares in return for past services performed by a shareholder for the corporation, you may wish to prepare the receipt form as explained, shown below. Have the shareholder submit a signed invoice for these services, marked "Paid in Full," showing the date of payment by the corporation. (This is the date you distribute the shares in return for these services; see "Distribute Your Stock Certificates," below.)

CAUTION

Tax issues to consider. The issuance of shares for performed services is not a common type of stock issuance transaction for newly formed corporations because of practical and tax considerations. First, most work done for the corporation will occur after your stock issuance. Second, most contractors or other professionals who have performed services will want cash (not shares of stock) as payment for their services. However, if one of the principals of your closely held corporation has performed services for the corporation prior to your stock issuance, this type of stock issuance transaction may make sense—after you, the corporation, and the shareholders check the tax consequences. Don't forget, as explained in Chapter 2, the issuance of shares for services is normally taxable to the shareholder. (Also, see "Potential Problems With Section 351 Tax-Free Exchanges" in Chapter 3.) Finally, to avoid unfairness to your other stockholders, be sure that the shareholder charges no more than the prevailing rate for the services performed.

Sample Receipt for Services Rendered

In consideration of the performance of the following services actually rendered to _[name of corporation]_ ,
 [name of shareholder] , the provider of such services, hereby acknowledges the receipt of
 [number of shares] shares of stock in _[name of corporation]_ as payment in full for these services, described as follows:

 [description of past services] _____ ❶

Date: _____ ❷

 [signature of shareholder] _____

Instructions

❶ Provide a short description of the services performed by the shareholder—for example, the dates, description, and value of (amount billed for) the work. As an alternative, simply refer to the attached bill for services, which should contain this information. (You can insert "see attached bill for services" in this blank on the receipt.)

❷ When you distribute the shares in return for the services, provide the date of issuance of the shares and have the shareholder sign the receipt.

Contract for Future Services

If you are issuing shares in return for a promise by a shareholder to perform future services (assuming your state allows this form of payment for shares; see "Payments for Shares" in Chapter 2, and the "Share Issuance" section of your state's BCA), you can prepare a short contract for future services to document the transaction. The following form, which we've provided online and in the receipts section of Appendix C, can be used for this purpose. Of course, you may also wish to prepare a complete employment or independent contractor agreement to more fully describe the services and terms associated with the promised work that the shareholder will perform.

Remember to check with your tax adviser before issuing shares for services—the shareholder may have to pay taxes on the shares-for-services transactions, and it may affect your ability to qualify for Section 351 tax treatment.

Sample Contract for Future Services

In return for the issuance of _[number of shares]_ shares of _[name of corporation]_ , _[name of shareholder]_ hereby agrees to furnish the following services to the corporation:

[description and schedule of services to be performed]

It is understood that the corporation may place the shares in escrow or make other arrangements to restrict the transfer of shares until the above services are performed in accordance with the above schedule. ❶

Date: _____ ❷

Signed: _[signature of shareholder]_____

Name of Corporation: _[name of corporation]___

By: _[signature of treasurer]_____, Treasurer

Instructions

❶ Many states that allow shares to be issued for future services specifically allow corporations to place these shares in an escrow account until the shareholder completes performance of the promised services. On completion, the corporation releases the shares to the shareholder. If your state allows the issuance of shares for future services but is silent on whether the corporation can place these shares in escrow pending the completion of the services, it should be fine to do so as long as the shareholder agrees to the escrow condition (as in the contract for future services, above).

❷ Have the shareholder and corporate treasurer sign the contract now, prior to any distribution of shares.

Issuance for Promissory Notes

If you are issuing shares in return for a promise of a shareholder to pay for the shares in the future, prepare the promissory note form we've provided online (see Appendix B) and in Appendix C, following the sample form and instructions below. Remember, your state must allow the issuance of shares for promissory notes. (See "Payments for Shares" in Chapter 2, and the "Share Issuance" or "Payment for Shares" section of your state's BCA.)

Our promissory note requires payment of equal monthly installments of principal and interest. You will have to consult a loan amortization chart (available from banks, real estate offices, and bookstores, as well as online sources such as www.nolo.com) to figure the amount of monthly payments: Just plug in the term of the loan, the principal amount, and the interest rate, and the chart tells you the total amount of the monthly payment. Our form can be used as is, or you can modify it to reflect your own repayment terms. For example, you may wish to require interest-only payments during the term of the loan, with a payment of the entire principal amount of the loan plus any accrued and unpaid interest at the end of the term. Or you may decide to eliminate monthly payments altogether, and simply require one complete payment at the end of the loan term. (If you need help figuring the payment amounts or writing your own note terms, see *The Corporate Records Handbook*, by Anthony Mancuso (Nolo); it contains various shareholder promissory note forms that include a range of repayment options.)

Instructions

❶ Specify a reasonable commercial rate. For example, the current prime rate plus two points might be what lenders are charging commercial clients. Check with your bank to see what it currently charges creditworthy customers.

❷ Normally, the number of monthly payments is the yearly term of the loan multiplied by 12, for example, 60 payments for a five-year note.

❸ Again, use a loan amortization chart to figure the amount of monthly principal plus interest payments.

❹ The shareholder should date and sign the note on the date when you distribute your stock certificates. (See "Distribute Your Stock Certificates," below.)

Sample Promissory Note

In consideration of the issuance of _[number of shares]_ shares of _[name of corporation]_ , _[name of shareholder]_ promises to pay to _[name of corporation]_ the principal amount of $ _[dollar amount of loan extended to the shareholder to buy the shares]_ together with interest at a rate of _[rate of interest]_ ❶ rate per annum. Payments are to be made in _[number of monthly installments]_ ❷ equal monthly installments of $ _[amount of monthly payment]_ , ❸ each payable on the _[day of the month when payments are due, for example "1st" or "15th"]_ day of each month, with the first installment due on _[date of first installment payment]_.

Date: _____ ❹

Signature: _[signature of shareholder]_ _____

Sample Form for Cancellation of Debt

The receipt of *[number of shares]* shares of this corporation to *[name of shareholder]* for the cancellation by *[name of shareholder]* of a current loan outstanding to this corporation, dated *[date of loan]* , with a remaining unpaid principal amount and unpaid accrued interest, if any, totaling $ *[loan balance]* ,❶ is hereby acknowledged.

Date: _____❷

Signature of Shareholder: _____ *[signature of shareholder]*

Receipt for Cancelling a Debt

If you issue shares in return for cancelling a debt owed by the corporation to a shareholder, you can prepare the receipt form shown above to document the transaction.

Instructions

❶ Show the total of the outstanding principal amount and accrued and unpaid interest (if any) owed on the loan. If you have a copy of the loan or other debt instrument (such as a promissory note), attach it to the receipt.

❷ When you distribute your stock certificates (see the next section), date the receipt and have the shareholder sign it.

Distribute Your Stock Certificates

Now it's time to distribute stock certificates to your initial shareholders. To complete this step, do the following:

- Have each shareholder (or both shareholders if the stock certificate is to be held jointly) sign his or her stock certificate stub. Indicate the date of stock issuance on each stub.

- Date each stock certificate and have your officers sign each one. Some states specify the officers who are required to sign certificates—normally, the president and secretary sign, but many states allow any two corporate officers to sign. (Check your state's BCA.)

- Impress your corporate seal in the seal space provided on the certificate. Remember, you are not legally required to seal your certificates, but many incorporators prefer to use the seal to make the certificates look official.

- Write the date of issuance for each shareholder in the stock transfer ledger (share register).

- Complete the date and signature lines on your receipts as explained in "Receipt for Specific Items of Property," above. Give each shareholder a copy of his or her receipt(s).

- Make sure to place all your completed stock stubs and completed copies of all receipts and any attachments—such as the closing balance sheet for a prior business, canceled notes, or a paid-in-full bill for services—in your corporate records book.

How to Sign Corporate Documents From Now On

Now that your incorporation is almost complete, there is one last point we wish to make that is central to the operation of your newly formed corporation. One of the reasons you decided to form a corporation was to limit your personal liability in business affairs. So, from now on, whenever you sign a document on behalf of the corporation, be certain to do so in the following manner:

[name of corporation]

By: _[signature of corporate officer]_

[typed name of officer] , _[title of officer]_

If you fail to sign documents this way—that is, on behalf of the corporation in your capacity as a corporate officer or director—you may be leaving yourself open to personal liability for corporate obligations. This is but one example designed to illustrate a basic premise of corporate life: From now on, it is extremely important for you to maintain the distinction between the corporation and those of you who are principals of the corporation. As we've said, the corporation is a separate legal "person," and you want to make sure that other people, businesses, the IRS, and the courts respect this distinction. (See "Courts Sometimes Pierce the Corporate Veil," in Chapter 2, for a short discussion of this point.)

Congratulations!

You have completed your last incorporation step. Please glance through the postincorporation procedures contained in Chapter 5 to see how they may apply to your corporation. ●

After You Form Your Corporation

Successfully organizing your corporation is just the first step in establishing and protecting its legal integrity. In this chapter, we briefly discuss the important steps you should take *after* forming your corporation. And we also explain the many good reasons why most jointly owned corporations should adopt a buy-sell shareholder agreement to help control what happens to the business if one owner dies or decides to leave. Due to the individual nature of each corporation and its business, as well as the wide diversity of employment and tax procedures in each state, it's not possible to discuss every possible ongoing tax or legal formality you will encounter. Rather, this discussion is intended to be a general guide to routine formalities and tax obligations that most corporations face. You can get most of the tax information and forms we discuss below from the IRS and your state tax and business registration agency websites.

Postincorporation Tasks

There are a few formalities that you should take care of shortly after you organize your corporation. Some apply to all incorporators; others are optional or may not apply to you at all. We tell you the circumstances under which each step must be taken.

File a Corporate Annual Report

Shortly after you file your articles of incorporation, you are normally required to file your first corporate report form with the state corporate filing office. In most states, this report must be filed each year. It's usually a cinch to complete an annual report form. Typically, the form will simply list and ask you to update the corporation's principal office and the names and addresses of its registered agent, directors, and officers. There will be a small filing fee.

Normally, the filing office will mail a report form to the principal office of your corporation in advance of the filing date. To plan ahead and to be sure you meet your state's filing requirements, you can to go your state corporate filing office website (see Appendix A), where you should find your state's annual report filing requirements, plus a downloadable form to use for your initial and ongoing report filings. Some states allow you to file your annual report online.

CAUTION

Watch out for penalties if you don't file reports. If you fail to file a report on time, state law typically says that your corporation can be assessed penalties. If reports are not filed for several years or more, your corporate charter can even be suspended until you make the required annual reports and pay any penalties. Among other things, if your corporation is suspended, it usually can't use the courts to sue or defend itself in a lawsuit. In short, make sure you comply with this required formality.

Register an Assumed or Fictitious Business Name

If your corporation will do business under a name other than the exact corporate name contained in your articles of incorporation, it makes sense in most states to register it as an assumed business name. Depending on the state, this second name will be called your "doing business as (dba)," "assumed," or "fictitious business" name. (See Chapter 4, Step 1, for more on corporate names.) Most states let you register an assumed name for your corporation.

EXAMPLE: If the name stated in your articles is "Acme Business Computers, Inc.," and you plan to do business under the acronym "ABC, Inc.," you may register "ABC, Inc." as the assumed or fictitious business name of your corporation.

However, we don't recommend that you adopt an assumed name in addition to your formal corporate name (see Chapter 4, Step 1), primarily because you need to establish a solid business identity for your real corporate name in most cases. Adding a second name dilutes your real corporate name, rather than strengthening it.

That said, registering your existing corporate name—the one stated in your articles—as an assumed or fictitious business name might be sensible. Why? Because registering an assumed name is one of many important ways to put others on notice that your business exists, and that they should not try to do business under a similar name.

If you do decide to register your corporate name as an assumed name, you will want to drop the corporate designator ("Inc." or "Corp.") because, under the assumed and fictitious business name statutes, your assumed name must be different from your formal corporate name.

EXAMPLE: Righteous Ron's Realty, Inc., could register "Righteous Ron's Realty" as an assumed corporate name.

CAUTION

Business name rules are complicated. Realize that registering an assumed name simply gives you a legal presumption that your corporation is the rightful owner of an assumed name. Even if you are first to register an assumed name for your corporation, if another business in your field can prove in court that it was the first to use the name, it will probably be awarded the right to use the name and to stop you from using the name as well. Another way of saying this is that other state and federal laws governing trade names and trademarks often have more force than the assumed name laws. (For a brief discussion of trade name and trademark laws, see Chapter 4, Step 1.)

State procedures for registering an assumed or fictitious business name vary. Your state's corporate filing office website (see Appendix A) should explain your state's registration procedure. In some states, you will register your assumed name with the state corporate filing office. In others, you will make your filing with the clerk of the county where the corporation has its principal office. In some states, you must file at both the state and county levels.

The registration process normally consists of three steps:

(1) File an assumed or fictitious business name statement with the state and/or county, declaring the formal name of the corporation, the corporation's address, and the assumed or fictitious name.

(2) Publish a notice of intent to use an assumed or fictitious business name in the county of the corporation's principal office. This publication normally must be made in the local newspaper for several consecutive weeks.

(3) File an affidavit of publication of the newspaper notice with the office where you made the assumed name filing.

The total cost to register an assumed name is modest: Filing and publication fees should total approximately $50.

File Final Papers on a Prior Business

If you have incorporated a prior business (transferred the assets of a business to the corporation in return for shares), the prior business owners should file all papers needed to terminate their prior business, including final sales tax and employment tax returns, if appropriate. Of course, you should close your previous business bank accounts and open the corporate bank accounts indicated in the bank account resolution of your organizational minutes. (See Chapter 4, Step 6.) In addition, if the old business holds any licenses or permits, you may need to cancel these and obtain new licenses or permits in the name of the corporation. (See "Obtain Corporate Licenses and Permits," below.)

Notify Creditors and Others of the Incorporation of a Prior Business

If you have incorporated a prior business, it is important to notify the creditors of the prior business and other interested parties— for example, suppliers, vendors, banks, and businesses with whom you have open lines of credit—of the incorporation of the prior business. You will want to do this in writing.

If you keep your business accounts current— that is, you pay bills and other debts as they become due—your creditors should not care that you are now doing business as a corporation. But if your prior unincorporated business owed significant debts when you incorporated—particularly if any of these debts were overdue—you can expect the creditor to call you and ask about the status of these debts after you send out notification

of your incorporation. If, as we assume, your corporation will pay the debts of the unincorporated business, just tell the creditor so. If, on the other hand, you incorporated to duck one or more debts of the prior business, watch out—the owners of the prior business will probably continue to be personally liable for the prior business debts. (See "Liability for the Debts of the Unincorporated Business" in Chapter 3.) If you intend to dispute any debts of the prior unincorporated business, you will need the help of a lawyer. (See Chapter 6.)

Prepare a short letter along the lines of the sample below. Your goal is to notify creditors that you have dissolved the prior business and that you are now doing business as a corporation. State the old name and address of the business and the new corporate name and address. Add whatever friendly remarks you feel appropriate to the closing of your letter ("We're still here, ready to serve you"). Place a copy of each mailed letter in your corporate records book. In some states, when you incorporate, you must comply with the state's Bulk Sales Act (or similar law), which requires you to publish a notice when you transfer the unincorporated company's assets and liabilities to your new corporation. Smaller businesses may receive exemptions to simplify or eliminate compliance with the Bulk Sales Act. You can search for your state's Bulk Sales Act online, or ask a local business lawyer for more information.

Instructions

❶ Normally, the corporate treasurer prepares and signs the letter, but any corporate officer may do so.

Sample Notice of Incorporation Letter

[date]

[name and address of your corporation]

Re: Incorporation of _[name of prior business]_

Dear _[name of company or individual] :_

I'm writing to let you know that our unincorporated business, _[name of prior business]_, was incorporated in _[state]_ on _[date your articles were filed]_ as _[name of corporation]_. This is a formal change that will help the business pursue its mission and the attainment of its goals with increased structure and efficiency.

We have enjoyed doing business with you in the past and look forward to continuing to do so in the future. Please call me at the telephone number shown below if you need additional information to update your records or accounts.

Sincerely,

[signature of officer] , _[title]_ ❶
[printed name of officer]
[officer's corporate telephone number]

Investigate Private Insurance Coverage

An item of business that should be near the top of your "to do" list after you incorporate is to check out the availability and cost of commercial liability insurance for your corporation. Corporations, like other businesses, should carry the usual kinds of commercial insurance to cover financial loss in the event of an accident, fire, theft, or other potential liability. Although the corporate form normally insulates shareholders from personal liability for business debts and judgments, it obviously won't prevent corporate assets from being jeopardized by these events. And since many entrepreneurs have much of their net worth tied up in their businesses, it will be no fun to have business assets taken to pay claims that could have been covered by insurance.

Your commercial policy should include coverage for business vehicles, inventory, and personal injuries on the premises. Additional coverage for product liability, or directors' and officers' liability (see "Directors" in Chapter 2), and other specialized types of insurance, may also be appropriate. To keep premiums down, many smaller companies purchase policies with reasonably large deductibles. (For a detailed discussion about business insurance, see Nolo's _Legal Guide for Starting & Running a Small Business_, by Fred S. Steingold.)

Obtain Corporate Licenses and Permits

Many businesses, whether or not they are incorporated, are required to obtain state or local licenses or permits before commencing business. This includes businesses that sell food or drink, provide professional services, emit toxic substances, and so on. You may need to pay fees and take out a bond to cover losses or injuries to the public. Of course, a license to practice a state-regulated profession requires meeting state education requirements and the passage of a state-administered test. The state agency that regulates your profession can explain any special licensing rules that apply to providing licensed services as a corporation.

An excellent resource for state licensing and permit rules is *The Small Business Start-Up Kit*, by Peri Pakroo (Nolo). It lists federal, state, and local start-up requirements that apply to all types of businesses.

Adopt a Shareholders' Buy-Sell Agreement

By now you're surely tired of incorporation paperwork and are ready to get down to business. Not so fast—there is one more postincorporation formality we want you to seriously consider. It involves the adoption of a shareholder agreement (commonly called a buy-sell agreement) to control who can own shares in your corporation in the future and how much people or the corporation must pay for them. In a nutshell, here's the problem.

When a shareholder in a closely held corporation dies, sells shares, gives shares away, or (in some cases) gets a divorce, there is the risk of bringing an outsider into the shareholder ranks.

Think about it: Do you really want to be forced to deal with another shareholder's spoiled son or hostile ex-husband? Remember, not only does a shareholder in a small corporation get to vote at annual meetings for the election of the board, that person has a say in all major decisions brought before the shareholders for a vote. These decisions may include significant structural changes to the corporation, such as amending the Articles of Incorporation or the corporate bylaws. But that isn't the worst part. A shareholder in a small corporation also may be able to attain a board position through an election. This is true because in most smaller corporations, a plurality—not a majority—shareholder vote is all that is needed to elect someone to the board. If an outsider is elected to the board, that newcomer will get a management vote equal to all other board members (each board member has one vote), thereby getting to participate in all major corporate decisions. (Even if you outvote the new board member, you'll still have to listen to him.)

You may be wondering why you should worry about these issues while your corporation is in the start-up phase. The answer is simple: You have a golden opportunity to deal with potentially explosive issues now, when everyone is in a good mood. By contrast, if you wait until an ownership change occurs or is imminent, you risk ending up in a dispute—and perhaps even a lawsuit.

Fortunately, armed with good information and forms, you can prepare a sound buy-sell agreement for your corporation. But this means doing the reading necessary to climb a reasonably steep learning curve. A good source of up-to-date information on this subject, designed for use by self-help incorporators, is Nolo's *Business*

Some Corporations Don't Need to Adopt a Buy-Sell Agreement

If you own 100% of your corporation, there is no need to prepare a buy-sell agreement. Similarly, if you and your spouse own the business together and you agree there is virtually no possibility that you will divorce, you may conclude that there is little reason to go to the trouble of creating a buy-sell agreement. After all, if one of you dies while you still own the business, chances are excellent that the other person will inherit the deceased spouse's shares—or that the shares will be left to a child or children according to a mutually agreeable estate plan.

A buy-sell agreement may also be unnecessary if shares are all owned by parents and their children in a very close-knit family, where all agree that the children will eventually be given or inherit the parents' interests.

The great utility of a shareholder buy-sell agreement is that it spells out whether the corporation and/or remaining shareholders get a chance, or are required, to buy the shares of a shareholder who stops working for the corporation, dies, divorces, or, under provisions in some agreements, becomes disabled. It also addresses the important issue of setting a price (or a procedure to place a price) on the shares when the corporation or shareholders buy shares under the agreement. This valuation issue is crucial, because one of the most potentially contentious issues involved in any share buy-back is how much the business is worth. In the absence of an agreed-on formula, the chances of a lawsuit are significant. If you doubt this even for a moment, consider how much an angry ex-spouse who receives shares in your corporation as part of a divorce may claim they are worth.

Buyout Agreements, by Bethany K. Laurence and Anthony Mancuso. This book takes you step by step through the process of adopting buy-sell provisions for your small corporation, limited liability company, or partnership, paying particular attention to the concerns and issues of the small, closely held business. Ready-to-use agreements are available online and at the back of this book to help you accomplish the task efficiently. (See Appendixes B and C.)

Of course, you may find other sources for a buy-sell agreement, including information designed for use by attorneys, at a business or law library. But no matter how you prepare your agreement, the range of legal and tax considerations involved means that it often makes sense to have a legal or tax adviser review your document before you adopt it.

Tax and Employer Registration Requirements

As you know, another basic corporate formality is reporting and paying ongoing income and employment taxes. To get the latest and complete business and tax reporting rules and forms, go to the following websites:

- For state corporate income or franchise tax filing requirements and forms, go to your state's corporate tax office website (see Appendix A).

- To find your state's business registration requirements and employment tax procedures and forms, go to your state's business registration and employment tax office. (Both of these areas are normally covered

Issues Covered in Shareholder Buy-Sell Agreements

Here are some of the basic issues normally addressed by corporate buy-sell agreements, and typical ways they are handled:

- **Buy-back price or formula.** Agreements specify a default price or procedure that will be used to value shares for purposes of any buyout covered in the agreement.

- **Buy-back payment method.** Agreements set out the terms for payment of the buy-back price. Typically, agreements provide for the payment of the buyout price in stages, with part cash paid at the time of buy-back, and the balance, plus interest, payable by the corporation in monthly installments.

- **Shareholder death.** Some agreements give the corporation or remaining shareholders a right to purchase the shares from a deceased shareholder's estate within a specified number of days from the date of the shareholder's death. Other agreements require the corporation, if financially able, to buy back the shares from the estate or heirs of a deceased shareholder on request by the representative of the estate or an heir.

- **Life insurance funding of buy-back.** Often, the corporation and/or shareholders are required to take out and pay for life insurance policies on each shareholder. If a shareholder dies, the cash proceeds from these policies are used to purchase the deceased shareholder's shares.

- **Shareholder tries to sell to an outside buyer.** Agreements often provide that either the corporation or the other shareholders have a right to buy the shares before an outside shareholder gets a chance.

- **Shareholder wants to give or transfer shares to relatives.** Some agreements restrict all gifts or other transfers of shares. Others allow gifts to family members, as long as certain conditions are met (for example, less than one-half of a shareholder's stock may be gifted to relatives).

- **Shareholder leaves the corporation.** Many agreements adopted by closely held corporations require the corporation to buy back shares held by a shareholder who quits the corporation. Other agreements simply give the corporation an option to demand such a buy-back, or let ex-shareholders demand a buy-back if they wish to sell the shares.

- **Current shareholder asks to be cashed out.** Some agreements let shareholders request a buyout of their shares, even if the shareholder remains an employee of the corporation.

- **Shareholder divorces.** Agreements often provide that if a shareholder divorces, and shares are transferred to the shareholder's ex-spouse by court order as part of a marital settlement agreement, the corporation can demand a buy-back of the shares from the ex-spouse. (Typically, spouses of shareholders also sign shareholder buy-sell agreements when they are adopted.)

- **Shareholder becomes disabled.** Some agreements require or permit the corporation to buy out the shares of a disabled shareholder, if one or two doctors sign a written statement of disability.

- **Shareholder has debt problems.** If a shareholder files for personal bankruptcy, many agreements require the corporation, if financially able, to buy the shares back from the bankruptcy trustee.

by one agency or office, often a subdivision of the main state tax agency.) You can probably find a link to the office on both your state's tax agency site and your state's corporate filing office site (see Appendix A).

- To obtain federal corporate income tax publications and forms, as well as federal employment registration and employment tax information and forms, go to the IRS website at www.irs.gov. We suggest all corporations obtain IRS Publication 509, *Tax Calendars*, prior to the beginning of each year. This pamphlet contains tax calendars showing the dates for federal corporate and employer filings during the year. Other particularly helpful publications include IRS Publication 15, Circular E, *Employer's Tax Guide*, and the *Publication 15 Supplement A and B*. Further federal corporate income tax information can be found in IRS Publication 542, *Corporations*, and Publication 334, *Tax Guide for Small Business.*

- An excellent small business resource for finding your state's other business and tax requirements is *The Small Business Start-Up Kit*, by Peri Pakroo (Nolo). Its appendix lists state business registration addresses and websites as well as business resource centers located in each state.

Ongoing Corporate Meetings

After forming your corporation, you should plan ahead for holding regular corporate meetings. We discuss the basic legal rules for holding annual and special meetings of directors and shareholders in "Directors" and "Shareholders" in Chapter 2. Your bylaws list the call, notice, quorum, and voting rules for annual and special directors' and shareholders' meetings. In this section, we discuss when and how to hold ongoing directors' and shareholders' meetings,

and provide a basic form you can use to prepare minutes for these meetings.

When to Hold Formal Corporate Meetings

You will wish to hold the following formal corporate meetings, remembering to prepare minutes and record them in your corporate records book:

An annual shareholders' meeting should be held each year to elect or reelect your board of directors. The date, place, and time of this meeting is scheduled in your bylaws. (See Chapter 4, Step 4, Article 2, Section 2.)

An annual directors' meeting is normally held just after the annual shareholders' meeting, when the directors accept their positions on the board for the upcoming year and discuss past corporate performance and upcoming business. You will also want to hold any additional directors' meetings scheduled in your bylaws, in addition to the annual directors' meeting.

Special directors' and shareholders' meetings may be called during the year to formally discuss and approve legal, tax, and business matters. You don't need to hold a formal corporate meeting to discuss routine business decisions, just those that you want to document with formal corporate minutes. Such decisions may include:

- amending corporate articles of incorporation or bylaws

- declaring dividends

- authorizing the issuance of additional shares of stock

- approving real estate construction, lease, purchase, or sale

- appointing key corporate officers and departmental managers and setting corporate salaries

- approving the terms of the loan of money to or from shareholders, directors, officers, and banks or other outsiders

- the commitment of substantial corporate resources

- the adoption of new corporate strategies or goals, or

- an immediate discussion and review of corporate performance.

Of course, many of these matters can be handled at annual or regular directors' meetings, but one or more of these decisions may come up during the year between regular meetings. If so, a special directors' meeting needs to be called. Special shareholders' meetings normally need to be called only when state law requires the ratification by shareholders of a director decision made during the year, such as the amendment of corporate articles or bylaws, or a change in stock rights or restrictions. Your state BCA lists any special shareholder ratification rules that apply in your state. (See the "Shareholder Meeting" section of your BCA.)

How to Document a Formal Corporate Meeting

You will want to call and provide notice of all directors' and shareholders' meetings as required in your bylaws and current state law. (Check your state's BCA for meeting rules.) At the meeting, the chairperson calls the meeting to order, then items of business are discussed and voted on (usually by voice vote at meetings

held by small corporations). At or shortly after the meeting, you should prepare formal minutes to record the matters discussed and approved at the meeting, showing the number of votes cast for and against each matter brought to a vote together with a description of the action taken or rejected by the meeting participants. State law does not specify how minutes should be prepared—you can simply draft your own to suit your needs. Below is a sample standard minutes form that you can follow to prepare minutes for any annual or special directors' or shareholders' meeting. The minutes form is available online and at the back of this book. (See Appendixes B and C.)

RESOURCE

For more minutes help and ready-to-use forms. If you are concerned about preparing minutes for annual and special meetings (and we think you should be, of course, now that you've incorporated), you owe it to yourself to see *The Corporate Records Handbook,* by Anthony Mancuso (Nolo). It helps you schedule, organize, and prepare all ongoing corporate paperwork, with specialized minutes forms for directors' and shareholders' annual and special meetings, plus more than 80 ready-to-use resolutions to plug into the minutes to describe the approval of common corporate legal, tax, and business decisions. It also contains forms to waive notice of meetings and approve decisions by written consent (without a meeting) for those times when you are too busy to comply with all the meeting requirements specified in your bylaws or state BCA.

Sample General Minutes of Meeting

Minutes of ___*[type of meeting: "Directors" or "Shareholders"]*___ Meeting
of
___*[name of corporation]*___

A _*[insert type of meeting, such as "special"]*_ meeting of the _*["directors" or "shareholders"]*_ was held on _*[date, time, and place]*_ for the purpose(s) of _*[purpose of meeting stated in the notice of the meeting]*_ .

*[name of corporate officer, usually the president]* acted as chairperson, and _*[name of corporate officer, usually the secretary]*_ acted as secretary of the meeting.

The chairperson called the meeting to order.

The secretary announced that the meeting was called by _*[if applicable, name of person who called the meeting]*_ .

The secretary announced that the meeting was held pursuant to notice as required under the bylaws of this corporation.

The secretary announced that the following _*["directors" or "shareholders"]*_ were present at the meeting, representing a quorum: _*[names of directors or names and shareholdings of shareholders present]*_ .

The secretary announced that the next item of business was the consideration of one or more formal resolutions for approval by the _*["board" or "shareholders"]*_ . After introduction and discussion, and on motion duly made and carried by the affirmative vote of _*["a majority" or other vote requirement (or list names of those voting for and against the proposal and, if a shareholders' meeting, each person's shareholdings)]*_ of _*["directors" or "shareholders"]*_ at the meeting, the following resolutions were adopted by the _*["directors" or "shareholders"]*_ entitled to vote at the meeting: _*[describe one or more resolutions adopted at the meeting]*_ .

There being no further business to come before the meeting, it was adjourned on motion duly made and carried.

*[signature of meeting secretary]* , Secretary

Lawyers and Accountants

Lawyers

If you form a straightforward corporation with just a few owners, one class of stock, and no special bylaw provisions, you probably won't run into any problems that require expert legal help. But if you wish to form a more complicated corporation, getting legal help or advice may be necessary before you file your articles of incorporation.

Throughout this book we have flagged areas of potential complexity where a degree of customization may be warranted—for example, complying with unique requirements of your state's securities law, adding a second class of stock to your articles, or adding special provisions to your bylaws. If any of these loom large for you, review them with an experienced business lawyer before filing your articles. The lawyer should have experience in small business incorporations in your state; should be prepared to answer your specific, informed questions; and should review—not rewrite (unless absolutely necessary)—any forms you have prepared.

Even if you have all your incorporation paperwork covered, it's not too early to find a lawyer to use later for ongoing business consultations. Once enmeshed in a crisis, you may not have time to hire a lawyer at affordable rates. Chances are you'll wind up settling for the first person available—and that's almost a guarantee you'll pay too much for possibly poor service.

Using a Legal Coach

Most readers will not want a lawyer who is programmed to take over all legal decision making and form drafting—this just builds up billable hours that few can afford. Instead, we suggest you find someone we call a legal coach: a professional who is willing to work with you, not just *for* you, when answering your particular questions and meeting your special corporate legal needs. Under this model, the lawyer helps you customize your legal paperwork—rather than writing on his or her own from scratch—and is available to help you later if a complicated corporate legal issue comes up that you can't handle by yourself.

Not all lawyers are comfortable taking a legal coach role, so you may need to interview several lawyers before finding a compatible adviser. When you call a lawyer, announce your intentions in advance: Tell the lawyer that you are looking for someone who is willing to review and perhaps customize the corporate formation papers you have prepared, or to handle specific legal questions. Mention that you are looking for someone who is willing to be flexible, point you in the right direction as the need arises, serve as a legal adviser as circumstances dictate, and tackle particular legal problems if necessary. In exchange for this, let the lawyer know you are willing to pay promptly and fairly.

When you find a lawyer who agrees to the arrangement you've proposed, ask to meet with him or her for a half hour or so. Expect to pay for this initial consultation. At the in-person interview, reemphasize that you are looking for a legal coach relationship. You'll also want to discuss other important issues in this meeting, such as the lawyer's customary charges for services, as explained further below. Pay particular attention to the rapport between you and your lawyer. Remember, you are looking for a legal adviser who will work with you. Trust your instincts and seek a lawyer whose personality and business sense are compatible with your own.

Using Different Levels of Legal Talent

Many lawyers are open to nontraditional business arrangements. In your quest for a lawyer, remember:

- **You don't need a big-time business lawyer.** Look for a lawyer with some small business experience, preferably in your field or area of operations. For the most part, you don't want a lawyer who works with big businesses (publicly held corporations, large limited partnerships, or investment pools, and the like). Not only will this person deal with issues that are far from your concerns, but he or she is almost sure to charge too much.

- **You don't need to start with a legal specialist.** Even if you have a very technical legal question, it's usually not necessary to seek out a legal specialist in an area such as insurance, banking, or securities law. Start by finding a good small business lawyer to act as your coach. Then rely on this person to suggest specialized materials or experts as the need arises. Again, finding a

lawyer with corporate experience is essential, but specialized legal involvement in narrower realms of business practice can wait until you actually need advice on a particular legal issue or problem.

- **Look elsewhere for tax advice, unless your lawyer also specializes in corporate taxation.** When it comes to corporate tax questions, we think a tax adviser with corporate experience is the best person to ask for help. (See "Accountants and Tax Advisers," below.) For other tax and financial decisions, such as the best tax year, accounting period, or employee benefit plan for your corporation, you'll find that accountants, financial planners, retirement and employee benefit plan specialists, and bank officers often have a better grasp of the issues than lawyers. And an added bonus is that although tax advice doesn't come cheap, it often costs less than legal advice.

How to Find a Lawyer

When you're ready to look for a lawyer, one excellent way to find one is to talk to people in your community who own or operate businesses of comparable size and scope. If you talk to half a dozen businesspeople, chances are you'll come away with several good leads. People who provide services to small businesses—such as bankers, accountants, insurance agents, or commercial real estate brokers—may also be able to provide the names of lawyers they trust to help them with business matters. In short, try to get a personal recommendation from someone who is qualified to evaluate small business lawyers, which probably excludes your sister who just hired a lawyer to increase her

child support. You can also check online for lawyers at Nolo's Lawyer Directory (www.nolo.com), which has information on lawyers by location and practice area.

Paying for Legal Help

When you hire a lawyer, get a clear understanding about how fees will be computed. For example, ask how you will be billed if you want to call the lawyer from time to time for general advice, to be steered to a good information source, or to have the lawyer review documents. Some lawyers bill a flat amount for a call or a conference; others bill to the nearest six-, ten-, or 20-minute interval. Whatever the lawyer's system, you need to understand it.

Particularly at the beginning of your relationship, when you bring a bigger job to a lawyer, ask specifically about what it will cost. If you feel it's too much, don't hesitate to negotiate; perhaps you can do some of the routine work yourself, thus reducing the fee for larger jobs.

EXAMPLE: You decide to add buy-sell provisions to your bylaws (see "Adopt a Shareholders' Buy-Sell Agreement" in Chapter 5). You buy a self-help resource and prepare a draft of your buy-sell provisions. The area is complicated enough that you decide to have your provisions checked by a small business lawyer you know. You call and ask the hourly fee for this review of your work. The fee seems acceptable and competitive, and you schedule an appointment to have the lawyer look over and customize your work (after the lawyer explains the reasons for doing so, of course).

It's a good idea to get fee arrangements in writing. (In several states, this is mandatory where a fee of $1,000 or more is expected.)

How Lawyers Charge for Legal Services

You can expect your lawyer to bill you in one of these ways:

- **By the hour.** In most parts of the United States, you can get competent services for your small business for $150 to $250 an hour, and often less. Newer attorneys still in the process of building a practice may be available for paperwork review, legal research, and other types of legal work at lower rates.

- **Flat fee for a specific job.** Under this arrangement, you pay an agreed-on amount for a given project, regardless of how much or how little time the lawyer spends. Particularly when you begin working with a lawyer and are worried about hourly costs getting out of control, it can make sense to negotiate a flat fee for a specific job, such as doing a prefiling review of your articles or a review of your bylaws. For example, the lawyer may review your articles and bylaws for $300.

- **Retainer.** Some businesses can afford to pay relatively modest amounts, perhaps $1,000 to $2,000 per year, to keep a business lawyer on retainer for ongoing phone or in-person consultations or routine business matters. Of course, your retainer won't cover a full-blown legal crisis, but it may take care of routine contract and other legal paperwork preparation and reviews.

- **Contingent fee based on settlement amounts or winnings.** This type of fee typically occurs in personal injury, products liability, fraud, and employment discrimination disputes, where a lawsuit will likely be filed, not in the corporate service area. Just so you know, however, the lawyer gets a percentage of the recovery (often 33% to 40%) if the client wins and nothing if the client loses. Even in the personal injury business, when a client gets sued, lawyers charge by the hour to defend a client, not a percentage of the money the lawyer saves the client if the defense is successful.

Resolving Problems With Lawyers

If you have any questions about a lawyer's bill or the quality of his or her services, speak up. Buying legal help should be just like purchasing any other consumer service. If you are dissatisfied, seek a reduction in your bill or make it clear that the work needs to be redone properly. For example, tell the lawyer that you need a more comprehensive lease or a better contract. If the lawyer you are dealing with runs a consumer-friendly business, he or she will promptly and positively deal with your concerns. If you don't get an acceptable response, find another lawyer pronto. If you switch lawyers, you are entitled to get your important documents back from the first lawyer.

Even if you fire your lawyer, you may still feel unjustly treated and overcharged. If you can't get satisfaction from the lawyer, write to the client grievance office of your state bar association (and send the lawyer a copy of your letter). Often, a phone call from this office to your lawyer will bring the desired results.

How to Look Up the Law Yourself

Many incorporators want to research legal information on their own. This book provides you with an easy way to do your own research by going to your state's online Business Corporation Act (BCA) as explained in Appendix A. It's a simple matter to look up corporate statutes in your state's BCA to get more information and the latest corporation rules that apply in your state.

Standard corporate forms and instructions used in your state to handle changes to your corporation's legal structure are provided online at your state's corporate filing office website. (See Appendix A.) Typically, this site offers forms for amending articles and changing your corporation's registered agent or office. You'll probably also find annual report forms (see "File a Corporate Annual Report" in Chapter 5) and other routine corporate filing forms used in your state.

You also can take advantage of a local law or business library to do your own legal research. County law libraries are open to the public (you will not be asked to produce a bar card before being helped), and they are not difficult to use once you understand how the information is categorized and stored. Libraries are an invaluable source of corporate and general business forms, corporate tax procedures and information, and the like. Research librarians will usually go out of their way to help you find the right statute, form, or background reading on any corporate or tax issue.

For more information about the laws that govern corporations and how to find them online or in the library, see "Corporate Statutes" in Chapter 2.

RESOURCE

An excellent legal research resource. If you are interested in doing self-help legal research, an excellent source of information on how to both find the law online and break the code of the law libraries is *Legal Research: How to Find & Understand the Law*, by Stephen R. Elias and the Editors of Nolo (Nolo).

RESOURCE

More help from Nolo. As mentioned throughout this book, Nolo offers resources of all kinds—both on the Web and off—to help you start your business and keep it healthy. (See "Nolo's Small Business Resources" in Chapter 1 for a detailed list of Nolo's most popular tools for small business owners, and remember to visit the Small Business area of Nolo's website at www.nolo.com.)

Accountants and Tax Advisers

As you already know, organizing and operating a corporation involves a significant amount of financial and tax work, and you'll need to make many important decisions about these matters. Throughout this book we have flagged areas of special consideration involving financial planning and corporate tax issues.

Generally, although we tend to use the terms tax adviser, financial consultant, and accountant interchangeably, you may wish to refer your initial incorporation tax concerns to a certified public accountant (CPA) with corporate experience. For general assistance and advice, a qualified financial planner may also be very helpful.

Once your initial incorporation tax questions have been answered, your corporation set up, and your books established, you may want to have routine tax filings and bookkeeping tasks performed by corporate personnel or independent contractors who have been trained in corporate bookkeeping and tax matters. (In many instances your accountant may either train or recommend these individuals.) Most corporations have their accountant or other tax return preparer handle at least their annual corporate tax returns.

For future financial advice, you may wish to contact an officer in the corporate department of the bank where you keep your corporate accounts. Banks are an excellent source of financial advice, particularly if they are corporate creditors—after all, they have a stake in the success of your business. Further, the Small Business Administration (www.sba.gov) can be an ideal source of financial and tax information and resources (as well as financing in some cases).

Whatever your arrangement for financial or tax assistance, you may wish to order the IRS and state tax publications listed in "Tax and Employer Registration Requirements" in Chapter 5 to familiarize yourself with some of the tax and bookkeeping aspects of operating a corporation.

When you select a tax adviser, the same considerations apply as when selecting a lawyer. Choose someone you know or someone who has been recommended by a friend with business experience. Be as specific as you can about the services you need, and find someone with experience in corporate taxation. Above all, find someone who will listen to and work with you, not simply charge high prices to give you one-sided, take-it-or-leave-it tax advice.

RESOURCE

Find a compatible tax adviser. Tax issues, in particular, are often cloudy and subject to a range of interpretations and strategies, particularly in the corporate arena, so it is absolutely essential that you discuss and reach agreement about the level of tax-aggressiveness you expect from your adviser. Some incorporators like to live on the edge, saving every possible tax dollar. Others are content to forgo contestable tax strategies to gain an extra measure of peace of mind. Whatever your tax comfort level, make sure you find a tax adviser who feels the same way you do, or who is willing to defer to your more liberal or conservative tax tendencies. ●

State Incorporation Resources

How to Locate Incorporation Resources Online

This appendix explains how to locate your state's websites that contain the legal and tax rules for forming and operating a corporation in your state. We show you how to locate the state corporate offices and other information online for any state through websites that maintain updated links with 50-state information.

State Corporate Filing Office Website

This is the state office where you file articles (or a similar document) to form a corporation. You can go to this site (or call the office at the telephone number listed on the site) to check the availability of your proposed corporate name and to reserve your name if you wish to do so. State corporate filing office websites typically provide downloadable articles, name reservation request forms, and the latest corporate filing fee information. Many websites allow you to reserve your name and form your corporation online from the website without having to prepare, print, and mail paper forms to the state corporate filing office.

To find your state's corporate filing office website, go to www.coordinatedlegal.com/SecretaryOfState.html. This provides a list of links to each of the 50 state offices. From your state's secretary of state office, you might need to search the tabs and menus to find the information on filing or finding a form that you need.

State Tax Office Website

This is the state office website where you can find state corporate and individual tax information and forms. Most states collect annual corporate income or franchise taxes, as explained on their sites.

To find your state's tax office website, go to the Federation of Tax Administrators website at www.taxadmin.org and click "State Tax Agencies" under the "Taxpayers & Preparers" tab, and finally, click on your state in the list.

State Securities Office Website

This is the state agency where you can find information and forms for complying with your state's securities laws requirements (and exemptions from these requirements) for selling shares in your corporation. The names of state securities offices vary widely.

To find your state's securities office website, go to the North American Securities Administrators Association (NASAA) website at www.nasaa.org, and click on the "Contact Your Regulator" tab. Click on your state's link to its security office website.

State Corporation Law Lookup Website

To find your state's Business Corporation Act (BCA) or similarly titled corporation law, visit the state law legal research area of Nolo's website at www.nolo.com/legal-research/state-law.html. Click on your state's name. This will bring you to your state's statutory lookup Web page. You will see either a list of state BCA headings with title and chapter numbers and the name of each state law or a search box that asks for a statute number.

If you are browsing through your state's BCA for a general subject, select the heading from the heading list in your BCA that seems most appropriate for the subject. For example, open the "Directors" heading to look for statutes about directors or directors' meeting requirements.

Then select the particular statute of interest listed under the heading. BCAs normally are not extremely long, so it should not be difficult to search through the heading or statute lists to find the subject areas you're seeking. With practice, you'll soon get to know how your BCA is organized, and future generalized searches should take less and less time.

Another 50-State Online Business Information Locator

The Wyoming Secretary of State publishes and maintains a listing of links to online resources of state agencies at http://soswy.state.wy.us/AboutUs/SOS50.aspx. If the links we provided above do not lead you to the online resource you are seeking, try using the Wyoming 50-state service. ●

How to Use the Downloadable Forms on the Nolo Website

This book comes with downloadable files that you can access online at:

www.nolo.com/back-of-book/NIBS.html

To use the files, your computer must have specific software programs installed. Here is a list of types of files provided by this book, as well as the software programs you'll need to access them:

- **RTF.** You can open, edit, print, and save these form files with most word processing programs such as Microsoft *Word*, Windows *WordPad*, and recent versions of *WordPerfect*.

- **PDF.** You can view these files with Adobe *Reader*, free software from www.adobe.com. Government PDFs are sometimes fillable using your computer, but most PDFs are designed to be printed out and completed by hand.

Editing RTFs

Here are some general instructions about editing RTF forms in your word processing program. Refer to the book's instructions and sample agreements for help about what should go in each blank.

- **Underlines.** Underlines indicate where to enter information. After filling in the needed text, delete the underline. In most word processing programs you can do this by highlighting the underlined portion and typing CTRL-U.

- **Bracketed and italicized text.** Bracketed and italicized text indicates instructions. Be sure to remove all instructional text before you finalize your document.

- **Signature lines.** Signature lines should appear on a page with at least some text from the document itself.

Every word processing program uses different commands to open, format, save, and print documents, so refer to your software's help documents for help using your program. Nolo cannot provide technical support for questions about how to use your computer or your software.

CAUTION

In accordance with U.S. copyright laws, the forms provided by this book are for your personal use only.

List of Forms Available on the Nolo Website

The following files are available for download at:

www.nolo.com/back-of-book/NIBS.html

Form Title	File Name
Request for Reservation of Corporate Name	NAMERES.rtf
Iowa Articles Instructions	IAARTINSTRUCTIONS.pdf
Iowa Articles of Incorporation	IAARTS.rtf
Nebraska Articles Instructions	NEARTINSTRUCTIONS.pdf
Nebraska Articles of Incorporation	NEARTS.rtf
Cover Letter for Filing Articles	COVERLET.rtf
Bylaws	BYLAWS.rtf
Incorporator's Statement	INCORPST.rtf
Minutes of First Meeting of Board of Directors	MINUTES.rtf
Stock Certificates	STOCKCERT.pdf
Bill of Sale for Assets of a Business	SALEBUSINESS.rtf
Receipt for Cash Payment	RECEIPTS.rtf
Bill of Sale for Items of Property	SALEPROPERTY.rtf
Receipt for Services Rendered	SERVICES.rtf
Contract for Future Services	FUTURESERVICES.rtf
Promissory Note	PROMISSORYNOTE.rtf
Cancellation of Debt	CANCEL.rtf
Notice of Incorporation Letter	NOTIFY.rtf
General Minutes of Meeting	GENMIN.rtf

Forms

Name of Form	Chapter/Step
Request for Reservation of Corporate Name	Chapter 4, Step 1
Iowa Articles of Incorporation With Instructions	Chapter 4, Step 2
Nebraska Articles of Incorporation With Instructions	Chapter 4, Step 2
Cover Letter for Filing Articles	Chapter 4, Step 2
Bylaws	Chapter 4, Step 4
Incorporator's Statement	Chapter 4, Step 5
Minutes of First Meeting of Board of Directors	Chapter 4, Step 6
Stock Certificates	Chapter 4, Step 7
Bill of Sale for Assets of a Business	Chapter 4, Step 7
Receipt for Cash Payment	Chapter 4, Step 7
Bill of Sale for Items of Property	Chapter 4, Step 7
Receipt for Services Rendered	Chapter 4, Step 7
Contract for Future Services	Chapter 4, Step 7
Promissory Note	Chapter 4, Step 7
Cancellation of Debt	Chapter 4, Step 7
Notice of Incorporation Letter	Chapter 5
General Minutes of Meeting	Chapter 5

Request for Reservation of Corporate Name

_____

_____

_____

_____

_____

Re: Request for Reservation of Corporate Name

Corporate Filing Office:

Please reserve the first available corporate name from the list below for my use.
My proposed corporate names, listed in order of preference, are as follows:

_____

_____

_____

I enclose a check for the required reservation fee.

Sincerely,

_____

_____

                 Signature

Iowa Articles Instructions

Articles of incorporation currently are not available online or from the state filing office (the state filing office site provides a link to a copy of the statute that lists the requirements for the contents of articles). The secretary of state provides other statutory forms, including an Application for Reservation of Name, which you may complete online. You can browse a tutorial on Iowa business organizations and formation procedures, plus links to various sections of the Iowa Business Corporation Act, from the site.

You must prepare articles of incorporation that meet the requirements of Section 490.202 of the Iowa Business Corporation Act, which you can read online at the Iowa corporate filing office website (see Appendix A). Your articles must contain the following:

- **A corporate name.** The name of an Iowa corporation must contain the word "corporation," "incorporated," "company," or "limited" or the abbreviation "corp.," "inc.," "co.," or "ltd." You can search the corporate database online from the state filing office website to see if your proposed name is already in use by another active Iowa corporation. An available corporate name may be reserved using the online form.

- **The number of shares the corporation is authorized to issue.** Iowa does not require a statement of par value. To create one class of common shares with equal rights and preferences, simply state the number of shares. The number of shares should at least be sufficient for initial stock issuance; you can authorize more if you wish because the filing fee is not based on the number of authorized shares. If you want to create special classes of shares, you must list them, together with the rights and restrictions associated with each.

- **The street address of the corporation's initial registered office and the name of its initial registered agent at that office.** Use a street address, not a P.O. box.

- **The name and address of each incorporator.** Only one incorporator is required, who need not be a director, officer, or shareholder.

Below is a sample articles form you can use to create one class of common shares. (We provide an RTF word processing version at www.nolo.com/back-of-book/NIBS.html.) The articles must be entirely typewritten or computer printed.

Articles of Incorporation

Pursuant to the Iowa Business Corporation Act, the undersigned incorporator submits the following Articles of Incorporation:

1. The name of the corporation is _[insert name of corporation]_ .

2. The corporation is authorized to issue one class of common shares. The total number of such shares it is authorized to issue is _[insert number here]_ shares.

3. The street address of the corporation's initial registered office is _[typically, the business address of the corporation is inserted here]_ , and the name of its initial registered agent at this address is _[typically, the name of an initial director or officer is inserted here]_ .

4. The name and address of the incorporator is _[insert name and address of incorporator, who dates and signs below]_ .

Date: _____

Signature of Incorporator:

_____

Submit an original and one copy of your articles, together with an SASE.

Online forms submission: You can file your Articles online by uploading a PDF version of your form to the Iowa Fast Track filing system (log in at https://filings.sos.iowa.gov/Account/Login). Note that you can convert a file to PDF by opening it in Google Docs, then saving it as a PDF file.

Filing fee: See the corporate filing office website (Appendix A).

Iowa Articles of Incorporation

Pursuant to the Iowa Business Corporation Act, the undersigned incorporator submits the following Articles of Incorporation:

1. The name of the corporation is _____ .

2. The corporation is authorized to issue one class of common shares. The total number of such shares it is authorized to issue is _____ shares.

3. The street address of the corporation's initial registered office is _____ , and the name of its initial registered agent at this address is _____

_____ .

4. The name and address of the incorporator is _____ .

Date: _____

Signature of Incorporator: _____

Nebraska Articles Instructions

Because Nebraska does not currently provide an official articles of incorporation form, you must prepare your own. You can upload and file your articles online at the Secretary of State's Business Services website. Your articles must meet the requirements of Section 21-220 (effective 1/1/2019) of the Nebraska Business Corporation Act, which can be viewed online from the Nebraska corporate filing office (see Appendix A), and contain:

- **A corporate name.** The name of a Nebraska corporation must include one of the following corporate designators: "corporation," "incorporated," "company," or "limited," or the abbreviation "corp.," "inc.," "co.," or "ltd." You can perform a free search of the Corporate and Business database for information on all entities, trade names, trademarks, and service marks (login required). To formally check name availability, you must email, fax, or mail your request to the office. You may reserve an available corporate name using the Application for Name Reservation form, available on the state filing office website.

- **The number of shares the corporation is authorized to issue and their par value.** Nebraska requires that your shares have a stated par value. Most incorporators make sure that the capital value of their authorized shares (number of shares × par value) is $10,000 or less in order to pay the minimum filing fee.

If you want to authorize more than one class of shares, you must list the designation of each class, the number of shares in each class and a statement of the par value of the shares in each class.

- **The street address of the corporation's initial registered office and the name of its initial registered agent at that office.** The registered agent must be a Nebraska resident and the registered office address must be in Nebraska. Use a street address, not a P.O. box. (You may include a P.O. box address if you also specify a street address.) Most incorporators use the street address of the corporation as the registered office address and designate one of the corporation's initial directors or officers as the agent at this registered office address.

- **The name and street address of each incorporator.** You need just one incorporator, who must sign your articles. He or she need not be a director, officer, or shareholder.

- **Any provision limiting or eliminating the requirement to hold an annual meeting of the shareholders if the corporation is registered or intends to register as an investment company under the federal Investment Company Act of 1940.** This provision is unlikely to apply to your corporation.

Below is a sample articles form you can use to create one class of common shares. (We provide an RTF version at www.nolo.com/back-of-book/NIBS.html.) The articles must be typewritten or computer printed.

Articles of Incorporation

Pursuant to the Nebraska Model Business Corporation Act, the undersigned incorporator submits the following Articles of Incorporation:

1. The name of the corporation is _[insert name of corporation]_ .

2. The corporation is authorized to issue one class of common shares, with a par value of $_[insert par value amount]_ per share. The total number of such shares it is authorized to issue is _[insert number here]_ shares.

3. The street address of the corporation's initial registered office is _[typically, the address of the corporation is inserted here]_ and the name of its initial registered agent at this address is _[typically the name of an initial director or officer is inserted]_ .

4. The name and street address of the incorporator is _[insert name and street address of incorporator, who dates and signs, below]_ .

Date: _____

Signature of Incorporator:

_____

Filing fee: See the corporate filing office website.

Online forms submission: You can file your articles online at the state filing office website by uploading a PDF version of the signed form to the website's Corporate Document eDelivery service. To convert your articles to PDF format, open your articles in Google Docs, then save the form as a PDF file.

Nebraska Articles of Incorporation

Pursuant to the Nebraska Model Business Corporation Act, the undersigned incorporator submits the following Articles of Incorporation:

1. The name of the corporation is _____ .

2. The corporation is authorized to issue one class of common shares with a par value of $_____ per share. The total number of such shares it is authorized to issue is _____ shares.

3. The street address of the corporation's initial registered office is _____ , and the name of its initial registered agent at this address is _____

_____ .

4. The name and address of the incorporator is _____ .

Date: _____

Signature of Incorporator: _____

Cover Letter for Filing Articles

_____

_____
_____
_____

_____
_____

Corporate Filing Office:

I enclose an original and _____ copy/copies of the _____,
_____ of _____ . Please file the
original document and return any file-stamped copies to me, at the above address.

This corporate name was reserved by the undersigned incorporator on _____,
_____ .

I enclose payment of required filing fees.

Sincerely,

_____

_____

ARTICLE 1. OFFICES

SECTION 1. PRINCIPAL OFFICE

The location of the principal office of the corporation will be within the state of _____ at an address fixed by the board of directors. The secretary of this corporation will keep a copy of the corporation's Articles of Incorporation (or similar incorporating document), these bylaws, minutes of directors' and shareholders' meetings, stock certificates and stubs, a register of the names and interests of the corporation's shareholders, and other corporate records and documents at the principal office.

SECTION 2. OTHER OFFICES

The corporation may have offices at other locations as decided by its board of directors or as its business may require.

ARTICLE 2. SHAREHOLDERS' MEETINGS

SECTION 1. PLACE OF MEETINGS

Meetings of shareholders will be held at the principal office of the corporation or at other locations as may be decided by the board of directors.

SECTION 2. ANNUAL MEETINGS

The annual meeting of the shareholders will be held each year on and at the following date and time:

_____ . At the annual shareholders' meeting, shareholders will elect a board of directors and transact any other proper business. If this date falls on a legal holiday, then the meeting will be held on the following business day at the same time.

SECTION 3. SPECIAL MEETINGS

Special meetings of the shareholders may be called by the individuals authorized to do so under the state's corporation statutes.

SECTION 4. NOTICES OF MEETINGS

Notices of meetings, annual or special, shall be given in writing to shareholders entitled to vote at the meeting by the secretary or an assistant secretary or, if there be no such officer, by any director or shareholder.

Notices of shareholders' meetings must be given either personally or by first-class mail or other means of written communication, addressed to the shareholder at the address of the shareholder appearing on the stock register of the corporation or given by the shareholder to the corporation for the purpose of notice. Notice of a shareholders' meeting must be given to each shareholder no less than 30 days prior to the meeting.

This notice will state the place, date, and hour of the meeting and the general nature of the business to be transacted. The notice of an annual meeting and any special meeting at which directors are to be elected will include the names of the nominees that, at the time of the notice, the board of directors intends to present for election.

SECTION 5. WAIVER OF NOTICE

The transactions of any meeting of shareholders, however called and noticed, and wherever held, are as valid as though undertaken at a meeting duly held after regular call and notice, if a quorum is present, whether in person or by proxy, and if, either before or after the meeting, each of the persons entitled to vote, not present in person or by proxy, signs a written waiver of notice or a consent to the holding of the meeting or an approval of the minutes thereof. If the waiver does not include an approval of the minutes of the meeting, it will state the general nature of the business of the meeting. All such waivers, consents, and approvals must be filed with the corporate records or made a part of the minutes of the meeting.

SECTION 6. LIST OF SHAREHOLDERS

Prior to any meeting of shareholders, the secretary of the corporation will prepare an alphabetical list of shareholders entitled to vote at the meeting that shows the address of each shareholder and number of shares entitled to vote at the meeting. This list shall be available for inspection at the principal office of the corporation by any shareholder within a reasonable period prior to each meeting and be made available for inspection at the meeting upon request of any shareholder at the meeting.

SECTION 7. QUORUM AND VOTING

Every shareholder entitled to vote is entitled to one vote for each share held, except as otherwise provided by law. A shareholder entitled to vote may vote part of his or her shares in favor of a proposal and refrain from voting the remaining shares or vote them against the proposal. If a shareholder fails to specify the number of shares he or she is affirmatively voting, it will be conclusively presumed that the shareholder's approving vote is with respect to all shares the shareholder is entitled to vote.

A majority of the shares entitled to vote, represented in person or by proxy, will constitute a quorum at a meeting of shareholders. If a quorum is present, the affirmative vote of the majority of shareholders represented at the meeting and entitled to vote on any matter will be the act of the shareholders, unless the vote of a greater number is required by law.

The shareholders present at a duly called or held meeting at which a quorum is present may continue to transact business until adjournment notwithstanding the withdrawal of enough shareholders to leave less than a quorum, if any action is approved by at least a majority of the shares required to constitute a quorum.

Notwithstanding other provisions of this section of the bylaws, if permitted by law and not prohibited by provision of the corporation's Articles of Incorporation (or similar incorporating document), shareholders may cumulate votes for the election of directors as provided in this paragraph. If permitted to cumulate votes in such election, a shareholder must state his or her intention to cumulate votes after the candidates' names have been placed in nomination at the meeting and before the commencement of voting for the election of directors. Once a shareholder has so stated his or her intention to cumulate votes, all shareholders entitled to vote must cumulate their votes in the election for directors. A shareholder cumulates votes by giving one candidate a number of votes equal to the number of directors to be elected multiplied by the number of his or her shares or by distributing such votes on the same principle among any number of candidates as he or she decides. The candidates receiving the highest number of votes, up to the number of directors to be elected, shall be elected. Votes cast against a candidate or which are withheld will have no effect in the cumulative voting results.

In any election for directors at a shareholders' meeting, upon the request of any shareholder made before the voting begins, the election of directors will be by ballot rather than by voice vote.

SECTION 8. PROXIES

Every person entitled to vote shares may authorize another person or persons to act by proxy with respect to such shares by filing a proxy with the secretary of the corporation. For purposes of these bylaws, a "proxy" is a written authorization signed by a shareholder or the shareholder's attorney-in-fact giving another person or persons power to vote with respect to the shares of the shareholder. Every proxy continues in full force and effect until the expiration of any period specified in the proxy or until revoked by the person executing it, except as otherwise provided by law.

SECTION 9. ACTION WITHOUT MEETING

Any action that may be taken at any annual or special meeting of shareholders, except for the election of directors, may be taken without a meeting and without prior notice if a consent, in writing, setting forth the action so taken, is signed by all the holders of outstanding shares entitled to vote on the action.

ARTICLE 3. DIRECTORS

SECTION 1. POWERS

The business and affairs of the corporation will be managed by, or under the direction of, its board of directors.

SECTION 2. NUMBER

The authorized number of directors is _____ .

SECTION 3. ELECTION AND TENURE OF OFFICE

The directors are elected at the annual meeting of the shareholders and hold office until the next annual meeting and until their successors have been elected and qualified.

SECTION 4. RESIGNATION AND VACANCIES

Any director may resign effective upon giving written notice to the chairperson of the board of directors, the president, the secretary, or the board of directors, unless the notice specifies a later time for the effectiveness of the resignation. If the resignation is effective at a later time, a successor may be elected to take office when the resignation becomes effective.

A vacancy on the board of directors exists in the case of death, resignation, or removal of any director or in case the authorized number of directors is increased, or in case the shareholders fail to elect the full authorized number of directors at any annual or special meeting of the shareholders at which directors are elected. The board of directors may declare vacant the office of a director who has been declared of unsound mind by an order of court or who has been convicted of a felony.

Vacancies on the board may be filled by the remaining board members unless a vacancy is required by law to be filled by approval of the shareholders. Each director approved to fill a vacancy on the board holds such office until the next annual meeting of the shareholders and until his or her successor has been elected and qualified.

SECTION 5. PLACE OF MEETINGS

Meetings of the board of directors may be held at any place, within or without the state, that has been designated in the notice of the meeting or, if not stated in the notice or if there is no notice, at the principal office of the corporation or as may be designated from time to time by resolution of the board of directors. Meetings of the board may be held through use of conference telephone, computer, electronic video screen communication, or other communications equipment, as long as all of the following apply:

(a) Each member participating in the meeting can communicate with all members concurrently.

(b) Each member is provided the means of participating in all matters before the board, including the capacity to propose, or to interpose, an objection to a specific action to be taken by the corporation.

(c) The corporation adopts and implements some means of verifying both of the following:

(1) A person communicating by telephone, computer, electronic video screen, or other communications equipment is a director entitled to participate in the board meeting.

(2) All statements, questions, actions, or votes were made by that director and not by another person.

SECTION 6. ANNUAL AND REGULAR MEETINGS

An annual meeting of the board of directors will be held immediately after and at the same place as the annual meeting of the shareholders.

Other regular meetings of the board of directors will be held at the times and places fixed from time to time by the board of directors.

SECTION 7. SPECIAL MEETINGS

Special meetings of the directors may be called by the individuals authorized to do so under the state's corporation statutes.

SECTION 8. NOTICES OF MEETINGS

Notices of directors' meetings, whether annual, regular, or special, will be given in writing to directors by the secretary or an assistant secretary or, if there be no such officer, by any director.

Notices of directors' meetings will be given either personally or by first-class mail or other means of written communication, addressed to the director at the address of the director appearing on the records of the corporation or given by the director to the corporation for the purpose of notice. Notice of a directors' meeting will be given to each director at least two weeks prior to the meeting, unless a greater period is required under the state corporation statutes for giving notice of a meeting.

This notice will state the place, date, and hour of the meeting and the general nature of the business to be transacted.

SECTION 9. WAIVER OF NOTICE

The transactions of any meeting of the board, however called and noticed or wherever held, are as valid as though undertaken at a meeting duly held after regular call and notice if a quorum is present and if, either before or after the meeting, each of the directors not present signs a written waiver of notice, a consent to holding the meeting, or an approval of the minutes of that meeting. If the waiver does not include an approval of the minutes of the meeting, it will state the general nature of the business of the meeting. All such waivers, consents, and approvals will be filed with the corporate records or made a part of the minutes of the meeting.

SECTION 10. QUORUM AND VOTING

A quorum for all meetings of the board of directors consists of a majority of the authorized number of directors.

Except as otherwise required under state corporate statutes, every act or decision done or made by a majority of the directors present at a meeting duly held at which a quorum is present is the act of the board.

SECTION 11. ACTION WITHOUT MEETING

Any action required or permitted to be taken by the board may be taken without a meeting, if all members of the board individually or collectively consent in writing to that action. Such written consents will be filed with the minutes of the proceedings of the board. Such action by written consent has the same force and effect as a unanimous vote of the directors.

SECTION 12. COMPENSATION

No salary will be paid directors, as such, for their services but, by resolution, the board of directors may allow a reasonable fixed sum and expenses to be paid for attendance at regular or special meetings. Nothing contained herein prevents a director from serving the corporation in any other capacity and receiving compensation therefor. Members of special or standing committees may also be allowed like compensation for attendance at meetings.

ARTICLE 4. OFFICERS

SECTION 1. OFFICERS

The officers of the corporation include a president, a secretary, and a treasurer, or officers with different titles that perform the duties of these offices as described in Sections 2 through 4 of this Article. Except as otherwise provided under state corporate statutes, any number of these offices may be held by the same person. The corporation may also appoint other officers with such titles and duties as determined by the board of directors.

SECTION 2. PRESIDENT

The president (or chief executive officer or alternately titled chief corporate officer designated by the board of directors) has general supervision, direction, and control of the day-to-day business and affairs of the corporation, subject to the direction and control of the board of directors. He or she presides at all meetings of the shareholders and directors and is an ex officio member of all the standing committees, including any executive committee of the board, and has the general powers and duties of management usually vested in the office of president or chief executive officer of a corporation, and other powers and duties as may from time to time be prescribed by the board of directors or these bylaws.

SECTION 3. SECRETARY

The corporate secretary (or other corporate officer designated by the board of directors to maintain and keep corporate records) will keep, or cause to be kept, at the principal office of the corporation, a book of minutes of all meetings of directors and shareholders. The minutes will state the time and place of holding of all meetings; whether regular or special, if special, how called or authorized; the notice given or the waivers of notice received; the names of those present at directors' meetings; the number of shares present or represented at shareholders' meetings; and an account of the proceedings.

He or she will keep, or cause to be kept, at the principal office of the corporation, or at the office of the corporation's transfer agent, a share register, showing the names of the shareholders and their addresses, the number and classes of shares held by each, the number and date of certificates issued for shares, and the number and date of cancellation of every certificate surrendered for cancellation.

He or she will keep, or cause to be kept, at the principal office of the corporation, the original or a copy of the bylaws of the corporation, as amended or otherwise altered to date, certified by him or her.

He or she will give, or cause to be given, notice of all meetings of shareholders and directors required to be given by law or by the provisions of these bylaws. He or she will prepare, or cause to be prepared, an alphabetical listing of shareholders for inspection prior to and at meetings of shareholders as required by Article 2, Section 6, of these bylaws.

He or she has charge of the seal of the corporation and has such other powers and may perform such other duties as may from time to time be prescribed by the board or these bylaws.

SECTION 4. TREASURER

The treasurer (or other officer designated by the board of directors to serve as chief financial officer of the corporation) shall keep and maintain, or cause to be kept and maintained, adequate and correct books and records of accounts of the properties and business transactions of the corporation.

He or she will deposit monies and other valuables in the name and to the credit of the corporation with the depositories designated by the board of directors. He or she will disburse the funds of the corporation in payment of the just demands against the corporation; shall render to the president and directors, whenever they request it, an account of all his or her transactions as chief financial officer and of the financial condition of the corporation; and have such other powers and perform such other duties as may from time to time be prescribed by the board of directors.

SECTION 5. APPOINTMENT, REMOVAL, AND RESIGNATION

All officers of the corporation will be approved by, and serve at the pleasure of, the board of directors. An officer may be removed at any time, either with or without cause, by written notification of removal by the board. An officer may resign at any time on written notice to the corporation given to the board, the president, or the secretary of the corporation. Any resignation takes effect at the date of receipt of notice or at any other time specified in it. The removal or resignation of an officer shall be without prejudice to the rights, if any, of the officer or the corporation under any contract of employment to which the officer is a party.

ARTICLE 5. EXECUTIVE COMMITTEES

SECTION 1. REGULAR AND EXECUTIVE COMMITTEES OF THE BOARD

The board may designate one or more regular committees to report to the board on any area of corporate operation and performance.

To the extent allowed under state corporate statutes, the board also may designate and delegate specific decision-making authority to one or more executive committees, each consisting of two or more directors, that shall have the authority of the board to approve corporate decisions in the specific areas designated by the board.

ARTICLE 6. CORPORATE RECORDS AND REPORTS

SECTION 1. INSPECTION BY SHAREHOLDERS AND DIRECTORS

The corporate secretary will make available within a reasonable period after a request for inspection or copying made by a director or shareholder or a director's or shareholder's legal representative the Articles of Incorporation (or similar organizing document) as amended to date; these bylaws as amended to date; minutes of proceedings of the shareholders and the board and committees of the board; the share register of the corporation, its accounting books, and records; and any other corporate records and reports. The requested records will be made available for inspection and copying at the principal office of the corporation within business hours. Any copying costs incurred by the corporation necessary to comply with a request for copies of records may be collected by the secretary from a requesting shareholder; the corporation assumes the cost of copies made for a requesting director.

SECTION 2. ANNUAL REPORTS TO SHAREHOLDERS

The secretary will mail a copy of any annual financial or other report to shareholders on the secretary's own initiative or on request made by one or more shareholders as may be required by state corporate statutes.

ARTICLE 7. INDEMNIFICATION AND INSURANCE OF DIRECTORS AND OFFICERS

SECTION 1. INDEMNIFICATION

The directors and officers of the corporation shall be indemnified by the corporation to the fullest extent permitted under law.

SECTION 2. INSURANCE

The corporation has the power to purchase and maintain insurance on behalf of any director or officer against any liability asserted against or incurred by the agent in that capacity or arising out of the agent's status as such, whether or not the corporation has the power to indemnify the agent against such liability under law.

ARTICLE 8. SHARES

SECTION 1. CERTIFICATES

The corporation will issue certificates for its shares when fully paid. Certificates of stock will be issued in numerical order, and state the name of the record holder of the shares represented by each certificate; the number, designation, if any, and class or series of shares represented by the certificate; and other information, including any statement or summary required by any applicable provision of state corporate statutes. Each certificate will be signed by the corporate officers empowered under state law to sign the certificates, and may be sealed with the seal of the corporation.

SECTION 2. TRANSFER OF SHARES

On surrender to the secretary or transfer agent of the corporation of a certificate for shares duly endorsed or accompanied by proper evidence of succession, assignment, or authority to transfer, it is the duty of the secretary of the corporation to issue a new certificate to the person entitled to it, to cancel the old certificate, and to record the transaction on the share register of the corporation.

SECTION 3. RECORD DATE

The board of directors may fix a time in the future as a record date for the determination of the shareholders entitled to notice of and to vote at any meeting of shareholders or entitled to receive payment of any dividend or distribution, or any allotment of rights, or to exercise rights with respect to any other lawful action. The record date so fixed will conform to the requirements of state law. When a record date is so fixed, only shareholders of record on that date are entitled to notice of and to vote at the meeting, or to receive the dividend, distribution, or allotment of rights, or to exercise their rights, notwithstanding any transfer of any shares on the books of the corporation after the record date.

ARTICLE 9. AMENDMENT OF BYLAWS

SECTION 1. BY SHAREHOLDERS

Except as otherwise provided by law, these bylaws may be adopted, amended, or repealed by the affirmative vote at a meeting of holders of a majority of the outstanding shares of the corporation entitled to vote.

SECTION 2. BY DIRECTORS

Except as otherwise provided by law, the directors may adopt, amend, or repeal these bylaws.

CERTIFICATE

This certifies that the foregoing is a true and correct copy of the bylaws of the corporation named in the title, and that these bylaws were duly adopted by the board of directors of the corporation on the date set forth below.

Dated: _____

Signature: _____, Secretary

Incorporator's Statement

The undersigned, the incorporator of _____, who signed and filed its Articles of Incorporation or similar organizing document with the state, appoints the following individuals to serve as the initial directors of the corporation, who shall serve as directors until the first meeting of shareholders for the election of directors and until their successors are elected and agree to serve on the board:

_____

_____

_____

_____

_____

Date: _____

Signature: _____, Incorporator

Minutes of First Meeting
of Board of Directors

Waiver of Notice and Consent to Holding
of First Meeting of Board of Directors

We, the undersigned, being all the directors of _____, hereby waive notice of the first meeting of the board of directors of the corporation and consent to the holding of the meeting at _____ on _____ _____ at _____ and consent to the transaction of any and all business at the meeting including, without limitation, the adoption of bylaws, the election of officers, the selection of the corporation's accounting period, the designation of the location of the principal office of the corporation, the selection of the place where the corporation's bank accounts will be maintained, and the authorization of the sale and issuance of the initial shares of stock of the corporation.

Date: _____

Signatures:

_____ , Director

_____ , Director

_____ , Director

_____ , Director

_____ , Director

Minutes of First Meeting of the Board of Directors

The board of directors of _____ held its first meeting at

_____ on _____, at _____.

The following directors, marked as present next to their names, were in attendance at the meeting and constituted a quorum of the board:

_____ [ ] Present [ ] Absent

_____ [ ] Present [ ] Absent

_____ [ ] Present [ ] Absent

_____ [ ] Present [ ] Absent

_____ [ ] Present [ ] Absent

On motion and by unanimous vote, _____ was appointed chairperson and then presided over the meeting. _____ was elected secretary of the meeting.

The meeting was held pursuant to written waiver of notice and consent to holding of the meeting signed by each of the directors. Upon a motion duly made, seconded, and unanimously carried, it was resolved that the written waiver of notice and consent to holding of the meeting be made a part of and constitute the first page of the minutes of this meeting.

ARTICLES OF INCORPORATION

The chairperson announced that the Articles of Incorporation or similar organizing document of the corporation were filed with the state corporate filing office on _____

_____. The corporate secretary was asked to place a file-stamped copy of the articles or filing receipt showing such filing in the corporation's records book.

BYLAWS

A proposed set of bylaws of the corporation was presented for adoption. Upon motion duly made and seconded, it was unanimously:

RESOLVED, that the bylaws presented to this meeting are adopted as the bylaws of this corporation;

RESOLVED FURTHER, that the secretary of this corporation is asked to execute a Certificate of Adoption of the bylaws, and to place the bylaws as so certified with the corporation's records at its principal office.

PRINCIPAL EXECUTIVE OFFICE

On motion duly made and seconded, it was:

RESOLVED, that the principal office of this corporation shall be located at _____

_____

APPOINTMENT OF OFFICERS

On motion, the following persons were unanimously appointed to the following offices:

President (CEO): _____

Treasurer (CFO): _____

Secretary: _____

CORPORATE SEAL

On motion duly made and seconded, it was:

RESOLVED, that the corporate seal impressed directly below this resolution is adopted as the corporate seal of this corporation. The secretary of the corporation is directed to place the seal with the corporate records at the principal office of the corporation, and to use the seal on corporate stock certificates and other appropriate corporate documents as the secretary sees fit.

STOCK CERTIFICATE

On motion duly made and seconded, it was:

RESOLVED, that the form of stock certificate attached to these minutes is adopted for use by this corporation for the issuance of its initial shares.

CORPORATE BANK ACCOUNTS

On motion duly made and seconded, it was:

RESOLVED, that the funds of this corporation be deposited with the following bank at the following branch office: _____ , located at _____ .

RESOLVED FURTHER, that the treasurer of this corporation is authorized and asked to establish one or more accounts with this bank and to deposit the funds of this corporation in these accounts.

RESOLVED FURTHER, that any officer, employee, or agent of this corporation is authorized to endorse checks, drafts, or other evidences of indebtedness made payable to this corporation, but only for the purpose of deposit.

RESOLVED FURTHER, that all checks, drafts, and other instruments obligating this corporation to pay money be signed on behalf of this corporation by any _____ of the following:

_____

_____

_____

RESOLVED FURTHER, that the bank is hereby authorized to honor and pay any and all checks and drafts of this corporation signed in this manner.

RESOLVED FURTHER, that the authority hereby conferred remains in force until revoked by the board of directors of this corporation and until written notice of revocation has been received by the bank.

RESOLVED FURTHER, that the secretary of this corporation is authorized to certify as to the continuing authority of these resolutions and to complete on behalf of the corporation the bank's standard form of resolution, provided that the form does not vary materially from the terms of the foregoing resolutions.

ACCOUNTING PERIOD

After discussion and upon motion duly made and seconded, it was:

RESOLVED, that the accounting period of this corporation shall end on _____ of each year.

PAYMENT, DEDUCTION, AND AMORTIZATION OF
START-UP AND ORGANIZATIONAL EXPENSES

On motion duly made, seconded, and unanimously approved, it was:

RESOLVED, that the treasurer of this corporation is authorized and empowered to pay all reasonable and proper expenses incurred in connection with the start-up and organization of the corporation, including, among others, expenses prior to the start of business necessary to investigate and create the business, as well as organization costs necessary to form the corporation, and to reimburse any persons making such disbursements for the corporation.

RESOLVED FURTHER, that the treasurer is authorized to elect to deduct and amortize, if appropriate, start-up and organization expenditures pursuant to and as permitted under Sections 195 and 248 of the Internal Revenue Code and as permitted under similar state tax provisions.

AUTHORIZATION OF ISSUANCE OF SHARES

On motion duly made and seconded, it was unanimously:

RESOLVED, that the corporation sell and issue the following number of its authorized common shares to the following persons, in the amounts and for the consideration set forth next to their names, below. The board also determined that the fair value to the corporation of any consideration for such shares issued other than for money is as stated below:

Name	Number of Shares	Consideration
_____	_____	_____
_____	_____	_____
_____	_____	_____
_____	_____	_____
_____	_____	_____

RESOLVED FURTHER, that the amount of consideration received by the corporation for each and any of the above shares issued without par value that is to be allocated to capital surplus is $_____ .

RESOLVED FURTHER, that the appropriate officers of this corporation are hereby authorized and directed to take such actions and execute such documents as they deem necessary or appropriate to effectuate the sale and issuance of such shares for the consideration listed above.

Since there was no further business to come before the meeting, on motion duly made and seconded, the meeting was adjourned.

_____ , Secretary

Certificate Number _____

for _____

Issued to: _____

Dated _____, 20 _____

From Whom Transferred

	No. Original Shares	No. Original Certificate	No. of Shares Transferred
Shares _____			
Dated _____, 20 _____			

Received Certificate Number _____

for _____ Shares

This _____ Day of, 20 _____

_____
SIGNATURE

Incorporated Under the Laws of _____

Number _____

Shares _____

This certifies that _____

_____ is the owner of _____ fully paid and

assessable _____ of the above Corporation transferable only on the books

of the Corporation by the holder in person or by duly authorized Attorney on surrender of this Certificate,

properly endorsed.

In witness whereof, the Corporation has caused this certificate to be signed by its duly authorized officers

and to be sealed with the Seal of the Corporation.

Dated: _____

_____,

_____,

_____,

Certificate Number _____

for _____

Issued to: _____

Dated _____, 20 ___

From Whom Transferred
_____

Received Certificate Number _____

for _____

This _____ Day of, 20 ___

	Shares	No. Original Shares	No. Original Certificate	No. of Shares Transferred
	Shares			
	Dated _____, 20 ___			

_____ Shares

SIGNATURE

Incorporated Under the Laws of _____

Number _____

This certifies that _____

_____ is the owner of _____ fully paid and

assessable _____ of the above Corporation transferable only on the books

of the Corporation by the holder in person or by duly authorized Attorney on surrender of this Certificate,

properly endorsed.

In witness whereof, the Corporation has caused this certificate to be signed by its duly authorized officers

and to be sealed with the Seal of the Corporation.

Dated: _____

_____ , _____

_____ , _____

_____ Shares

Certificate Number _____

for _____

Issued to: _____

Dated _____, 20 _____

	Shares _____	
Dated _____, 20 _____		
No. Original Shares	No. Original Certificate	No. of Shares Transferred

---

From Whom Transferred _____

for _____

This _____ Day of, 20 _____

Received Certificate Number _____ Shares _____

SIGNATURE _____

Incorporated Under the Laws of _____

Number _____

This certifies that _____ is the owner of _____ fully paid and assessable _____ Shares _____ of the above Corporation transferable only on the books of the Corporation by the holder in person or by duly authorized Attorney on surrender of this Certificate, properly endorsed.

In witness whereof, the Corporation has caused this certificate to be signed by its duly authorized officers and to be sealed with the Seal of the Corporation.

Dated: _____

_____,

_____,

Certificate Number _____

for _____

Issued to: _____

Shares _____

Dated _____, 20 _____

Dated _____, 20 _____

No. Original Shares	No. Original Certificate	No. of Shares Transferred

From Whom Transferred

Received Certificate Number _____ **Shares** _____

for _____

This _____ Day of, 20 _____

_____
SIGNATURE

Number _____

Incorporated Under the Laws of _____

This certifies that _____

is the owner of _____ fully paid and

assessable _____ of the above Corporation transferable only on the books

of the Corporation by the holder in person or by duly authorized Attorney on surrender of this Certificate,

properly endorsed.

In witness whereof, the Corporation has caused this certificate to be signed by its duly authorized officers

and to be sealed with the Seal of the Corporation.

Dated: _____

_____,

_____,

_____,

Shares _____

Certificate Number _____

for _____

Issued to: _____

Dated _____, 20 _____

Shares _____

Dated _____

No. Original Shares

No. Original Certificate

From Whom Transferred

Received Certificate Number _____

for _____ Shares

Dated _____, 20 _____

No. of Shares Transferred

This _____ Day of, 20 _____

SIGNATURE

Number _____

Incorporated Under the Laws of _____

This certifies that _____ is the owner of _____ fully paid and assessable _____ of the above Corporation transferable only on the books of the Corporation by the holder in person or by duly authorized Attorney on surrender of this Certificate, properly endorsed.

In witness whereof, the Corporation has caused this certificate to be signed by its duly authorized officers and to be sealed with the Seal of the Corporation.

Dated: _____

_____ ,

_____ ,

_____ ,

Shares _____

Certificate Number _____

for _____

Issued to: _____

Dated _____, 20 _____

	Shares	No. Original Shares
	Dated _____, 20 _____	No. Original Certificate

From Whom Transferred

_____

	No. of Shares Transferred

Received Certificate Number _____

for _____ Shares

This _____ Day of, 20 _____

SIGNATURE

Incorporated Under the Laws of _____

Number _____

This certifies that _____

_____ is the owner of _____ fully paid and assessable _____ of the above Corporation transferable only on the books of the Corporation by the holder in person or by duly authorized Attorney on surrender of this Certificate, properly endorsed.

In witness whereof, the Corporation has caused this certificate to be signed by its duly authorized officers and to be sealed with the Seal of the Corporation.

Dated: _____

_____,

_____,

_____ Shares

Certificate Number _____

for _____

Issued to: _____

Dated _____, 20 _____

From Whom Transferred _____

Received Certificate Number _____

Shares _____

for _____

This _____ Day of, 20 _____

Shares _____	for _____
Dated _____, 20 _____	

No. Original Shares	No. Original Certificate	No. Original Transferred	No. of Shares Transferred

SIGNATURE

Incorporated Under the Laws of _____

Number _____

_____ Shares _____

This certifies that _____

_____ is the owner of _____ fully paid and

assessable _____ of the above Corporation transferable only on the books

of the Corporation by the holder in person or by duly authorized Attorney on surrender of this Certificate,

properly endorsed.

In witness whereof, the Corporation has caused this certificate to be signed by its duly authorized officers

and to be sealed with the Seal of the Corporation.

Dated: _____

_____ , _____

_____ , _____

_____ , _____

Incorporated Under the Laws of _____

Number _____

This certifies that _____

_____ is the owner of _____

_____ of the above Corporation transferable only on the books of the Corporation by the holder in person or by duly authorized Attorney on surrender of this Certificate, properly endorsed.

In witness whereof, the Corporation has caused this certificate to be signed by its duly authorized officers and to be sealed with the Seal of the Corporation.

Dated: _____

_____, _____

_____, _____

_____, _____

Shares _____

Certificate Number _____

for _____

Issued to: _____

Dated _____, 20 _____

Number _____ Shares

Dated _____, 20 _____

No. Original Shares	No. Original Certificate	No. of Shares Transferred

---

From Whom Transferred _____

Received Certificate Number _____

for _____ Shares

This _____ Day of, 20 _____

SIGNATURE

Certificate Number —————

for ————————

Issued to:

Dated ————————, 20 ——

From Whom Transferred

| Shares ———— | Dated ————, 20 —— | Received Certificate Number ———— |
| No. Original Shares | No. Original Certificate | No. of Shares Transferred | for ————————
This ———— Day of, 20 —— |

———————— Shares

SIGNATURE

Incorporated Under the Laws of ————————

Number ————

This certifies that ————————

———————————— is the owner of ————————

———————— fully paid and assessable ———————— of the above Corporation transferable only on the books of the Corporation by the holder in person or by duly authorized Attorney on surrender of this Certificate, properly endorsed.

In witness whereof, the Corporation has caused this certificate to be signed by its duly authorized officers and to be sealed with the Seal of the Corporation.

Dated:

————————,

————————,

Shares ————

Bill of Sale for Assets of a Business

This is an agreement between:

_____

_____

_____,

herein called "transferor(s)," and _____, a corporation, herein called
"the corporation."

In return for the issuance of _____ shares of stock of the corporation, transferor(s) hereby
sell(s), assign(s), and transfer(s) to the corporation all right, title, and interest in the following property:

All the tangible assets listed on the balance sheet attached to this Bill of Sale and all stock
in trade, goodwill, leasehold interests, trade names, and other intangible assets [except
_____ of _____, located at
_____].

In return for the transfer of the above property to it, the corporation hereby agrees to assume, pay, and
discharge all debts, duties, and obligations listed on the balance sheet attached to this Bill of Sale
[except _____]. The corporation agrees to indemnify and hold
the transferor(s) of this business and their property free from any liability for any such debt, duty, or
obligation and from any suits, actions, or legal proceedings brought to enforce or collect any such debt,
duty, or obligation.

The transferor(s) hereby appoint(s) the corporation as representative to demand, receive, and collect
for itself any and all debts and obligations now owing to_____. The transferor(s)
further authorize(s) the corporation to do all things allowed by law to recover and collect any debts
and obligations and to use the transferor's(s') name(s) as it considers necessary for the collection and
recovery of these debts and obligations, provided, however, without cost, expense, or damage to the
transferor(s).

Date:_____

_____, Transferor

_____, Transferor

_____, Transferor

Date: _____

_____, Corporation

By:

_____, President

_____, Treasurer

Receipt for Cash Payment

Receipt of $_____ from _____ representing payment in full for _____ shares of the stock of this corporation is hereby acknowledged.

Dated: _____

Name of Corporation:_____

By: _____, Treasurer

Bill of Sale for Items of Property

In consideration of the issuance of _____ shares of stock in and by
_____ , _____ hereby sells, assigns, conveys, trans-
fers, and delivers to the corporation all right, title, and interest in and to the following property:
_____ .

Date: _____

_____

Receipt for Services Rendered

In consideration of the performance of the following services actually rendered to _____ ,

_____ , the provider of such services, hereby acknowledges the receipt

of _____ shares of stock in _____ as payment in full for these

services, described as follows:

_____

_____

_____

_____

Date: _____

_____

Contract for Future Services

In return for the issuance of _____ shares of _____,
_____ hereby agrees to furnish the following services to the corporation:

_____

_____

_____

_____

_____

It is understood that the corporation may place the shares in escrow or make other arrangements to restrict the transfer of shares until such time as the above services are performed in accordance with the above schedule.

Date: _____

Signed: _____

Name of Corporation: _____

By: _____, Treasurer

Promissory Note

In consideration of the issuance of shares of _____,
_____ promises to pay to _____ the principal
amount of $ _____ together with interest at a rate of _____ rate per annum.
Payments are to be made in _____ equal monthly installments of $_____, each
payable on the _____ day of each month, with the first installment due on _____.

Date: _____

Signature: _____

Cancellation of Debt

The receipt of _____ shares of this corporation to _____ for the cancellation by _____ of a current loan outstanding to this corporation, dated _____, with a remaining unpaid principal amount and unpaid accrued interest, if any, totaling $ _____, is hereby acknowledged.

Date: _____

Signature of Shareholder: _____

Notice of Incorporation Letter

_____

_____

Re: Incorporation of _____

Dear _____ :

I'm writing to let you know that our unincorporated business, _____, was incorporated in _____ on _____ as _____. This is a formal change that will help the business pursue its mission and the attainment of its goals with increased structure and efficiency.

We have enjoyed doing business with you in the past and look forward to continuing to do so in the future. Please call me at the telephone number shown below if you need additional information to update your records or accounts.

Sincerely,

_____ , _____

_____

_____

General Minutes of Meeting

Minutes of _____ **Meeting**

of

_____

A _____ meeting of the _____ was held on _____ for the purpose(s) of _____ . _____ acted as chairperson, and _____ acted as secretary of the meeting.

The chairperson called the meeting to order.

The secretary announced that the meeting was called by _____ .

The secretary announced that the meeting was held pursuant to notice as required under the bylaws of this corporation.

The secretary announced that the following _____ were present at the meeting, representing a quorum: _____ .

The secretary announced that the next item of business was the consideration of one or more formal resolutions for approval by the _____ . After introduction and discussion, and on motion duly made and carried by the affirmative vote of _____ _____ of _____ at the meeting, the following resolutions were adopted by the _____ entitled to vote at the meeting: _____ .

There being no further business to come before the meeting, it was adjourned on motion duly made and carried.

_____ , Secretary

Index